For Loraine,

Thank you for being the illustrator of my new book "Tabasco the Saucy Racoon" who you'll meet again in this book when I meet the owner of Tabasco Sauce. As you can see I've only had one illustrator before — Robert Bateman — but I hope you and I will have a long collaboration in future books that will immortalize my animal companions.

Written in Langley when we meet in person for the first time,

November 15, 2005

LOOKING FOR THE WILD

Books by Lyn Hancock

Pacific Wilderness
There's a Seal in My Sleeping Bag
The Mighty Mackenzie
There's a Raccoon in My Parka
Love Affair with a Cougar
An Ape Came Out of My Hatbox
Tell Me, Grandmother (co-author)
Northwest Territories: Canada's Last Frontier

LOOKING FOR THE WILD

Lyn Hancock

Foreword by
Roger Tory Peterson

Illustrations by
Robert Bateman

1986
Doubleday Canada Limited
Toronto, Canada

Canadian Cataloguing in Publication Data

Hancock, Lyn, 1938-

  Looking for the wild

ISBN 0-385-25063-0

1. Natural history - North America. 2. North
America - Description and travel. I. Title.

QH102.H36 1986 574.97 C86-094036-5

Library of Congress Cataloging-in-Publication Data

Hancock, Lyn.
  Looking for the wild.

1. Natural history — United States. 2. Natural
history — Canada. 3. Nature conservation — United
States. 4. Nature conservation — Canada. 5. United
States — Description and travel — 1981- .
6. Canada — Description and travel — 1981- .
7. Hancock, Lyn — Journeys — United States — Description
and travel — 1981- . 8. Hancock, Lyn — Journeys —
Canada — Description and travel — 1981- .
9. Peterson, Roger Tory, 1908-   — Journeys — United
States — Description and travel — 1981- .
10. Peterson, Roger Tory, 1908-   — Journeys — Canada —
Description and travel — 1981- . I. Title.
II. Title: Looking for wild America.

QH104.H26   1986   333.95′16′0973   86-16652
ISBN 0-385-25063-0

To Tess Kloot, for her support and enthusiasm

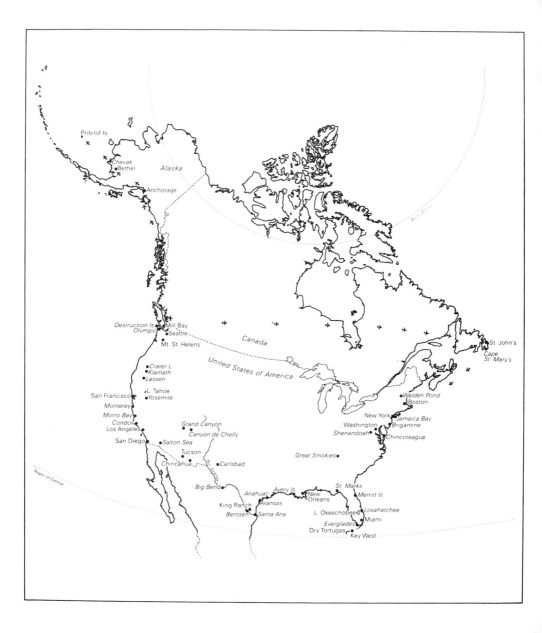

Pribilof Is.

Chevak
Bethel   *Alaska*

Anchorage

Arctic Circle

St. John's
Cape
St. Mary's

Destruction Is. Mill Bay
Olympic   Seattle
                  Mt. St. Helens

Canada

United States of America

Crater L.
Klamath
Lassen

L. Tahoe
Yosemite

San Francisco

Walden Pond
Boston

Monterey
Morro Bay
Condor
Los Angeles

Grand Canyon
Canyon de Chelly

New York
Washington
Shenandoah

Jamaica Bay
Brigantine
Chincoteague

San Diego

Salton Sea
Tucson
Chiricahua   *Carlsbad*

Great Smokies

Big Bend

Tropic of Cancer

Anahuac   *Avery Is.*
King Ranch   *Aransas*
Bentsen   *Santa Ana*

New
Orleans

St. Marks
Merritt Is.

L. Okeechobee   *Loxahatchee*
Everglades   Miami
Dry Tortugas
Key West

Contents

Foreword

More than thirty years have passed since James Fisher and I made our 30,000-mile odyssey around the perimeter of North America. After traveling for 100 days, from Newfoundland to the Bering Sea by way of the highlands of Mexico, we put it in a book, *Wild America*, which made the bestseller list for several weeks.

It had been our intention to make the same journey some years later so as to compare things as we found them then to the way they are today. Unfortunately, James Fisher lost his life on the M1 highway while driving much too fast to his home in Ashton after a late evening with friends at his London club. *Wild America Revisited* would have to be written without him as co-author. But without James, what better traveling companion than my wife, Ginny? Her eyes would be the fresh ones, seeing many of America's wild places for the first time.

However, it was inevitable that *Wild America*, published in 1955, should already have inspired others to follow our trail. One British couple, just retired from colonial service in southeast Asia, did things in reverse, starting on the west coast and proceeding eastward. Toward the end of their journey they stopped at our home in Old Lyme. I recall their visit well because in a woods down near the Sound we found a Brown Creeper's nest, the only one I had ever seen in our part of Connecticut.

Another young Englishman, Stuart Keith, fresh out of Oxford, received the book as a Christmas present, and after reading it said to his brother Anthony, "We've simply got to do that!" Having the time and the resources they traversed much of our route in 1956, all except the Mexican part. Their goal was to top our list of birds seen in one year. They ticked off 598 north of Mexico, quite a few more than our 572 but, frankly, Fisher and I had not planned our trip solely to run up a record list. However, with the addition of nearly 130 Mexican specialties we had finished with 701, 401 of which were lifers for James.

Stuart Keith had a book in mind, something like *Wild America*, but it was put aside and never finished after he accepted a chair at the American Museum. Later, the forests and broad savannahs of Africa beckoned him.

Apparently *Wild America*, as well as Stuart Keith's challenge, had sparked the competitive spirit of several other young, hardcore birders who were determined to see more birds than we did.

Ted Parker, whose ears are second to none and who is now working in Peru, raised the ante above 620 until another hardy young obsessive, Kenn Kaufmann, by bumming rides and living on inexpensive cat food, put the mark at 650.

Since then record after record has fallen. Jim Vardeman, risking family and business, and by spending embarassing amounts on air travel, hit 699; just one short of his goal of 700. Even that record toppled when Benton Basham of Tennessee, with the help of his network of ornithosleuths, racked up 711 between the first of January and the end of December, 1984.

Thus it is no surprise that bird tourism, a recent spinoff of the birding game, should take the ball and run with it. Several entrepreneurs, such as Victor Emanuel, had already taken tour groups to the Tortugas, Texas and other birding hotspots, but Gus Yaki of Toronto was the first to advertise a guided tour completely around the continent, a repeat of the trip Fisher and I had made thirty years earlier. Gus invited me to participate, but because of several irrevocable commitments, I could not spare the three months to do this. However, I did join Yaki's intrepid little party briefly in the Pribilofs where I was leading a Lindblad tour with Peter Alden.

Ginny and I were already deep in our own project, *Wild America Revisited*, although it would be spaced over several years rather than within a consecutive three-month period, and it would include a few key spots that Fisher and I had not visited.

One of the travelers in Yaki's group was Lyn Hancock, a young writer from Perth, Australia. She was already familiar with some of the wilderness areas of western Canada where she had lived for several years, but most of the wild spots south of the border were as new to her as they had been to James Fisher.

I have found much pleasure in reading what she has to say about our continent's wild heritage because she brought Aussie eyes to what she saw, quite in contrast to my American viewpoint or James Fisher's British eyes. Gus Yaki, as guide and mentor, had been to many of these places before; he knew just where things were, and who to contact for local guidance.

Thirty years have seen many changes; the proliferation of people, motorcars and traffic have made their inroads on the wild side of America. But, because of the groundswell of interest in the environment and its preservation, some spots remain the same, unviolated. A few places, because of management, are even better.

Lyn Hancock, an engaging writer, has entertained us before in *There's a Raccoon In My Parka*. She handles details and dialogue so well that we feel we know her and some of her companions rather intimately. We share their enthusiasms and can clearly visualize what they have seen. I know that her readers will be fascinated by what she has to say.

After a suitable lapse, perhaps when the new western *Field Guide* has been put to bed, Ginny and I will put the finishing touches on our own book, *Wild America Revisited*. By then there will have been other things to tell, other changes, other insights.

Roger Tory Peterson
July, 1986

Preface

For one hundred days in the spring of 1953, renowned American artist, writer, and ornithologist Roger Tory Peterson and naturalist-writer James Fisher, perhaps Britain's best-known authority on birds, traveled thirty thousand miles around the North American continent looking for Wild America. Peterson wanted to show Fisher as many different New World habitats and species as possible, especially birds. Together they wrote a book on their travels, the classic *Wild America*, which was published in 1955. It has since become the bible of North American nature lovers. In it, British-born Fisher said that never had he seen such wonders or met landlords so worthy of their land. He marveled that Americans had the power to ravage their country, yet they had made it a garden.

I found his words strange, picturing instead congested freeways, sprawling cities, harnessed rivers, cleared forests, and acid rain; thinking of extinct or near-extinct species such as the ivory-billed woodpecker, the dusky seaside sparrow, the Eskimo curlew, the California condor, the eastern panther, or declining species like the grizzly bear or the Alaskan fur seal.

If you believed the message that the media delivered, the environmental picture was gloomy indeed. Glimmers of light were rarely publicized: open cut mines revegetated, farms reforested, private land for sanctuaries donated; species like the gray whale, elephant seal, sea otter, and whooping crane reestablishing, the cattle egret and house finch expanding their range.

Thirty years after Peterson and Fisher, a small band of professional naturalists and amateur nature lovers, including myself, would travel the same route, visiting the same places for the same one hundred days and would note the changes that had been wrought to the various landscapes and their inhabitants. We were looking for answers to the questions, are we winning or losing in our efforts to save planet Earth, its wilderness and its wildlife? What has happened to Wild America in the last thirty years?

Being an optimist, I was interested in seeking out the agencies who had a positive effect on the environment, in places like Audubon sanctuaries and national wildlife refuges, and people like the bird watcher in Mississippi who persuaded a whole city to reserve its prime waterfront for birds. And in writing about the journey, I wanted to appeal not only to the serious conservationist but also to the diffident: to a driver taking his kids on the road for a family vacation, motivating them to watch for birds and panthers rather than license plates; and to a backpacker usually more interested in making miles than in reveling in moments along the way. I would write about people as well as animals. Ours would be more than the usual tourist route. We would travel from Newfoundland in Canada to the Dry Tortugas west of the Florida Keys, across to California, and then north to the remote Pribilof Islands in Alaska.

Alaska — its fur seals and its seabirds — would be my personal mecca. Twenty-one years before, I had come to Canada as a schoolteacher, married a wildlife biologist studying bald eagles, and was suddenly thrust into a world of animals, not only at home but out in the wild. An Alaskan fur seal born on the Pribilofs and washed ashore outside my home in British Columbia stimulated a deeper interest in marine mammals, which led me to study them along the coasts of Washington, Oregon, and California. Since then I had collected murres and puffins on Washington and British Columbia islands for the New York Zoological Society, and had helped to raise peregrine falcons in captivity. Cougars I cared for in Canada became a lifelong passion; I studied them all over the United States. Curiosity about the natural world led me to adventures all over North America and a strong urge to share these experiences resulted in eight books and countless articles. It was for this reason that I was invited to record this trip.

I had driven the route before, once as a teacher with a busload of other teachers, twice with my parents visiting from Australia, and part of it several times with my biologist husband. I had "done" America as a tourist, as an author, as a film maker. Now I would do it again as a naturalist with other naturalists, a total of thirty people from around the world, each with his or her own special interest. Sometimes our group would be as few as four; other times it would be as large as twenty-one.

Our leader was Gus Yaki, a remarkable man who describes himself as "just someone who likes nature." He is justly famed as the founder of Nature Travel Service, a service for nature lovers who roam the world with him. He was the one who conceived and organized the Wild America tour.

Born in 1932 in Sandwith, Saskatchewan, one of many tiny rural communities on the prairies that no longer appear on modern maps, Gus has always been interested in what makes the world tick. One time he was pointing out different ducks on the water with one hand, a warbler in the bush with the other, and at the same time mentioning to his guests that there was a robin's nest in a tree above and a *Taraxacum officinale* plant on the ground. A couple of newcomers who had never before been in his company looked on in amazement. Finally one young man said, "How long have you been interested in this type of thing?"

Gus paused, then said, "Ever since I was an embryo."

Gus has no need to advertise his services. As one guest said, "his grapevine has as many and far-reaching tentacles as a kudzu vine." He has a loyal following of self-described "Gus-o-philes" who have gone on as many as sixty trips with him. As one Gus-gal said, "I have spent as much time with Gus as with my children." We would be meeting many of his guests during our travels around North America—naturalists with specialized knowledge of each local area.

Two other naturalists par excellence would be joining us for part of the time: Roger Tory Peterson himself, dean of America's birders, and Robert Bateman, Canada's foremost wildlife artist. Through his numerous field guides, nature books, articles, films, radio and television programs, paintings, and directorships of many wildlife and conservation organizations, Roger Tory Peterson has turned on millions of North Americans to an interest in birds and general appreciation of the natural world.

Robert Bateman, who now lives on Saltspring Island, British Columbia, just over the water from my own home in Mill Bay, is more than a top wildlife artist with Robert Redford looks, paintings on exhibition around the world, reproductions in thousands of homes, and books that are bestsellers. He is a teacher, an ardent naturalist, and a dedicated conservationist, as well as a warm friend. The special feature that sets his art apart from that of other wildlife painters is his attention to landscape. What others paint as background, Robert Bateman will emphasize as foreground. For him, the feeling of the land is all-important; sometimes the animals are secondary.

With so many diverse interests and individual talents, our search for Wild America promised to be a rewarding one. Unfortunately, because of their heavy schedules, Peterson and Bateman could be with us for only part of the time. But from them and my other companions, especially the enthusiastic Tess Kloot, I savored again the joy I remembered from my first travels around America, as Peterson had done through James Fisher's eyes on that first journey years ago. And I found there were still wild places and magic moments in the wilderness.

I arrived in St. John's, Newfoundland, on the evening of April 7, 1983, to begin my search for Wild America. Although it took only eight hours by plane to cross the continent from my home on the Pacific to the Atlantic, it would be three months through America and another month through Canada before I returned home to the Pacific.

Never have I seen such wonders or met landlords so worthy of their land. They have had, and still have, the power to ravage it; and instead have made it a garden.

— James Fisher in *Wild America*, 1955

Northern Gannet
Sula bassanus

Chapter One
Off to Newfoundland
April 12–16

"Dearly beloved, as we are gathered together in the bus," Gus intoned facetiously from the wheel of his rented van as we left St. John's and turned southwest across the Avalon Peninsula, "let's start reading *Wild America*." Although we had all read and reread Peterson and Fisher's book before, we were to read it again daily on the trip.

April 12, the first day of our expedition, set the routine for the next one hundred days. Bird walk before breakfast. Read what Peterson and Fisher did on the same day thirty years before. Explore their destinations and add more of our own. Lunch on the trail usually overlooking some body of water, park, sewage lagoon, or cemetery, all good birding places. Explore again in the afternoon. Dinner and check-in to a motel on the edge of town, again preferably in some birdy area. Reread Peterson and Fisher at night to compare and contrast our experiences. Bird walk again at midnight — for dedicated types like Gus Yaki and Tess Kloot and Miss Smith.

Tess Kloot from Australia is a wonderful and remarkable person. Pint-sized, exuberant, strongly Aussie-accented, Tess had got into bird watching late in life when she heard a blackbird singing. She is the coauthor of two bird books, has a special Bird Room in her house, and is as passionately fond of birds as she is of her children (or as I, another Aussie, teased, her "chooldren"). She would be with us almost all the way. As James Fisher sought the differences between Europe and North America but found instead similarities, so Tess sought the similarities between Australia and America and would discover vast differences.

Miss Smith is a single-minded, determined, very independent lawyer who had given up a successful practice in British Columbia to travel the world after birds. She had already driven Peterson's route around America on her own but was prepared to do part of it a second time to gain new insights from Gus.

One of the most important activities of the day — besides birding, forever now a verb — was updating our bird list. Birders usually keep lists of birds they see in a day, in a year, in a lifetime. Birders to whom the list is the thing are called bird twitchers, because they twitch from one place to another in an all-out effort to add just one more bird to their list.

We too added interest to our trip by counting numbers and species. Whenever Fisher found a new bird, he would shout "Tally-ho!" When Tess did, she sometimes got carried away and came out with "Wacko" in fair dinkum Down Under lingo. Each night we recorded our sightings in columns against a checklist published by the American Ornithologists' Union.

I recorded other things too — even people — in my field notebooks, on my tape recorder, on messy scraps of paper. My neck was permanently hung round with cameras, lenses, tape recorder, notebook, and, when I could find time to use them, binoculars. Tess kept bringing me a succession of pens on chains that went around my neck with everything else.

Although birding was our predominant interest (for an increasing number of people, it is their connection to the natural world), we had wider aims — the search for wildness in America and the effect of humankind on that wildness. And although our group was committed to looking for Wild America, I knew that each of us would have to come to terms with what we meant by wildness. For some it is a thousand miles of tundra, for others a strip of forest beside a highway. In places no longer wild, we would need to look for ways in which people were working to bring back some of that wildness.

Newfoundland is an appropriate place to start, for the discovery of North America began here with the Vikings in about 1001 A.D. The province's people strive to maintain an older, traditional lifestyle based on fishing and sealing. Newfoundland is appropriate too in its geography. With its glaciated landscapes, wind-stunted vegetation, and subarctic climate, Newfoundland contrasted sharply with the rest of our journey south to summer.

With steady rain, monochrome scenery, birds hidden or not yet arrived, it was rather a dreary drive across the barrens and boreal forests of the Avalon Peninsula. Perhaps because of this landscape, Newfoundlanders have colorful villages with even more colorful names, like Famish Gut, Empty Basket, Gripe Point, Bleak Joke Cove, Leading Tickle, Heart's Desire, Heart's Content, Heart's Delight, and Cupids. You can brighten many a foggy day by imagining the stories behind such names as Run-By Guess, Come By Chance, Seldom Come By, and Nancy O. And from the salt boxes of the farthest fishing coves to the row houses or elegant townhouses of innermost St. John's, Newfoundlanders paint their homes in vivid purples, greens, yellows, reds, oranges — whatever colors of paint, some say, are on special that day.

A stream of memorable pictures passed by: houses like Neapolitan ice cream clothing the steep hillsides of each tiny cove; spruce poles leaning neatly against their walls for fences, firewood, or flakes (fish drying racks); rows of cod and capelin hanging out to dry by lace-curtained windows; sheep and goats lazing in the middle of the road. Every time Gus braked to point out a bird, I would rush to squeeze in a photograph.

The island of Newfoundland is relatively sparse in its native flora and fauna, although numbers and species have increased in the past thirty years. It is an island in an isolated position on the lee side of North America and has only recently emerged from the last Ice Age, less than ten thousand years ago. Its rocks, part of the Appalachian system that extends to the southern United States, are very old and hard. They are slow to break up and, scoured by glaciers, produce thin, coarse soil. Much of Newfoundland's soil is thought to have been dumped onto the Grand Banks to the southeast, enriching the fishing grounds there but impoverishing the island. A harsh climate and off-shore sea ice, which retard spring and shorten the growing season, along with the poor soil, keep Newfoundland's plant species to a minimum. And this year, spring was later than usual.

Newfoundland, however, has lost less wild habitat than most places in North America, and it has gained species. Some were introduced accidentally, others were planned. From Europe by sailing ship came insects, weeds and roadside plants, house mice and Norway rats, earthworms, slugs, and woodlice. From the mainland came green frogs, snowshoe hares, moose, and mink. Since Peterson and Fisher made their trip, spruce grouse, ruffed grouse, mallard ducks, evening grosbeaks, chipmunks, cinereous shrews, the European skipper butter-fly, and the ubiquitous starlings have joined Newfoundland's fauna.

Gus — a tireless teacher, with one hand cupped to his mouth as a megaphone while he steered with the other — kept up a running commentary. He pointed out diversity amid the apparent monotony: countless bogs and ponds that in summer come alive with birds like greater yellowlegs, mergansers, and black ducks; the wind-stunted, bushy-topped spruce trees once used as stovepipe and chimney cleaners by inventive fishermen, and the heathland dotted and clumped with sheep laurel, partridge-berry, and Labrador tea.

We stopped at Butterpot Provincial Park, a favorite picnic spot in summer. It was therapeutic to get out of the van and become intimate with the land, to feel the spongy sphagnum under my feet, to see the glitter on the tamarack backlit by a fitful sun. Today we were on the lookout for a willow ptarmigan — the bird Newfoundlanders call a partridge — although they were at a low point in their population cycle. I wanted to find a moose. Half a dozen were introduced to Newfoundland in 1878 and 1904, and the population has since increased to 50,000. But Gus pointed out dryly, "That 50,000 could be hiding behind 500,000 spruce trees." And they were.

Although we did not see willow ptarmigan that day, we did see other birds. Tiny blotches on telephone lines became red crossbills in the telescope. Dots in the sky circling tightly like balls on an unseen string were pine siskins perhaps in courtship flight. Blobs on rock piles like helmeted sentries focused into horned larks. Staccato flutters in woodlots landed to become golden-crowned kinglets, dark-eyed juncos, pine grosbeaks, and the captivating black-capped and boreal chickadees. "Chickadees are birds that charm everyone," said Gus admiringly. "They will take food from your hands. In Britain, one of their kind, the blue tit, learned to take the caps off milk bottles to get at the cream that rises to the top of unhomogenized milk."

Because Newfoundland (excluding Labrador) is an island, some species differ in appearance, behavior, or song from their mainland cousins. American robins, for example, are darker in color (perhaps because of higher humidity), and they rarely seem to nest around houses. Another oddity we saw was a white-winged crow. We were to record several other albinistic characteristics during our journey.

About thirty-five miles from St. John's, we stopped at Salmonier Nature Park, a one-hundred-acre enclosed area within a three-thousand-acre wilderness reserve, designed to provide people with a cross-section of Newfoundland wilderness. Kevin Moore, the acting manager, led us over the long, winding trails of Salmonier to show us animals we had little time to look for in the wild: moose, caribou, red foxes, lynx, and snowy and boreal owls.

"At Salmonier," Kevin explained, "we have enclosed pieces of the wild but have made barriers unobtrusive, so people see wildlife in as near a natural setting as possible. Mammals in particular are difficult to see in the wild — that's why I became a birder — so we've got to show them in a place like this. Hopefully, the people who get turned on to enjoying wildlife here will get turned on to general conservation." Not all wildlife at Salmonier is enclosed. Visitors can see the free-roaming caribou of the Avalon Wilderness Area through telescopes at the caribou viewing tower.

We headed next for Cape St. Mary's Seabird Sanctuary at the southwestern tip of the Avalon Peninsula. Newfoundland has unique and outstanding seabird colonies. They are spectacular and easily accessible.

All but one are islands, which inhibit predators such as fox and mink, and which have steep cliffs to create strong air currents for birds to launch themselves out to sea. Cape St. Mary's is not an island, but it has a couple of miles of steep cliffs for seabirds to nest on.

The skies promised something like sunshine as we roller-coastered over the headlands and around the coves south of Placentia Bay. Peterson and Fisher had had to trek in ten miles to Cape St. Mary's from St. Bride's, with a pack pony to carry their gear. We had it easy in our comfortable van. But despite a now-automated lighthouse, and a visitor center to handle the thousands of people who now take guided tours of the sanctuary between May 24 and Labor Day weekend, the land and the birds were much the same, and we had it all to ourselves.

We left the van at the lighthouse and followed a narrow trail through public sheep pasture along the cliffs. We stepped into another world — an Arctic tundra world — lush, green, and spongy underfoot, pregnant with excitement overhead.

You hear them long before you see them — an incredible din of cries and whines, croaks and squawks, growls and gargles. "It's like a symphony," said Tess, "an undercurrent of guttural roars, the bass tones, and above those, the screams, the tenor tones." Then the wind shifts, you round a bend in the headland or drop behind a hill, and the din stops abruptly, like a radio shut off. Only the sound of surf crashing far below remains.

You see them long before you recognize them — a blizzard of birds wheeling, whirling in the air, rafts of dark shapes bobbing, clogging the waters offshore. Then the mist lifts and you get a quick glimpse of The Stack, a giant rock chimney severed from the land by a narrow chasm covered with gleaming white pearls. Then the pearls lift from the cluster to become snowflakes, and you know that you are seeing a veil of northern gannets, large pelicanlike birds that set up their summer homes each year at Cape St. Mary's, Newfoundland's largest gannet colony, the second largest in North America.

The swirling fog hides the stage again, but the music continues. Such sounds led Jacques Cartier and other early sailors to find and explore the New World colonies. The cries of kittiwakes, murres, and puffins at Baccalieu Island acted as navigation aids to guide sailors to a safe landing on the fog-shrouded coast. Once upon a time a man could be publicly whipped for disturbing seabirds on Baccalieu. Unfortunately, the birds on other islands were disturbed to the ultimate when their flesh and eggs provided fresh food for men on boats long stuck at sea, their feathers were sold for decoration and mattress stuffing, their bodies were rendered for oil and then burned for fuel or taken for fish bait. By about 1802 the great auks on Funk Island, the last North American rookery, were destroyed, and the species was soon extinct.

While Gus, Tess, and Miss Smith pushed on expectantly toward The Stack, Jim Buschman, the other photographer in our group, lollygagged behind with me to photograph alpine bistort and bunchberry sprouting from lichened black rocks at our feet. Common loons still in winter plumage skeined across the sky. Rafts of gorgeous harlequin ducks, starkly plumed common eiders, long-tailed oldsquaws, and razorbills with their Jimmy Durante beaks, rode the whitecaps out to sea.

You need binoculars and telephoto lenses to capture these, but once at The Stack, you are so close to the nesting birds, only 50 feet away, that you feel you can reach out and touch them. Don't — the narrow chasm between you and them has taken more than one life. However, there is no need to stand giddily peering 260 feet down into an abyss. Just curl up in a natural rock armchair, scalloped by erosion for your comfort, and watch the gannet show.

It was impossible not to feel the excitement when we visited — in the air, on the land, in the water. Three thousand murres, penguinlike and immaculate, standing side-by-side, layer-upon-layer along the shelves of rock; twenty thousand black-legged kittiwakes, delicately pretty birds some call tickle-lace, nuzzled in pairs beside them; and at least three thousand pairs of gannets. More would arrive later.

While Gus leaned dizzily over the cliff edge counting numbers and species, the rest of us remained amazed by the awesome spectacle on The Stack — thousands of gannets in their most spectacular plumage, gleaming white except for jet-black wing tips, saffron-washed heads and blue-tinged eyes. Tess noticed bright green stripes on their ankles. Jim pointed out the blue-black stripe under their beaks, a symmetrical design that reminded him, when they put their heads up, of rocket ships taking off.

Hatched here, accustomed to people, seemingly safe on their isolated rock top, the gannets went about their business oblivious to our excitement. They had enough of their own. With back-pedaling wings, splayed-out feet, and tail used as a rudder to slow them down, incoming birds landed, jostled to their nesting site, and dropped seaweed, moss, or pieces of stick. Pairs of gannets, mated for life, bobbed up and down, bowed to each other, faced-off chest to chest, and clashed bills. Sometimes we did not know if the birds were making love or war. "That's not an expression of hostility," explained Gus. "It could have originated that way, but now that they're mates, they recognize each other and clap beaks to reinforce contact."

Some of the gannets were sky-pointing, stretching their necks and pointing their bills to the sky. Gus commented, "That means one's about to take off, so he wants to tell those around him, 'Don't jab me as I go.' It can also mean that his mate is nearby and he is sky-pointing to signal, 'Hi, honey! I'm here.' "

The most spectacular gannet display is its dizzying plunge-dive into the sea to feed. Six feet of white wings fold and the gannet turns into a torpedo, cleaving the water's surface to toss spray ten feet high. As one plummeted into the ocean, Gus explained that air cells between its skin and the muscles of its neck and shoulders inflate to cushion the impact, and its bill clamps shut. A gannet does not spear fish on the way down. Its eyes are positioned in front so it can gauge depth accurately and come up at a fish from below. It gulps down its catch when it breaks into the air again.

Most of the gannets at Cape St. Mary's were fishing far from The Stack, but Jim and I tried to photograph their flight as they wheeled around the cliff face, all going in the same direction. At the time of our visit, courtship and nest sprucing were in vogue. Three weeks before, only two hundred pairs of gannets had come to Cape St. Mary's from their wintering quarters at sea along the southeastern coast of the United States. Now in mid-April we counted roughly three thousand pairs, about the same as Peterson and Fisher had done on the same day thirty years before. Soon more than five thousand pairs would be nesting at this gannetry.

Although gannet colonies in North America have decreased to six since the exploitive years of the early explorers, the gannets at Cape St. Mary's appear to be increasing. The previous year, Bill Montevecchio and John Wells, two Newfoundland ornithologists, had discovered fifty chicks on the mainland close to The Stack, a "biologically significant" event. Now over a hundred pairs nest there, despite disturbance by people, foxes, sheep, weasels, and dogs.

A solitary murre sat atop a boulder in the middle of The Gannet Stack, but the gannets appeared unperturbed. They own the rock now, but back in 1880 murres were the original nesters. Like gannets, murres spend most of the year at sea. Then, beginning in April, breeding murres fly in to spend their summers on land. They stand on cliff ledges like books in bookcases hundreds of feet high. In line, facing the cliff, with white breasts, black backs, and two white wing borders like buttons on their tail feathers, murres remind me of men in tuxedos lined up at a urinal. (Although in the wild murres have no occasion to walk, the ones which I describe in my book *There's a Seal in My Sleeping Bag* that incubated under my sweater, hatched in a tent, and then followed me as their official mother, Konrad Lorenz–style, walked very well.)

There are two kinds of murres in Newfoundland, common and thick-billed. Thick-billed murres differ from common murres in having slightly larger bodies, stouter bills, and an obvious white line on their upper mandibles. About 17 percent of the common murres at Cape St. Mary's were in their ringed or bridled phase, that is, their eyes were circled with a fine white ring that ran backward like a streak.

One murre looked a kingpin of the gannetry, although the other murres were lined up in more usual fashion along ledges on the mainland cliffs. They were close to us, but we needed a boat to see the whole colony. As we strolled the headlands, we saw only a fraction of them. Gus, with no fear of heights, saw more by bending over the cliff edge. At this time, not all breeding murres had arrived. Gus counted about 2,500 common murres, but no thick-billed ones. Later in the season there would be about ten thousand pairs of common murres and perhaps a thousand pairs of thick-bills.

Although thick-billed murres winter in Newfoundland, they are chiefly birds of the High Arctic. Only since the early 1950s have they been known to nest in Newfoundland. Peterson and Fisher recorded the first substantial colony of nesting thick-bills at Cape St. Mary's.

Men eat murres. Newfoundlanders call them turrs and shoot up to half a million of them annually. There are no bag limits, and some hunters kill five hundred at a time, easy pickings from powerboats with automatic shotguns. Newfoundland is one of the few places in the world where it is legal for nonnatives to kill seabirds without restriction.

Almost all of the scientific research into the natural history of Newfoundland has been done since 1950, the same year the Newfoundland Natural History Society was founded by legendary ornithologist Leslie Tuck and one year after Leslie Tuck was appointed as the province's first Dominion wildlife officer. His name stands above all others in bringing knowledge of Newfoundland's natural history to the public eye.

Leslie Tuck was there at the airport to meet James Fisher in 1953, and he personally escorted Fisher and Peterson to Funk Island, the former home of the great auk and still one of Newfoundland's most important seabird colonies. Seabirds, especially murres, were Les Tuck's passion. Although he died in 1979, he is still remembered fondly by ornithologists studying seabirds today in Newfoundland, including David Nettleship, Bill Montevecchio, William Threlfall, John Piatt, John Wells, and Bruce MacTavish, who are continuing his unfinished work. We met some of these men at Memorial University and accompanied them on field trips.

Places we really wanted to visit were Gull, Green, and Great islands in the Witless Bay Seabird Sanctuary. These islands have the largest concentration of seabirds in eastern North America, the largest breeding concentrations of the parrotlike puffins and pretty kittiwakes in the western Atlantic, and the second-largest colony of murres.

Even though the Witless Bay sanctuary is less than twenty miles from St. John's and only a few miles from shore, it is not as accessible as Cape St. Mary's. To reduce human disturbance, visitors need a special permit from the Wildlife Division of the Department of Tourism if they wish to land on Gull Island. Only in exceptional circumstances are they allowed to land on Green or Great islands.

You can see the birds from the water by boat without harming them if you keep at a safe distance and use binoculars: shelves of black-legged kittiwakes and clouds of great black-backed gulls and herring gulls; skeins of whirring murres and razorbills circling the cliff line; black guillemots exploding from crevices at the shoreline; Atlantic puffins launching themselves from grassy hummocks at the skyline. To see the diminutive storm petrels, you must wait till evening, when under the cover of darkness, birds who have spent the day at sea return to their mates deep inside burrows. Then the night is full of ghosts, dark whirring shapes and a medley of underground sounds. The night flight of the petrels is unforgettable.

We could not get a boat to the islands because the bay was full of ice: not until mid-May would fishermen be ready to take us out to the islands. The height of the bird watching season in this sanctuary is the last two weeks of June and the first two in July; by the second week in August almost all the seabirds have gone.

We stopped for lunch by a deserted fish-processing plant in the village of Witless Bay and set up the scope. The kittiwake cliffs of Gull Island, only three miles away, were easily visible. And in between, wherever there was ice-free water, bobbed hundreds of common eiders and oldsquaws not yet departed for their northern breeding grounds.

I looked for puffins. They had been coming in since early April to find their mates, select their sites, and dig out their burrows. But they would not be laying eggs till late May and early June, and it would not be till early July that the chicks hatched and the colony become galvanized into frenzied feeding activity.

Of North America's 310,000 Atlantic puffins, 225,000 nest on the three islands of Witless Bay. Like its other alcid cousins, this chunky "sea parrot" can race through the water after fish and catch them with its pincerlike bill. (Having had to pull a protesting puffin from a burrow, I well know the power of its scimitarlike beak.) It jerks the fish to the roof of its mouth and secures it to a series of spiky serrations with its tongue. Amazingly, a puffin can already be carrying several fish crossways in its bill when it catches even more. Unfortunately for the puffin, it is often easier to get hold of a fish in the water than to keep it on the way back home. Scavenging gulls constantly patrol the colony to badger incoming puffins and snatch fish destined for the chicks in the burrows.

Rapidly increasing gull populations, especially in Witless Bay, are causing problems for puffins. Bill Threlfall told us that the numbers of herring gulls, great black-backed gulls, and black-legged kittiwakes have risen sharply since 1966, probably as a result of human sewage, garbage, and offal from proliferating fish-processing plants. Gulls thrive on mankind's wastes, but some researchers feel that gulls also pick on puffins, pirating their fish and chicks.

There are other problems for the puffins of Witless Bay. Their preferred food — and that of other alcids, as well as cod and whales and man — is a greenish silver, sardine-sized fish called capelin. When the capelin come ashore to spawn on high tides in June and July, fishermen wade into the water to take them by the truckload. The capelin fishery expanded in 1972 to international status, survived five years of over exploitation, then crashed in 1978. The puffins on Great Island had a bad year in 1981, when the capelin fish, a puffin's normal diet, failed to come inshore. David Nettleship called the breeding season "an almost total failure."

However, since 1981 the puffins seem to be faring well. Bill Threlfall said that "in 1982 there were more capelin around than fishermen had seen in twenty years." Up to a point, populations can remain stable in the face of such fluctuations, but they also become more vulnerable to other factors, such as in the case of puffins and murres, toxic chemicals, oil pollution, and drowning in fish nets.

From Witless Bay we continued down the coast to Cape Race, stopping wherever the road overlooked the sea to look for birds. It was a drab and wintry world, the low tide grounding icebergs in the mud, the fog hovering, ready to hide our views. No brightly colored houses relieved these landscapes. Then in the middle of the windswept barrenlands we found a lonely shack labeled Seventh Heaven.

We left our rambling gravel road and clambered joyously over the tilted, table-top, wave-polished rock that shelved into the sea at Cape Race, one of the most forbidding places in Newfoundland. It is the closest point of land to where the "unsinkable" *Titanic* went down exactly seventy-one years ago to the day of our visit. Amid the black boulders and crashing, spuming surf were common eiders, oldsquaws, American black ducks, purple sandpipers, and ruddy turnstones. The sun shone for one glorious moment in a tiny cove, and there bobbing on the waves of that deserted beach swam one lone dovekie, the smallest of Newfoundland's seabirds. Tess was in birders' heaven.

Next morning Bill Montevecchio and John Piatt took us on a trip to Cape St. Francis, north of St. John's.

On Water Street in St. John's — the oldest in North America, the guide books said — a man was selling dead harp seals from his truck. "The best flippers, the biggest flippers in many years, the biggest, fattest, sassiest pups," proclaimed the signs. Yet most sealing vessels lay idle in the keyhole harbor. Few boats had bothered to butt their way through the unprecedented ice this year, and anyway, there was little market for seal pelts. Markets had collapsed because of the lobbying of protesters, and Newfoundlanders were bitter.

Ice conditions were the worst since the turn of the century. The harbor was clogged and giant icebergs scintillated on the skyline whenever the sun shone. The ice caused problems for more than sealing ships. Already fifty white-beaked dolphins had been crushed to death by huge ice pans. Four to five hundred killer and humpback whales had been trapped in shallow water as ice stretched headland to headland and cut off the bays.

Bill and John's colleagues in the whale rescue team from Memorial University were angry that the world — aroused by subjective, selective media coverage — censured Newfoundland for hating seals and whales when many Newfoundlanders, including fishermen, do their best to save such entrapped creatures every year. Headlines grab more attention when teary-eyed, virginal white baby seals drip blood from hunter's clubs, or ice-entrapped and net-imprisoned whales die from fishermen's gunshot wounds. A story about the death of the last

Eskimo curlew is much more engrossing than the current comeback of the seals and whales.

Compared with thirty years ago, marine mammals on the North Atlantic coast are doing quite well, either maintaining or increasing their once-dwindling numbers. The 800 humpback whales between Nova Scotia and the Gulf of Maine in 1952 have increased to 4000 in 1985. About 200 right whales (so called because they float when dead) now thrive in the Bay of Fundy; a few years ago, they were on the brink of extinction. Nevertheless, seals and whales continue to compete with people for the same codfish and capelin, and they increasingly enmesh themselves in nets. Some people's patience runs thin, the pendulum swings, and again the animals are threatened with overhunting or environmental mismanagement.

There are fewer eagles, merlins and peregrine falcons today, according to Bill Threlfall. But there are more seals, more whales, more gulls, more kittiwakes, more fulmars, more gannets, and in some places like Witless Bay, more puffins and common murres. More starlings, more mallards, more Canada geese, more ruffed grouse, more evening grosbeaks. More moose. There are harlequin ducks breeding for the first time in Newfoundland. Black-headed gulls and manx shearwaters are breeding for the first time in North America.

Then why do the scientists feel, in the words of Bill Threlfall again, that "seabirds are now in greater danger of extinction due to oil development, commercial fishing, and hunting, than at any time in their history," including the days of the great auk? Perhaps because seabirds are always vulnerable and because of what has happened elsewhere in the past. Toxic chemicals in the Gulf of St. Lawrence have devastated double-crested cormorant colonies, caused growth deformities and locomotory defects in young gannets, and reduced the number of razorbills by half. Heavy metal poisoning along the New England coast has caused a decline in the tern populations. Hunting, oil fouling, and drowning in fish nets have reduced common and thickbilled murre species in the eastern Canadian Arctic. The inability of puffins to find capelin — either because the capelin population crashed after 1977 or because they schooled in deep water, beyond the puffins' diving range — caused less than half the normal number of puffin chicks on Great Island to be fledged in 1981. It could happen again.

Scientists fear the threat of oil above all. Les Tuck estimated that half a million seabirds die annually from exposure to oil, not just spectacular and headline-grabbing spills like that of the *Torrey Canyon* but the regular and illegal discharge of refined oil by tankers or lubricating oil by trawlers and cargo ships. John Piatt wrote that "more seabirds die from oil pollution in Newfoundland waters than anywhere else in eastern North America." For especially vulnerable seabirds like murres and puffins, a single drop of oil can be their death, plastering their feathers, destroying their natural insulation and bringing their skin into direct contact with the frigid sea. Even holding a murre with greasy hands can destroy its feathered insulation. Recently, scientists have begun to think that oil ingested while the birds preen also reduces female fertility, impairs the growth of chicks, and makes all birds more vulnerable to environmental stress.

Will people make a difference? And if so, whom? Industrialists? Governments? Scientists? Or ordinary people who just like looking at a butterfly, a dovekie, a baby harp seal?

We spent our last day in Newfoundland with Bill and Fiona Day, who had shared their home with us all week. We went looking for the natural world in the streets of St. John's. Most people who saw us cruising the oldest and most grandiose houses and gardens in the city would think we were studying history or architecture.

Wrong. We were looking for pine grosbeaks, strikingly plumaged wine colored birds. We did not find any grosbeaks, but we did see four starlings on a chimney and three boreal chickadees on a hedgerow. Out at Long Pond past the university, Miss Smith "got" a dozen ring-billed gulls.

We took another trip to Signal Hill, an island of Newfoundland "wilderness" within the city. Most people drive up Signal Hill (as we had done before) to see the view, to visit Cabot Tower built in 1898 to commemorate John Cabot's landing on Newfoundland's shores in 1497, or to see where Marconi received the world's first wireless signals sent across the Atlantic from England.

We rambled across its windswept heathlands looking for willow ptarmigan among the mountain alder, dwarf birch, and Labrador tea. Gus pointed out how plants in this acid soil restrict their moisture intake by having hard, leathery, narrow, or curled-up leaves. Tess was intrigued by the massive mats of mountain cranberry that the Newfoundlanders call partridge-berry and gather annually for sauces, jams, and jellies. Signal Hill was one of the very few sites in Newfoundland where Scottish heather had become naturalized.

Suddenly three willow ptarmigan, two males and a female, exploded from the bushes with a loud whirr of wings and resounding cackles.

The cock birds, already in rusty brown breeding plumage, were vying for a mate. The object of their attention was still wearing much of her winter white.

Herring gulls laughed overhead, but the loveliest sound of all was the song of the fox sparrow, one of the most abundant birds in Newfoundland and one of the earliest to arrive in the spring.

After five days of mostly birding, we were ready for a break. But not Gus. That night he took us to dinner in an old restored house on Duckworth Street. At the entrance, we were all straining in the dark to see some paintings in a next-door window when he said dryly, ''I hope you've got your binoculars. There are some starlings sleeping above you.''

Willet
Catoptrophorus semipalmatus

Chapter Two
The Northeast
April 17–May 1

"Keep your eyes open for your first American bird," said Gus, as our plane emerged from the fog that had followed us from Newfoundland. The tarmac spread like a carpet along the entrance of the harbor to present the city of Boston, backdropped by smokestacks, expressways, and more than twenty skyscrapers. Thirty years before, there had been only one. Would Wild America still be nearby?

"*Larus marinus*," said Tess Kloot gleefully, her binoculars pressed against the window as we landed. "Great black-backed gull."

"Herring gulls and starlings," called Miss Smith as we stepped through the sliding glass doors and into the parking lot.

Gus had a strong distaste for cities and other artifacts of human civilization. The only reason we were in Boston now — and were soon to be in New York and Washington — was the fact that Roger Tory Peterson and James Fisher had gone there thirty years before.

"This is not my forte," he said as we packed our gear in his big blue van, our home for the next sixty days, "but we have another guest to pick up from the airport this evening, so we'll have to stick around."

Jim Buschman had left us in Newfoundland, but Marjorie Dufton joined us at the airport. A retired teacher-librarian from London, Ontario, Marjorie had come for the plants. She wanted to see the redbud and the dogwood in their full flowering glory. She would have to be patient. The woods and the marshes were largely yellow, brown and bare. Spring in New England was still a promise.

For flowers, that is, but not for birds. Next morning the path to our motel in Boston was strewn with mockingbirds and robins. We woke in the morning to a dawn chorus of cardinals, black-capped chickadees, northern flickers, song sparrows, swamp sparrows, mourning doves, and a catbird. "Twenty species before breakfast!" exclaimed Tess. We saw almost half the number of species that we had seen in a week in Newfoundland. But on our first full day in New England, the sounds of birds in Concord, Massachusetts, were in danger of being drowned out by the sounds of singing of another sort, of brass bands and marching girls. Americans, with flags flying, street parades, and pageantry, were noisily celebrating the events of April 1775, the first two battles of the Revolution between John Hancock's Minutemen (farmers who were ready to leave their plowshares and fight at a minute's notice) and approaching British troops.

Beginning today, after each morning's early bird walk we would head for the nearest diner for breakfast, but our chief reason was to phone the local Bird Hot Line. We took turns at the telephone trying to scribble down the names of unusual birds and unfamiliar places where they were to be seen. The Audubon Bird Hot Line for East Massachusetts is only one of many such hot lines all over the country where bird watchers can take advantage of local knowledge.

As Peterson had remarked in *Wild America*, it was appropriate for bird watchers to begin a cross-country trek in this part of Massachusetts, because the Nuttall Ornithological Club of nearby Cambridge is the oldest bird club in America. The Nuttall Club led to the American Ornithologists' Union, which led to the National Audubon Society. He said that Massachusetts boasts more bird watchers per square mile than any other state, and probably produces more experts.

We met one such expert at Great Meadows National Wildlife Refuge in Concord. Our conversation with Mary Romanow of the Brookline Bird Club took place at the top of a tower while we were scoping wood ducks. She told us that the Brookline Club, with 1300 members, is the most active bird club in the United States, perhaps in the world.

"There's a ton of birds coming in at Cape Cod and there are forty-four ospreys at Westport — isn't that great?" Mary bubbled enthusiastically. "Make sure you pop in to Mt. Auburn Cemetery in Cambridge before you leave the area." Many people go to Mt. Auburn to see the graves of Henry Wadsworth Longfellow or Oliver Wendell Holmes, but bird watchers go to catch warblers coming through on spring migration.

So far, with spring late, we had not seen a single warbler. We had tried for warblers in the Concord Cemetery, but only turned up — near the graves of Louisa May Alcott and Henry David Thoreau — ten white-breasted nuthatches and one tufted titmouse.

Wildlife refuges were more rewarding. The National Wildlife Refuge system begun by President Theodore Roosevelt in 1903 has been called "the last line of defense for America's wildlife." The 432 federal wildlife refuges in the United States represent every major ecosystem in the country, from broad-leaved deciduous forests and semitropical barrier islands to prairie potholes and fragile tundra. Many say there is nothing even remotely comparable to them in magnitude and diversity anywhere else in the world.

At first, refuges were managed exclusively for the preservation of wildlife. Fisher in 1953 was much impressed by Americans as custodians of their wild country and its inhabitants. But starting in the 1950s, the refuges were opened up to sports hunting, fishing and trapping, cattle grazing, and oil and gas exploration. In the 1980s they were further beleaguered by timber harvesting, farming, haying, concessions and, unfortunately, people — too many people. The fifty or so wildlife refuges scattered throughout the densely populated north-eastern United States constitute less than one half of 1 percent of the whole system in area, yet they receive almost 15 percent of the total visitors.

The Great Meadows Refuge at Concord was virtually deserted when we arrived. History had preempted birding for the day, although some children dressed in eighteenth-century costume — and carrying binoculars — were obviously trying to partake of both. The purpose of the 3000 acres of Great Meadows is to protect wetland habitat for migrating birds such as ducks and geese and shorebirds. We saw many of these, but the most memorable sighting was unexpected — a partially albino male song sparrow with a white body, a dusky head and wings, and a reddish tail. We added it to our list of other oddities, which now included an albino robin and a starling with a blue tail, perhaps painted.

We moved on to Concord's other attraction (some would say main attraction), Walden Pond, the home of the famous nineteenth-century philosopher Henry David Thoreau, who retreated there between 1845 and 1847 to live in solitude and contemplation of nature. Ironically, it is a lot less wild than Great Meadows. We lunched at Walden Pond, but so did hundreds of others. Now a National Historic Monument, Walden Pond attracts over 600,000 visitors a year. They trample vegetation and erode the pond's shoreline. For James Fisher too there had seemed no wildness left in Walden.

Gus drove next to the Atlantic Ocean at Newburyport, Massachusetts, to look for migrant birds stopping down at the Parker River National Wildlife Refuge on Plum Island after their winter in the South. We were surprised to find that we were almost the only people there. But birds were there en masse. I understood why they had landed after we got out of the van and felt the brute force of the Atlantic Ocean. It was almost impossible to stand against the blasting wind and the driving rain. The sea boiled white as rolling ramparts churned into shore and sent billows of spray bouncing skyward. I left my companions to the birds of pools and marshes and took the boardwalk to the beach. I wanted to see the Atlantic Ocean, to feel what the birds felt as they were buffeted through wind and wave. The sand blasted my face, and I had to push the wind away as if it were a wall, but I reveled in the wildness that was this day in America.

I was bird watching too. A medley of sanderlings scurried just beyond wave-reach till, lifted by the wind—or was it by intent?—they flew down the shore in one body.

On the marsh, flocks of Canada geese were grazing (this is one species that has never heard of the ecological depression), and northern harriers were hovering over the reedgrass. Shuffling about on its golden slippers was a white-plumed snowy egret, a bird related to the herons which we would be seeing much more of later as we went south. ''He looks as if he's just washed his hair and can't do a thing with it,'' Tess chortled.

But it was mainly a day for gulls — ring-billed gulls, great black-backed gulls, herring gulls, Bonaparte's gulls (my favorite), Iceland gulls. I spotted the rare little gull (*Larus minutus*), the smallest of the gulls. It is a Eurasian bird, a gull of the Old World that, like the black-headed gull, seems to be colonizing the New World. It has bred in Ontario, Michigan and Wisconsin.

The following day, April 20, we started south along the coast through Massachusetts, Rhode Island, and Connecticut, toward New York City. In contrast to the day before, the sun was out, the air felt warm, and the waves were a mere slap at the sea's edge. Weeping willows making fans of filmy green against blue skies meant that warblers could stop for the insect hatch. Mute swans were already nesting in the marshes, and a great egret stalked with stately steps on its black slippers. Like the golden-slippered snowy egret, it was expanding its range north along the coast and was probably breeding too. Spring's promise was about to be fulfilled.

We headed across the Pine Barrens toward New Bedford, Massachusetts. Once an almost continuous forest of pitch pine with stands of southern white cedar rising from swamps, the Pine Barrens since Peterson and Fisher's time has been crossed by a network of divided freeways. We sent a mental greeting to Roger Tory Peterson when we passed his house in Old Lyme, Connecticut. He was in Britain giving a lecture, so we spent the evening in Norwalk instead with Anna and Walter Byrom, naturalist friends of Gus's. Meeting the locals, one of the most rewarding aspects of our expedition, was a good way to get updated information on local conditions.

According to the Byroms, woodlands have increased in Connecticut in the past three decades as former farms have been abandoned and present farms have been forbidden development. And perhaps there are more eagles now as well, since the use of pesticides has been reduced. The Byroms said that one pair nesting in northeast Connecticut is being closely monitored. People take a more positive attitude toward predators than they did thirty years ago, and the state had just introduced fines of $500 for those who dare disturb eagles.

We continued south again the next day. Increasing signs of current civilization warned us that we could not put off big cities any longer — a maze of freeways and overpasses in perpetual motion; lines of cars, trucks, trailers, rushing like frenetic snakes beside us, away from us, toward us; dioramas of green signs bombarding us from the side, from the front, from above, like decks of cards unfolding for an instant, then whisked away; bridges soaring into the sky over smokestacks, and bridges spanning estuaries over boat basins.

Gus, who dislikes cities, warned us not to open doors to strangers. As navigator, I pored nervously over the map. Tess warned Gus that she would be hanging onto his coattail.

Perhaps we were being too harsh in our indictment of cities. Connecticut and New York State from Highway 95 was scarcely Wild America in the pristine sense, yet certainly there were pockets of wildness, or at least attempts to simulate wildness. And surprisingly, when we arrived we found that there was wildness in New York City too — Central Park, where famous early ornithologists saw their first birds and where present-day birders go to see their first warblers; the Battery Gardens, which we overlooked from our hotel room; and roof-top gardens, seen from the Empire State Building, had real trees. Long Island, extending 120 miles into the Atlantic Ocean and right in the middle of the Atlantic Flyway, attracts almost all of the 412 bird species reliably recorded in the New York City area. New Yorkers have only to stay in New York to see the vast majority of North American birds.

And if they want to see the rest of the natural world, they have only to go to the American Museum of Natural History, which now covers twenty-five acres. Peterson and Fisher had commented enthusiastically on interpretive devices such as individual phone lectures, the planetarium, and the 3-D Cinerama. There is now also a four-story-high screen called Naturemax, the most recent method of bringing into the museum the sights and sounds of the natural world on film.

Next morning we left the blue jays and mockingbirds of Manhattan and drove into Brooklyn. "I'm glad to say I've been here," said Tess, "but I'm also glad to leave." Gus as usual was oblivious to people and buildings and vehicles. He kept calling out fascinating facts like "See that tree on the boulevard? It's the Tree of Heaven, you know, the one from the novel, *A Tree Grows in Brooklyn*. It can withstand heavy air pollution."

Surprisingly soon, we left the highrises behind and drove onto a sandy hook of land at the entrance to New York Harbor—Jamaica Bay National Wildlife Refuge, a unit of Gateway National Recreation Area and part of the National Park System.

As I stood by the tern nesting area of the West Pond Trail and looked around me, I realized why Jamaica Bay is so special. To the west over New York Harbor was the longest single-span bridge in the world: to the north was the clutter and congestion of the Manhattan skyline; to the east was the thundering air traffic of John F. Kennedy Airport. Jamaica Bay is the only national wildlife refuge in the heart of a city. It is adjacent to the most densely populated metropolis in the United States, one of the most highly developed commercial and industrial regions in the world. Yet it shows how abused natural resources can be renewed.

There was no Jamaica Bay National Wildlife Refuge when Peterson and Fisher did their trip. Park ranger David Avrin told me that in 1953 the air was polluted, the waters were almost dead, many species had disappeared. This gateway to New York and New Jersey could have been developed as a seaport, a subdivision, or a shopping centre—or it could be managed as a wildlife refuge. Thanks to Robert Moses, a powerful New York bureaucrat, and Herbert Johnson, a dedicated horticulturist, and despite a shoestring budget, dikes were built, fresh water was created, plants attractive to wildlife were grown — and Jamaica Bay became a refuge.

Established officially in 1972, it has allowed millions of American city dwellers to enjoy a national park experience at their doorstep, not to mention the more than 315 bird species that have resided in or migrated through the refuge. Located under the Atlantic Flyway and having saltwater marshes, freshwater ponds, and uplands planted with trees and shrubs, Jamaica Bay is specially attractive to birds, and the rare is becoming commonplace. Common and least terns, black skimmers, piping plovers, egrets, herons, and the glossy ibis have chosen to breed. The avocet, two godwit species, all three phalarope species, the buff-breasted sandpiper, and the Eurasian curlew sandpiper and ruff have chosen to visit.

We passed a thick pole topped by a platform, one of two man-made nesting sites for ospreys, or fish hawks. Eastern Long Island in New York State once had one of the greatest concentrations of breeding osprey populations along the Atlantic coast. Since the pesticide DDT was banned in 1971, ospreys have begun to breed again on the East Coast, but bird watchers are still waiting for the first osprey to nest at Jamaica Bay.

There was a real feeling of spring in the air, and even of summer for those of us more used to northern climes. The yuccas were blooming, purple periwinkle and whitlow grass flowering, caterpillars hatching, yellow-rumped warblers flitting amid the fragrant bayberry, Canada geese already with young. Some birds that should have been winging their way north were still lingering.

As we left Jamaica Bay, fishermen were bringing in catches from the pier, bird watchers were consulting their field guides, schoolchildren were listing signs of spring. Such public interest augured well for the continued coexistence of people and wildlife in the country's largest urban-area refuge.

We spent that night and the following morning in New Jersey with local naturalists who are not only enjoying their hobby but are helping to conserve natural areas by donating money and time to various projects and by passing on their love of the natural world to other people, especially children. White-haired Midge Rowley treated us to a grand breakfast in her 200-year-old home overlooking an enchanting garden of spring flowers; energetic Vi Debbie teaches nature study to girl scouts, YWCA groups, senior citizens, and night school students; gracious Irma Johnson, a real Southern belle from Kentucky, flew up to join our expedition. We were to meet Midge, Vi, and another of Gus's guests, Gerry Breitenback, again in Alaska. These are the kinds of people whose bird-watching hobby stimulates them to support agencies like the Nature Conservancy, which in New Jersey has kept many thousands of acres of wild land wild. The Nature Conservancy had only just begun in 1953 when Peterson and Fisher made their trip.

Midge Rowley and Vi Debbie came with us on the drive down the

New Jersey coast. Vi's favorite birding spot was Brigantine National Wildlife Refuge. "Going to Brigantine is like dying and going to birders' heaven," she said ecstatically, getting in the car to lead the way.

As Jamaica Bay is to New York City, so Brigantine is to Atlantic City. Its 6,603 acres of salt marsh and barrier beach (out of a total area of 20,229 acres) is designated a National Wilderness Area, but the sights and sounds of civilization are very close. Philadelphia is sixty miles away, Atlantic City eleven miles away, the Garden State Parkway six miles away, and the busy Intracoastal Waterway cuts through the middle of the refuge.

In 1953 Peterson despaired that such little pockets of wildness were fast disappearing, that the sand dunes, barrier islands, and estuaries of the New Jersey coast were inundated by beach shacks, billboards, and hot dog stands, that the wild beaches of Barnegat and Brigantine were almost completely built up, and that only ten miles of seashore — Island Beach State Park — remained intact. Since then, groups like the Nature Conservancy and the National Audubon Society have acquired additional land for Barnegat and Brigantine, helping to make them more attractive to wildlife.

The Brigantine refuge was established in 1939 primarily for the protection and management of waterfowl passing through on the Atlantic Flyway. Spring and fall are still the best times to see the spectacular concentrations of ducks and geese (in November more than 100,000 birds on 1,600 acres) but there is lots to see in any season. More and more waterfowl are stopping to spend the winter at Brigantine, and many birds, such as the Canada goose, gadwall, northern shoveler, and ruddy duck, species that traditionally nested west of the Mississippi, are now nesting there in spring and summer.

We arrived at Brigantine on April 23, between the peak of the northbound duck and geese migration (March 20 to April 15) and the peak of the shore and wading birds gathering (April 20 to May 30). Brigantine seemed to be brimming over with birds. We counted sixty-three different species. But Vi was disappointed. "This is a dead day," she kept wailing as we drove slowly around the perimeter of the artificial pools on an elevated dike, stopped often to set up the scope for a closer look, and then climbed the tower for a wider view.

We had seen the first of the northbound brant a few days before at the Parker River National Wildlife Refuge on Plum Island. Now on the New Jersey coast we saw thousands of brant, the little goose with the black neck and the white stern ("Brant have pants," says Gus). Brigantine sees 90 percent of the wintering brant population and has been especially good to brant. About 1930, a blight suddenly struck the eelgrass, their chief winter food, and within a year or two most of it had disappeared. Beds of ribbonlike eelgrass have now recovered, but in the meantime brant have found a new food source, sea lettuce, to tide them over their winter vacation.

Large, showy waders like ibis, herons, egrets, and bitterns have now come north to nest at Brigantine. We were lucky to see the little blue heron, the Louisiana heron, the black-crowned night heron, and the American bittern. I enjoyed watching great egrets and snowy egrets, their chest and tail feathers blowing in clouds around them, strutting through the mud. Stiffly, like automatons, they poked their bills into the water. Suddenly one would spike a long mud worm, drop it when it wiggled, latch onto it again, wash it, gulp it down, reposition it like a person clearing his throat, gulp it down again, then lean forward in the water for a long stiff drink.

A high-pitched *pill-will-willet* drew my attention to a flying willet landing next to a small flock of long-legged gray sandpipers. Suddenly something sparked their attention and they rose into the air en masse, their drabness magically transformed. As all fifteen birds banked low over the water like a fan opening and closing, I marveled at the striking black and white bands of their wing pattern. I was to see many more willets in the weeks to come, and I always reveled in that remarkable change from nondescript to spectacular.

Tess and Gus added another part-albino to our oddity list, two black-bellied plovers, each with a white chest, an unusual characteristic that could not be explained as a mere change of costume between seasons.

The after-lunch period is usually the slow period of the day for birding, so that is when Vi took us to the upland area by the West Tower for some botanic wandering. The air was full of the aromatic smell of budding sassafras twigs and the purple mint, creeping Charlie (whose alias, Gill-on-the-ground, is a connection I cannot fathom). "This is what we do with the kids," laughed Vi, plastering a set of winged maple seeds on her nose. "See, a Pinnochio nose." The winged seeds of the red maples were a sign that spring in New Jersey was well under way, even if many of the birds had not yet left Brigantine for their northern nesting grounds.

Although Brigantine is mostly for the birds, there were plenty of signs of other wildlife: fox scats, dinner-plate-sized horseshoe crab carapaces, raccoon and deer prints, and the sounds of chorus frogs and spring peepers. The snapping turtles seemed still to be hibernating, but painted turtles were out swimming, a muskrat sunbathed on a bank, several eastern cottontail rabbits dived into the brush, and gray squirrels chattered from trees as we passed underneath.

Most people come to Brigantine to sight ospreys and peregrine falcons, raptors whose comeback on the New Jersey coast from near extinction is cause for celebration. We saw both. An osprey plunged into the water after a fish and emerged from the halo of splash with its quarry held lengthwise along its body, for better cleavage through the air. A pair of peregrine falcons circled the dike.

We passed a hacking station, a big wooden box on a platform set on top of four telephone poles, where falcons had been bred in captivity and fed till they could fend for themselves. They had migrated perhaps as far south as Central or South America, then returned to where man had put them to fledge, and were now ready to breed. A couple of months after our visit, three young peregrine chicks were successfully hatched at Brigantine.

Roger Tory Peterson can take heart in the return of the peregrine to the New Jersey coast. In fact, the coastal marshes of New Jersey's Island Beach State Park were the site of the first successful release of captive-bred falcons. In 1976 Paul McLain, deputy director of New Jersey's Fish and Game Division and Supervisor of its Endangered Nongame Species Program, headed a team that put three captive-bred peregrine chicks in a cage on top of a telephone pole. The birds came from Dr. Tom Cade's raptor breeding facility, the famed Hawk Barn of Ithaca, New York. Dr. Cade had tried the year before to release captive-bred chicks into the wild by hacking them on cliffs where peregrines had nested before; but the young birds, undefended by parents, were attacked and eaten by great horned owls. There was another problem. Birds raised by humans are imprinted to humans and are not likely to mate with their own kind. To avoid human contact, the hacked birds were fed from a chute that could be tripped by remote control.

Why all this trouble? Prior to the 1950s an estimated 350 to 400 pairs of peregrines bred east of the Mississippi River. The next decade saw their decline caused by a proliferation of DDT and other chemicals in the environment. These pesticides are most damaging when concentrated in animals at the top of a food chain — raptorial birds like eagles, hawks, ospreys, and peregrine falcons. The chemicals cause the female to lay thin-shelled eggs which are crushed easily by the brooding parent. By 1960 it was generally agreed that nesting peregrines east of the Mississippi were extinct. Twelve years later DDT was finally banned, at least in the United States.

For decades, falconers (who fly birds for sport) had been trying to breed falcons in captivity. I had been trying to do it myself in association with falconer friends in Canada. Several individuals had success, but it was not until the experiments of Dr. Heinz Meng, a professor at the New York State University, Dr. Tom Cade, director of the Laboratory of Ornithology at Cornell University, and Richard Fyfe of the Canadian Wildlife Service in Wainwright, Alberta, that success was achieved on a large scale. By the early 1980s peregrines hatched in captivity and hacked in the wild were returning to raise their own young. In the spring of 1983, as we searched for Wild America, two adult peregrines, Scarlett and Beauregard, hatched four healthy chicks — on the ledge of a thirty-three-story building in Baltimore, Maryland. They were the first peregrines to breed in an urban environment for thirty years. A year later, two pairs of peregrines nested successfully on bridges in New York City.

Currently, more than 100 captive-bred peregrine chicks continue to be released each year on towers, skyscrapers and traditional cliff sites between Ontario and South Carolina, and the breeding population appears to be doubling annually. It is expected that by the end of 1986, fifty to sixty pairs of adult falcons should be nesting in eastern North America.

Dr. Cade's aim is to have 175 pairs nesting east of the Mississippi River by 1990. This is about half the number of pairs estimated to be present before DDT started wreaking such havoc. DDT continues to be a problem because wintering peregrines still pick it up in Mexico and Central America, where the chemical is still in use. However, substantial numbers of both eastern and western peregrines seem to be reproducing in spite of it. The newsletter of the Peregrine Fund, a nonprofit organization dedicated to reestablishing peregrines in the wild, reports that an average of more than two young have been hatched for each nesting attempt since wild peregrines began breeding again in 1979. So the currently popular image of man the destroyer is being turned around, at least as far as the peregrine recovery is concerned.

Cape May, at the border of New Jersey and Delaware, has the reputation of being one of North America's top birding hot spots. The town is most famous as a junction for migratory birds, especially hawks. It was the New Jersey Audubon Society's bird observatory in Cape May State Park that we would be exploring.

At the peak of the fall migration, hundreds of birders gather at Cape May Point to make an annual census of migrating hawks and owls along the Atlantic Flyway. In 1977, in one day, 81,597 birds of prey were recorded at the point. Cape May also gives its name to the Cape May warbler. This warbler, the only one with chestnut cheeks, was named for Cape May because it was there in 1809 that the first specimen was seen, shot, and described by early ornithologists. Ironically, it was another fifty years before a second one was recorded there. Unknown at that time, drab plumaged juveniles of this species are present each autumn.

As it turned out, we found more birds by driving the streets than by standing on the sand dunes — perhaps because there were more of one than the other. Access to the beach along Cape May was continually impeded by residences and resorts. The best birding was at a sanctuary in the heart of town. Not that we could get inside — this one is strictly for the birds; people are not permitted to enter. "Stone Harbor Bird Sanctuary, Home of the Herons," says the sign. It is a twenty-one-acre, bush-lined marsh registered since 1947 as a natural landmark and is unique in being the only heronry in the United States sponsored by and located within a town. The sanctuary is totally surrounded by houses. We had to "get" what birds we could by walking around its edges. Still, there was something supernaturally splendid in peering through the fog and the leafing juneberry branches to see great egrets looking like ghosts as they sat displaying showers of white feathers in their own private domain.

Chincoteague National Wildlife Refuge occupies the lower third of Assateague Island, a sixty-mile-long barrier island straddling Maryland and Virginia. The refuge was the setting for Marguerite Henry's famous children's novel, *Misty of Chincoteague*, and is one of the most popular refuges in the United States. It hosts 1.5 million visitors a year. Local citizens, sensitive to the damage done by dune buggies and other off-road vehicles, are fighting those who would increase such access to its ten miles of beach.

Most people know Chincoteague for its wild ponies, which are thought to be descendants of mine horses surviving the shipwreck of a sixteenth-century Spanish galleon. Each year in the last week of July, the ponies are rounded up from the southern end of Assateague Island to swim at low tide across to Chincoteague Island, where some of the foals are sold at a public auction. The rest swim back to Assateague. The refuge is also famous for its oysters and clams, as well as an oyster museum. We found birds in abundance at the refuge, fifty-six species before breakfast.

Chincoteague offers year-round interpretation programs to get people involved in wildlife: counting deer at night in January, migrating hawks in September and all birds at Christmas, viewing waterfowl at Thanksgiving, collecting storm-tossed shells in winter, even helping transplant loggerhead turtles. The refuge conducts daily wildlife safaris by boat and bus.

We elected to walk with Gus through the pinewoods. The trees were alive with tweets, chirps, whistles, lisps — and the sound that all bird watchers try to make to attract birds out of the bush. "Pish! Pish!" While "pish-ing" in the Chincoteague pinewoods, we bumped into the advance guard from the Outdoor Club of the University of Montreal, who told us excitedly of seeing a dickcissel. This bird, about the size of a house sparrow, used to breed along the eastern seaboard between Massachusetts and South Carolina. It is occasionally seen in winter at bird feeders in the company of sparrows, but it winters mainly between Mexico and South America. It spends its summers raising young and cracking seeds in fields in the American prairie states between the Rockies and the Appalachians. So seeing a dickcissel on a barrier island beside the Atlantic Ocean was certainly worth adding to one's rarity list.

And then, in unison as if led by the same conductor, all kinds of gulls landed on the pavement in front of us. They faced into the wind as if to say, "Well, we're here. Now which one of us did you want?"

Hawk-eyed Gus picked out our quarry immediately, a black-headed gull, except that it did not have either a black head or a brown head — it had a white head. And it was not an adult, it was an immature. Well, knowing the differences, not just between species but between ages and sexes as well, is what makes the experts so expert. Gus and I crept out of the van and closed in to take a picture of the rare European visitor. None of the other gulls appeared perturbed.

We stalked sparrows and gulls until it was time to leave Chincoteague and the Atlantic Ocean, at least for a time. While the others were packing the picnic supplies away, I rushed across the dunes for a farewell look at the long sweep of sand and the foaming, smoking waves.

Driving west to Washington, D.C., spring was finally in full flood: fields of lush green grass, dogwoods flowering in pink and white, and to Marjorie's delight, magnificent magenta blooms on the eastern red-bud trees. Gus was grappling with the map, but he still had time to point out purple martins nesting near houses, cedar waxwings feeding in a flowering cherry tree, turkey vultures and peregrines circling overhead, and as we swept into the sky ourselves on the four-mile-long Chesapeake Bay Bridge, a solitary royal tern.

Gus was prepared to drive past the architectural splendors of the nation's capital, but we'd have to see a bird before he would stop. Thanks to Washington's other claim to fame, its many parks and gardens, we did — Bonaparte's gulls by the Tidal Basin, Caspian terns by the Washington Memorial, ospreys over the Lincoln Memorial, rough-winged swallows at the Jefferson Memorial, and house finches at the Department of Justice.

Washington's famous cherry blossoms had wafted away three weeks before. Marjorie had missed the city's annual rite of spring, but she could still find an artificial spring of tulips and daffodils massed by every monument and a wild spring in Rock Creek, Plummer's Island, and along the Chesapeake and Ohio Canal.

Rock Creek Park, 1,754 acres of natural woodland following Rock Creek, is one of those "fingers of wilderness penetrating Washington's heart" that James Fisher had extolled. Rock Creek, once described by President Theodore Roosevelt as "wild as a stream in the White Mountains," now gurgles brownly past playgrounds, tennis courts, biking, riding, and jogging paths, old forts, an art barn and a grist mill, not to mention the National Zoo. Hardly wild, but Gus used its nature trails as a setting for his talk about plants.

I was fascinated by the shapes and colors of tree trunks. The blue-gray bark of the American hornbeam looked like flexed muscles. The splotched yellow, brown, and white of the American sycamore looked like leopard skin.

"Here's a Japanese barberry bush," Gus said, waving me toward him. "These yellow flowers are beautiful. Tickle their stamens and they snap shut. This is their way of getting cross-pollinated. When a bee visits the flower, it gets slapped by the stamen."

One is never at a loose end in the bush. The trees were flowering but not yet thickly leaved, making it easier to spot birds amid the branches, especially the red flashes made by woodpeckers and northern cardinals.(A week later we would have to identify most birds by sound.) We followed them as they flitted through the branches, listening to the *hee hee hee* of the tufted titmouse, the *tea daddy tea daddy tea daddy* of the ruby-crowned kinglet, the *drink your teeee* of the rufous-sided towhee, the *chee* wheeze of the blue-gray gnatcatcher. "Some of them are no bigger than blowflies," marveled Tess, straining to keep each tiny flicker focused in her binoculars.

Although many people know Rock Creek, we had difficulty finding Plummer's Island, the island in the Potomac River where Peterson and Fisher had enjoyed their spring picnic in 1953 with the cream of Washington's custodians of the natural world, the people whose passion it was "to keep wild America wild." Plummer's Island, described by Fisher as "one of the most intensively botanized, zoologized, ecologized wild islands in the world," was established as a nature preserve way back in 1901 by the Washington Biologists' Field Club.

The island is located between locks ten and eleven on the Chesapeake and Ohio Canal. The 185-mile-long canal was opened in 1828 as an economical transportation route to link the commercial establishments of the East with the frontier resources of the West. Eventually flooding did it in. And flooding from the recent record rains that had preceded us all along the East Coast made it impossible to get to Plummer's Island. Marjorie and Miss Smith decided to stroll the towpath, but Gus, Tess, and I trekked to the Potomac. Tall, bare tree trunks stood in the muddy water drowned to their knees, their thighs, their chests. Even the flowering woodlands were in flood. We swished knee-deep through lush green fields of appendage water-leaf kaleidoscoped with blue phlox, yellow ragwort, Virginia bluebells, sessile trillium, and lacy-leaved white bleeding heart-like squirrel corn, which really did have niblets of "corn" when we dug them up.

As we drove back to Washington for a rendezvous with some of Gus's guests from former trips, we wondered how much had changed since Peterson and Fisher were here together picnicking on Plummer's Island. Local knowledge again helped to answer those questions. Nancy and John (with their cat, Walden) Pond and Elizabeth and Henry Allen joined forces to treat us to a wonderful dinner from their combined gardens. Henry, who has walked ninety miles of the C. and O. Canal, said that despite opposition from conservationists who wanted "more canoes and fewer cars," the farmland along the Potomac did give way to parkways and overpasses and beltways. However, the towpath was restored and the canal in 1971 became a national historic park. One hopes that with the increasing numbers of canoeists, hikers, cyclists, fishermen, and bird watchers, there is still room for the birds.

Peterson in 1953 had found at least 400 pairs of black-crowned night herons nesting in the wild above captive night herons in the zoo at Rock Creek Park. The wild herons had been stimulated to nest by their captive brethren. ''Herons still nest there,'' said Elizabeth, ''but in much smaller numbers. I spotted eighteen to twenty large, twiggy nests on the outside of the cage, which now, by the way, houses bald eagles.'' Black and turkey vultures were also attracted to the zoo by the magnet of free meat put out for the captive birds. ''You still see them around,'' added Elizabeth, ''but in tens now, not hundreds.''

At the nature center in Rock Creek Park, you press a button and a board lights up to show twenty dots, representing twenty animals that once lived along the Potomac before pioneer days. One by one, the lights go out. Today, birders have increased manyfold in Washington, headquarters of dozens of conservation agencies. One can hope that in this showplace of parks and gardens, the birds and other wildlife will increase too.

Although we agreed with Roger Tory Peterson that Washington was a satisfying city for a naturalist, we were all glad to be zinging west along the freeway toward the mountains — especially Gus. At intervals between telling jokes and pointing out broad-winged hawks riding the thermals, he prepared us for Appalachia. For the next few days while driving through Virginia, North Carolina, and Tennessee, via the Sky-line Drive of Shenandoah National Park, the Blue Ridge Parkway, and Great Smoky Mountains National Park, we would be exploring about 600 miles of the 1,600-mile-long Appalachian Mountain chain. It was a recycled wilderness — wilderness that since pioneer times had been logged, farmed, hunted, mined, and eroded. Now, as cut-over forests were growing back, worn-out fields were being revegetated, and some wildlife species were reappearing, the wilderness was being restored by both man and nature.

Less than a hundred miles west of Washington we climbed the foot-hills of the Appalachian Piedmont to the famous Blue Ridge, a wall of very old, very resistant rocks upon which a highway had been built. The Skyline Drive and Blue Ridge Parkway are not freeways scarred by billboards and businesses like other freeways in North America, but scenic country roads that undulate along the crest of the Appala-chian Mountains, swinging from side to side to give views of immacu-late storybook farms in green valleys and vistas of parallel ridges and hills rolling away to the hazy horizon. Most people in the eastern United States live within two days' driving distance of Appalachia, yet from our highway in the sky on this end-of April day, few other vehicles traveled with us, and we had the illusion of being far removed from civilization.

We swung in and out of spring according to elevation: sometimes down to 600 feet among the just-budding deciduous hardwood trees, the serviceberry, magnolia, redbud, buckeye, tulip, and flowering dogwood, other times up to 5000 feet among dark coniferous evergreens, the Fraser fir and red spruce; sometimes down along streams among groves of dripping hemlocks, other times on open ridges among pine and oak and hickory. Still, spring of any kind was very late this last week of April, and the view from the van was of rather a drab brown world.

Gus's nature travelogue never stopped. "These rocks are among the oldest on earth. Once, they may have been higher than the Alps or the Rockies, but over the ages they have been worn down by erosion. Once, their slopes were covered with trees, but for 200 years they have been heavily logged and burned. Many of the trees you see now were probably saplings when Peterson and Fisher came through. In another thirty years, though, they'll be forest giants — for this part of the world anyway."

At the southern end of the Blue Ridge Parkway in the Great Smoky Mountains National Park where the Appalachian forests reach their climax — a mere 780 square miles in area — famed naturalist-writer Edwin Way Teale says that there are more species of native trees than in the whole of Europe (131), almost half the total of bird species for Great Britain (200, including in spring a galaxy of wood warblers), fifty kinds of fur-bearing animals, eighty kinds of fish, more salamanders than exist in any other area of the world (about thirty), 1,300 flowering plants, 330 mosses and liverworts, 230 lichens, and twenty six orchids. And more species are being discovered all the time.

Why such abundance and variety? As Peterson explains so succinctly, the trees of the Appalachians survived the "Big Ice" because these mountain ran north to south, not east to west, as in Europe. When the Ice Age came to an end, some of the hardier trees spread northward again via the valleys, while others climbed the mountains. In addition, the old Appalachians have such diverse landforms within them — coves, or naturally terraced valleys, near the foot of mountain slopes: balds, or grassy openings, near the summits of mountain peaks: sphagnum bogs; steep shaly barren ridges; gaps and gorges where wind and water have cut passes through the mountains—that there is a range of habitats to attract and create a variety of species.

It is all very well to know the virtues of Appalachia in theory, but to find them for ourselves, we had to get out at the various viewpoints and look, or stop at the different trailheads and walk. The park ranger at the Dickey Ridge Visitor Center in Shenandoah National Park said that she had been waiting a month for the flowers to be out and was still waiting. However, at places like the Fox Hollow Nature Trail, Hawksbill Gap, Big Meadows Visitor Center, Smart View, Rocky Knob, Mabry Mill, and Mount Mitchell State Park (the highest point in eastern America), we found enough of interest to please us all.

There were always surprises sprouting from dead leaves, flitting amid "dead" twigs, or moving against dull skies. Treasures like a pipevine swallowtail butterfly on a blue phlox, or a woodlot of painted trilliums for Marjorie ("You're trampling the trilliums!"), a yellow-bellied sapsucker for Tess ("I thought a name like that must be made up"), boxwood for Irma ("There's a southern mystique about boxwood. It speaks of home and mother and family"), a field sparrow singing in a tree ("It has a *pink* bill!"), and for me, a red-tailed hawk flying by with a vole in its claws, and six rufous-red ruffed grouse strutting sedately down the road ("Lovely birds with the rich colors of our malleefowl," said Tess).

There were manmade treasures too — zigzagging split rail fences, gracefully arched stone bridges, abandoned log cabins, and restored gristmills. Stopping to look at these reminders from the pioneering days made me think back to Wild America when it was forested east of the Mississippi, when mountain people came West to hunt and log and farm, when lumber companies came in to cut what was left of the last primeval forests. Wild America here would have disappeared forever had it not been for the chestnut blight of the late 1920s, the subsequent end to raising razorback hogs that thrived on chestnuts, the establishment of national parks in the 1930s, and the displacement of most of the mountain people. There are still some chestnuts, some hogs, some farms, some mountain people, but Appalachia is returning to its roots. Perhaps not the same — why should it be? — but a Wild America we will have to live with and learn to appreciate.

As I looked west to Kentucky and West Virginia past fields that looked filmy and unreal, as if recently given a pale green watercolor wash, past endless waves of blue ridges — navy blue, mulberry blue, slate blue — fading to gray in the distance, I thought of hardwood forests there that had been mined naked, of forty to fifty bird species reduced to less than ten. But I remembered that the strip-mined sites had returned to grassland, that horned larks, eastern meadowlarks, red-winged blackbirds, savannah sparrows, grasshopper sparrows, and vesper sparrows had responded to the new habitat and had come to live here. Weedy species perhaps, less diversity certainly, but a Wild America nevertheless.

It was almost midnight when we stopped for the night at Asheville, North Carolina. We were now close to the best-kept wilderness of all, the Great Smoky Mountains National Park, straddling North Carolina and Tennessee. The name comes from the smokelike haze that envelops these mountains, a haze caused by both people and nature. We had been looking over this sea of billows and troughs all along the Blue Ridge Parkway, but in the Great Smokies it was more intense. And so were our expectations of spring.

"Be near Asheville, North Carolina, the third week in April, and you will see the warblers pour across the mountains," Ludlow Griscom, famed field ornithologist, had told Edwin Way Teale. And that is how I expected to see them, a wall of warblers like colorful butterflies flitting northward from the Caribbean, from Central and South America, keeping pace with unfolding buds and expanding leaves, resting in the still bare branches, feeding on the hatching caterpillars. And I expected to see wildflowers. "Come to the Smokies the last week of April for a wildflower pilgrimage," said the travel brochures. "Springtime in the Appalachians is like nowhere else in the world."

Two million tourists a year visited the Great Smokies in 1953; closer to ten million poured through the park's gates in 1983. By the billboards, hotels, and souvenir shops, by the noise and garishness, it seemed to me that they were coming for resort recreation rather than warblers and wildflowers. "The Most Photographed View in the Smokies," said the sign. But when we left our vehicle and focused the free telescope by the overlook, our view was of a dull clump of buildings on a far hill, a ghost town needing advertisement. "Welcome to the World's Largest Bingo," said the sign at Cherokee. "Stay at the Tomahawk Hotel," or "Visit the Wigwam Craftshop," said others. The Cherokees had learned to live in a land not of wilderness but of white society's dollars.

We knew we had reached the national park when the billboards ran out. It was Wildflower Weekend and the masses were there — not wildflowers as much as people, hundreds of them to a group, walking behind park naturalists. They were of all ages, all walks of life: some needed sticks, others wheelchairs. "People return year after year even though they have seen it all before,'' said Irma, having been here with Gus before. Admittedly, not all were interested in picking out plants or watching birds. One young man was photographing his car parked by a waterfall.

So far it had been a disappointing spring. Nature had gone by her own idiosyncrasies, not by the calendar. The current of warm water known as El Nino had upset the ecological balance everywhere, Newfoundland and New England included. In 1983 this ''dislocation of the world's largest weather system flung high winds, rampaging floods, and the misery of drought around the world,'' according to *National Geographic*. Now we saw its effects in the Appalachians. ''I've never seen the Smokies so devoid of flowers at this time of year,'' sighed Irma, for whom Appalachia is almost home territory.

Even the warblers were sparse. This could have been caused by El Nino or other factors far away in Central and South America. Ornithologists such as J. W. Terborgh were predicting that forests in the tropics, where the migrating birds wintered, were being cleared at such an alarming rate that they would be gone completely by the end of this century. And since the densities of wintering birds are much greater than their summer densities, the clearing of one acre of tropical forest is the equivalent of removing five to six acres of breeding habitat. In an attempt to test the theory that fewer migrants were returning to the Appalachians to breed, another ornithologist, George A. Hall, studied a virgin tract of red spruce and hardwood forest and found that indeed both the number of species and the number of birds had declined over the years of his study. Hall could not give precise reasons, but he ruled out pesticides, cowbird parasitism, and fragmentation of the northern habitat. He suggested that the most likely cause for the decline was removal of the tropical forests.

It may be surprising to non-naturalists, but we found most of our birds and plants in areas associated with people, in sunlit clearings on the edges of woods such as the Oconaluftee and Sugarlands visitor centers, and the Pioneer Farmstead, a reconstructed open-air museum.

''Everything is here,'' enthused Marjorie, turning her back on the Pioneer Farmstead. While the others went off to the woods, I poked around the farmhouse, the woodshed, blacksmith shop, corn crib, and sorghum mill, and was rewarded by the sight of barn swallows feeding their young on a ridge pole.

When I caught up with the others, each was spellbound by spring in the glade and along the river. Marjorie was burying her cameras in the colorful flowers. Gus was pointing out two of his favorite bushes and trees to Irma and Miss Smith. "The silverbell is one of the nicest trees in the Smokies. Look at these pendants of white bells. And this yellow-root bush is a lovely thing. Most people don't notice it, but note its drooping clusters of tiny prune-colored, star-shaped flowers." Sometimes Gus sounded like a tape recorder or a Delphic oracle, but he certainly knew his stuff. Tess of course was wandering with her outsize binoculars in her own little world of birds, entranced by two male indigo buntings ("looking as if they'd just been dipped in inkpots") hopping after a more drably dressed female, by white-throated sparrows lisping in a tangle of Japanese honeysuckle, a Louisiana water thrush tail-bobbing in the river, a pileated woodpecker bouncing between the trees. I kept running into the ubiquitous tufted titmouse calling *Peter, Peter, Peter*. I don't know if I was more intrigued by its name, its pointed crest, or its beady black eyes.

But it is the woodland wildflowers that have center stage in early spring. Taking advantage of warmer air and maximum light before the canopy of another year's leaves closes over them, the first flowers of spring erupt from woodland floors, woodland swamps, and woodland streams, not yet the massed tapestries of color—pink mountain laurel, purple rhododendron, flaming azaleas—that clothe the slopes in later spring, but delicate individual buds and blossoms that make contrasts more compelling.

Yellowy brown hoods burn from the juicy green leaves of skunk cabbage. Jacks, looking like greenish candles, peer from the striped canopies of Jack-in-the-pulpits. White sundials rise out of the crinkly green leaves of bloodroot. Luminescent magenta stars are cradled against the rich green leaf stars of red trillium. Delicate white cars nod above the fernlike leaves of Dutchman's breeches. Mauve petals wave above the dark green liver leaves of hepatica. Fine pink lines etch the white petals of the wide-leaved spring beauty. Miniature green stars of club moss sprout out of oak leaves, like a cedar forest on the ground. Violets, blue, yellow, and white, push like tiny lights through brown beech leaves.

Tess and I sang "On Top of Old Smoky" vigorously, if not tunefully, as we headed up to Newfound Gap by the highway across the park. "Vegetatively speaking, we're going north to Canada," said Gus, "leaving behind spring wildflowers and flowering broad-leaved hardwoods and climbing up to spruce and fir country."

Theoretically, each hundred feet of elevation means one day's retreat from spring. Spring creeps slowly up the mountains, taking from six to eight weeks to reach the summits. We in our van would be telescoping that journey, climbing to the ''top of old Smoky,'' Clingmans Dome — at 6,643 feet, the second-highest peak in the Appalachians — in less than an hour. As Gus pointed out, it would be like taking a trip fifteen hundred miles to the north in Canada.

At Newfound Gap, the highest point on the transpark highway, we found El Nino had struck again; the road to Clingmans Dome was closed by unseasonable snow. Instead, we hiked part of the Appalachian Trail which crosses the road at Newfound Gap. Few have hiked the 2,000-mile trail between Maine and Georgia in its entirety, but thousands have sampled sections for an hour, a day, or a week. As we stepped from one protruding root to another on the much eroded trail, it was clear that this section was highly popular.

The warblers were awaiting us at Sugarlands Visitor Center. Not miles of them, as Edwin Way Teale describes, but more than we had seen on our way south. Some were planning to stay for the summer, others were just stopping to refuel en route to more northerly nesting grounds. Two warblers in particular looked outstanding. The Blackburnian warbler was named after a Mrs. Blackburn, who collected stuffed birds and was a patron of ornithology. The back of this warbler's head and back is black and its throat is a burning orange. The hooded warbler is perhaps the most striking warbler of all. James Fisher described its black head and yellow mask very aptly when he said that ''it looked as if they had pulled black Balaklava helmets too far down on their breasts to stretch a great gap through which their yellow faces peered.''

The creature I most wanted to see — or even hear — was the cat with many names, the eastern panther, or, as it is known in different parts of North America, the cougar, puma, or mountain lion. Having studied cougars in the wild and raised them in captivity in the West, where they are common (although not commonly seen), I was anxious to get from researchers in the East the latest information on their search for the eastern panther. The park ranger at Rocky Knob on the Blue Ridge Parkway had told me of a hot line by which panther sightings were reported to Donald Linzey of the Virginia Polytechnic Institute in Blacksburgh, Virginia. Bob Downing, a biologist with the U.S. Fish and Wildlife Service, told me from Clemson, South Carolina, that his funding for the search had run out, but that he and Linzey were going to carry on by themselves.

In referring to the animals thought to be extinct in the Appalachians since 1900 — the eastern panther, timber wolf, eastern bison, and eastern elk — Roger Tory Peterson commented in *Wild America* that "a few mountain lions, even in this modern era, would not be a bad idea." He added that the "half-starved and runty" deer in Pennsylvania and West Virginia might even benefit from some predatory selection. Attitudes to panthers have much improved since then. Die-hard hunters and farmers still want to exterminate them, but there is considerable interest everywhere in increasing their numbers.

Although there is one small population of eastern panthers in Florida, no one knows for sure if the cat exists elsewhere in the East or is extinct. People like Bob Downing and Donald Linzey believe that there are so many sighting reports (fifty-six between 1900 and 1981) that small numbers must be surviving in the coastal swamps and restored forests by living on the white-tailed deer, whose numbers are probably higher now than they were when the Pilgrims landed. Admittedly, some of the sightings when checked turn out to be house cats, hoaxes, or released captive panthers and many sightings remain unsubstantiated. But Bob points to the panthers killed in Pennsylvania in 1969, in Tennessee in 1971, in West Virginia in 1974, in Virginia in 1978, and in North Carolina in 1981. "How many have to be killed before skeptics believe in the cat's existence?"

It is still a seesaw situation in the Smokies. Stuart Coleman, the resource management specialist who collects panther sightings in the national park, said that there have been eight to twelve reports a year for the past four years. "The trouble is, we have no pug marks, no scats, no reliable photographs, no bodies. And many people report black panthers, when ours are tawny. I think it comes from watching too much TV."

"Well, black or blackish cats are reported in South America, Florida, New Brunswick, Manitoba, even British Columbia," I replied, ever hopeful. "I know some scientists are skeptical, but specimens reported to be black have been collected in Florida and South America. Still, I know what you mean. The black panther of India is more likely to be known to the general public than the tawny eastern panther here."

Stuart was recording sightings, even putting out synthetic scent stations near the Cades Cove Visitor Center to see what animals might be attracted, but he was not in favor of putting panthers back in the Smokies. "The park is only about sixty miles wide and thirty miles long, too small a sanctuary, and panthers don't recognize road signs, so if they were transplanted here, they would end up damaging somebody's livestock, fouling up somebody's deer hunt, and scaring people. It's not practical."

Nevertheless, Stuart would like to know for sure if the eastern panther still exists. "If it's extinct, our policy allows for western cougars to be introduced, but not otherwise."

Stuart was pessimistic when I asked him about the changes to the natural world in the past thirty years. "I don't think we're winning. There are too many introduced non-native species like the European wild boar. Boars are now through 85 percent of the park, a tremendous disturbance. To give you an idea of the damage boars cause, imagine seeing the forest floor after a rototiller runs over it two or three times followed by a hundred inches of rain. Then the balsam woolly aphid from Europe is infecting the Fraser fir, a relic from the Ice Age. And the introduced rainbow trout is beating out the native brook trout."

He was concerned that the Great Smoky Mountains National Park was like a bufferless island, with summer homes built slap against its boundaries, causing less wild habitat for native wildlife. He was worried that pollution limits were being exceeded, that acid rain was damaging the trees.

After a noisy night in Gatlinburg, a resort town at the northern entrance to the park, it was a relief to visit the homes of the Stupkas and Baldwins. Peterson and Fisher had visited with these naturalists in 1953, so perhaps I would discover from them if we were winning or losing in our battle to conserve a more natural world. Their homes, signposted Wildlife Sanctuaries, were only five miles from Gatlinburg, but they were at the end of a gravel road with unsurpassed views over the highest peaks of the Appalachians, all of them mile-high mountains. "We're looking along thirty-five miles of border between North Carolina and Tennessee," said Glidden Baldwin when he welcomed us to his sanctuary.

The neighboring Stupkas were away. Arthur Stupka, now in his mid-seventies, was the first park naturalist in a national park east of the Rockies. It was he who had laid out all the trails in the Great Smokies. Arthur had recently re-married — on Valentine's Day — and was away with his bride on his honeymoon.

The Baldwin house was alive with bird song when we arrived. White-throated sparrows were bathing in a pool by a sign labeled "Chipmunk Crossing," yellow-bellied sapsuckers were drilling an oak tree, white-breasted nuthatches and Carolina chickadees were flitting around the hemlocks, an American goldfinch was vying with a ruby-throated hummingbird at the bird feeder, a couple of fence lizards were skittering over the woodpile. The bonanza, especially for Tess who comes from a country without any, was three of nature's hammerheads — the red-bellied, the downy, and the hairy woodpecker, all males.

Both Glidden and Flora Baldwin are optimistic types, so apart from saying that gray foxes had vanished primarily because of an influx of humans to the area, they took a positive view of man's effect on the natural world, a view no doubt stimulated by seeing that world from their eyrie in the skies.

We spent our last day in the Appalachians hiking the trail to the Ramsay Cascades. Glidden said that thirty years ago, Peterson and Fisher could drive halfway along the Ramsay Prong (a prong is a fork in a river). Now man was trying to reverse the usual exploitation-of-nature theme. Some of the roads were permanently closed, parking lots had been revegetated, roads had reverted to trails.

It was four miles to the top of the cascades. Miss Smith decided to hike to the end of the trail while the others, with differing interests and hiking speeds, sauntered along with Gus. Always attracted by what was around the next corner, I chose to follow Miss Smith.

This was the Trail of the Big Trees so loved by Fisher. More than twenty different trees in the Smokies have set all-time records for size and growth — the Canada hemlock, silverbell, red spruce, yellow buckeye, and mountain ash — but accustomed to the coastal forests of British Columbia, the California redwoods, and the Western Australian hardwoods, I was not as impressed as perhaps I might have been. However, these were taller and wider than any trees we had encountered elsewhere in eastern North America.

As I rushed along the narrow, twisting footpath (really a root path) and crossed and recrossed the bubbling stream, there was no time to stop and turn over rocks and logs to look for the salamanders for which the Great Smokies are renowned. But I could not resist taking quick photos of the striped pipsissewa, the showy orchis, and the strikingly leaved rattlesnake plantain.

And then around the next bend, across the next stream, and over the rickety bridge, we reached our destination, the Ramsay Cascades. The sign read: "Climbing beyond this point is hazardous. Four deaths from falls here since 1971. Please don't be next."

It was a pretty area and well populated with people picnicking, but I had no time to explore. Miss Smith, for whom this was the last day on the trip, opted to stay to enjoy the waterfalls that plunged over the rock ledges. I decided to scramble back along the trail four miles to join the Baldwins and the rest of the group for a farewell dinner to the Smokies.

Ivory-billed Woodpecker
Campephilus principalis

Chapter Three
The Southeast
May 1–15

Irma Johnson, Marjorie Dutton, and Miss Smith left us in Atlanta, and we picked up Emily Hamilton from Toronto. Emily, with her peaches-and-cream complexion, looked fragile and walked with a cane (a result of a recent hip operation), but she had rafted the Nahanni River and had hiked through Nepal. She acted like somebody who could handle Wild America. She was well prepared for the trip: she was dressed immaculately for the tropics in white slacks, white blouse, white hat, and white shoes; she had each day's itinerary neatly organized with maps — current maps *and* maps of thirty years ago when Roger Tory Peterson and James Fisher had traveled; she knew the number of miles between our destinations, and she had prepared background information on our objectives. Emily was an amateur botanist whose special aim for our expedition was to find the rare Florida torreya, a member of the yew family.

Emily referred to Peterson and Fisher as "the boys," and after a few days with her, Tess Kloot and I did too. " 'The boys' didn't talk about *Torreya taxifolia*," she said in her slightly English-accented voice, "but I would like to see it. It is found only along the Apalachicola River west of Tallahassee. So while you look for the ivory-billed woodpecker, I'll look for the Florida torreya."

"And I'll look for the Florida panther," I smiled as I helped Emily into the van.

But first we had Georgia on our mind.

Signs of a southern landscape were all around us. The kudzu vine, introduced since Peterson and Fisher's time, according to Tess "shrouded trees, fences, and roadside slopes like a giant cobweb." There were paddocks of black-trunked pecan trees, orchards of new-leaved peach trees, even some of last year's cotton — and roses, roses, roses, the official flower of Georgia. Spring had decided to stay. Deciduous trees were fully clothed, the redbud was in leaf, elm trees had winged seeds, magnolias were magnificently flowered — and people were wearing swimsuits.

We fell asleep that night in Thomasville to the high-pitched churring of crickets and an orchestra of frogs: swamp chorus frogs that kept changing the tune, stopping, starting, adding more notes as if they had made a mistake, rehearsing, then returning to their original theme. I was captivated by the variety of their songs: short, sharp notes back and forth like a whipsaw, continuous thrumming like playing a comb, dancing up and down the scale like xylophones. Emily reminded us how fascinated "the boys" had been too.

Next morning we were guided around Thomasville by Leon Neel, one of the foresters who had guided Peterson and Fisher in 1953. We saw 300- and 400-year-old trees in a unique forest on the Greenwood Plantation, one of the few virgin longleaf pine forests left standing. This private estate of the John Hay Whitney family is a remarkable success story of cooperation between private enterprise and government agencies. Since the 1940s it has been managed by selective cutting and controlled burning to provide aesthetically pleasing trees, excellent timber, some of the best bobwhite quail hunting in the world, a haven for nongame species like the endangered red-cockaded woodpecker, and a garden of wildflowers that includes more than ten rare orchids. It was multiple use in action, and it worked. So far.

"The family would like to save this as a national monument," Leon explained as we drove along the red sandy track of Pinetree Boulevard through trees that looked planted, not pristine. "But conservation is expensive, and one wonders how long the family can afford not to harvest all these pines."

The family's policy has been fortunate for the red-cockaded woodpecker, who needs such mature, well-spaced pine trees for nesting. Leon took us to three of them. Half a dozen birds were having a tremendous game, tearing from one tree trunk to another, calling noisily, so seemingly quarrelsome that one sees why an early ornithologist called this woodpecker *Picus querulus*.

We could identify the nest hole by its surrounding circle of resin. The red-cockaded woodpecker has the unique habit of drilling holes through the bark of a living pine tree to wound the cambium layer and cause the pitch to flow freely. It returns to the same tree year after year until it can no longer make the gum flow. Perhaps this is to protect its nest hole from predators such as snakes. The canny woodpecker always chooses a tree that already is rotten at the core. Its other habit, extracting worms that bore into the ears of corn, makes it welcome at Greenwood Plantation, which is a farm as well as a forest.

"What a lovely fragrance the resin gives!" exclaimed Tess while we continued our efforts to freeze the chattering, chasing birds in our lenses.

In the next minute, we found two more things to remember Greenwood by: blue grosbeaks for Emily and Bachman's sparrows for Gus Yaki, life birds for both of them. "You don't often see this shy sparrow," said Gus, trying to focus one in his scope, "and its numbers are declining, especially in the northern parts of its range."

Scattered through the pine forest were saw-palmetto ("I don't think you'll find a lovelier plant in the south," said Leon), bracken and cinnamon ferns, wild azaleas, lilies, grass-pink orchids, and the orange milkwort called yellow bachelor's-button. I tried to catch a black-masked fox squirrel in my camera as it scampered off through the trees. "You see something new every five minutes," said Emily contentedly as we meandered back to the van.

Florida — Land of Flowers, Vacation Paradise, Retirement Haven. Florida — where ten million people live and five million more are expected by the end of the century. Florida is wild, but much of that wildness has been packaged to attract tourists to Monkey Jungles, Parrot Jungles, Orchid Jungles, Sea Worlds, Disney Worlds, Cypress Gardens, Tropical Gardens, Aquariums, Seaquariums, Serpentariums. Plants, reptiles, birds, mammals, even the knees of cypress trees, put on shows to entertain those who try to escape northern winters by flocking to this lush subtropical neon-plastic retreat.

Despite the commercialism of "Cheesecake Florida," as James Fisher called it, there are other Floridas. The real Florida, says the Department of Natural Resources, is found in its eighty-eight state parks, which represent almost every type of habitat found in the state — beaches, offshore islands, springs, rivers, lakes, woodlands, open prairies. The real Florida, says the Department of the Interior, is found in the federal wildlife refuges and national parks. The real Florida, says the Florida Trail Association, is seen along 1,000 miles of hiking trail, which stretches from one end of the peninsula to the other. The real Florida for birders may be found anywhere — in a saw-palmetto thicket, in a suburban garden, or even in the air above a troupe of scantily clad water-skiing maidens.

We spent the night at one outstanding private tourist attraction that has a bit of all Floridas — the four thousand acres of Wakulla Springs Wildlife Sanctuary. It has glass-bottom boat rides over the world's largest and deepest spring, and cruises down the Wakulla River through jungle gardens with a Disney-style commentary that includes Henry, a pole-vaulting fish, but it is not commercialized in the worst sense.

We arrived at Wakulla in time for the last boat ride of the day — and the last four seats. As we left the dock, everything happened at once. It was like Disneyland with free entertainers who played themselves, like a zoo with caged spectators.

An anhinga, cousin of the cormorant but with a black, furry body and feathered wings and tail, jumped out of the water and stood spread-eagled to dry itself on a branch. An anhinga is sometimes called a snakebird because often when it swims only its head and long, slender neck are seen out of the water, making it look like a snake. It is also called a water turkey, because when it soars in the air it fans out its tail the way a turkey does.

No sooner had I quickly clicked off a shot of the anhinga than a female limpkin landed on a shallow nest of eelgrass anchored on the water's surface. This long-billed, white-spangled brown bird dropped a shiny apple snail in front of her single four-week-old young who gobbled it greedily, shell and all. If the chick had been much younger, she would have worked at the shell with her bill to release the soft body inside. Fortunately, there seemed plenty of snails, the main diet of this gangly bird, to satisfy its avid appetite. Reeds and cypress knees were clustered with the snails' egg masses, which looked like pinkish white pearls. The limpkin is called the crying bird because of its eerie wail at night, a sound that some say is like a woman lost forever in the swamps, and others say is like the call of the Florida panther.

Edwin Way Teale in 1951 called the Wakulla River the Limpkin River because it was the only place he knew where "these rare shy birds can be seen in numbers close at hand." Two years later, Peterson estimated that twenty-five pairs of limpkins nested along two miles of the same river. The limpkin is common at Wakulla but elsewhere it is rare, restricted to west and central Florida, and Georgia. It was once found all over the state, until almost wiped out by hunting. Now it is making a comeback.

There were birds wherever we looked: pied-billed grebes diving underwater; gaudy red-billed common moorhens with chicks splashing behind; regally colorful wood ducks sitting above them in nest boxes; black vultures draped in trees like huge black fruits or sailing gracefully overhead; then, surprisingly close, an osprey diving to catch a bass. The cooperative boatman was continually trying to get me into the best position to take pictures. The tameness of birds in this sanctuary makes it an obvious mecca for wildlife photographers.

The birds performed well, but it was the alligators that thrilled most of the visitors. All aboard craned forward when the boatman announced baby alligators and one-year-olds clinging to logs. Adult alligators with tails swishing back and forth like fins drifted disarmingly peacefully beside our boat. One alligator that has become a legend at Wakulla Springs is 200-year-old Joe, who was killed in 1966. His assassin has never been found, despite a reward of $5,000. China and the southern United States are the only two places on earth where alligators are native. Once endangered, they are now protected and increasing in Florida.

Next day we drove to St. Marks National Wildlife Refuge, 100 square miles of marshes, swamps, pine-oak uplands, and water along the Gulf of Mexico. "Get your bird books out," said Gus. "Peterson and Fisher saw 125 different species of birds in a day here, and mostly New World species. Note that the farther south we get, the more uniquely American birds we see."

St. Marks was established in 1931 to provide habitat for wintering populations of waterfowl and for birds using the Mississippi Flyway on spring and fall migration. The largest concentrations of waterfowl are seen from mid-November to mid-January, and Gus, who comes to Florida most years, was forever commenting on how few birds we were seeing in spring as compared to winter. Certainly, many of the ducks and geese had already left for the north, but we managed to see at least seventy-five species of birds on our day at St. Marks.

The National Audubon Society has reported that wetlands (the marshes, swamps, bogs, meadows, potholes, and sloughs that are essential habitats for waterfowl) are disappearing at the astonishing rate of 458,000 acres a year. The U.S. Fish and Wildlife Service estimates that remnant tracts of native grasslands are being lost at the rate of 2 percent annually. Both agencies agree that ongoing losses in breeding, migration, and wintering habitat have resulted in alarming declines in some waterfowl species such as mallards, pintails, blue-winged and cinnamon teal, dusky and cackling Canada geese, white-fronted geese, and black brant in western North America, and black ducks in eastern North America. Deborah Holling, a park naturalist at St. Marks, agreed, adding that ring-necked ducks and American wigeon have declined dramatically, at least in their use of the refuge.

The Audubon Society considers that there has also been a thirty-year decline in redhead and canvasback ducks. It has a Blue List, or early-warning system, for identifying declining species. The list is based largely on the Christmas Bird Count, compiled on one day each year when armies of avian observers all across the continent go out and count birds. The Blue List for 1982 recorded declining numbers of roseate terns, least terns, least and American bitterns, wood storks, fulvous whistling-ducks, and piping plovers, and local declines in numbers of great egrets, snowy egrets, yellow-crowned night herons, and glossy ibises.

Gus told us how he felt about the issue. "Thirty years ago, there was a lot more water on the prairie, where most of these waterfowl nest. But many of the prairie potholes were drained for farms, fewer eggs were hatched, so fewer ducks come south. I believe the trouble is also due to overhunting. Limits are too high for many of the popular species, and many dead or injured birds are not recovered. Lead shot often kills long after it is fired from a shotgun. When it falls into a marsh it is often picked up by a duck thinking it is food. If food is scarce, that lead pellet will kill the duck. What is needed is a total ban on lead shot, using steel instead."

Although refuges were originally established to be sanctuaries for wildlife (the first was established at Pelican Island, Florida, in 1903), hunting has been permitted since the 1950s where numbers of waterfowl warrant. Some hunters may not have an ecological conscience, but hunters generally spend a lot of money to conserve waterfowl habitat by paying taxes and buying licenses and joining organizations like Ducks Unlimited, which work to buy and restore waterfowl habitat.

And many species are increasing in number — mallards and wood ducks, most subspecies of Canada geese, most snow geese, most white-fronted geese, Ross's geese, eastern brant, tundra and trumpeter swans, reddish egrets, and cattle egrets. As we saw driving down the Atlantic coast, the breeding ranges (if not the numbers) of the glossy ibis, snowy egret, cattle egret, Louisiana heron, willet, black-necked stilt, and American oystercatcher are expanding northward. Some naturalists believe this range expansion could be due to the birds losing habitat in one area and going elsewhere to find a replacement.

Certainly, wetland habitat continues to disappear, and protected lands such as government wildlife refuges and private sanctuaries continue to be assailed by threats both within and outside their borders. But people are cooperating increasingly to do something about these dangers. The U.S. Fish and Wildlife Service in conjunction with the Canadian Wildlife Service has launched a comprehensive continent-wide management plan to conserve wetlands and waterfowl. This program will continue into the next century. In Florida, the Audubon Society has inaugurated a program whereby sponsors endow memorial wildlife sanctuaries to conserve land for all wildlife, including waterfowl. Many other agencies, both public and private, are making the acquisition and conservation of wetlands a top priority.

Getting at the truth is confusing, especially because all the facts upon which judgments must be made have not yet been discovered and all the factors are not yet known. Agriculture, industry, and recreation may be the main offenders, but they are not the only ones.

At the entrance to St. Marks refuge, Gus called, ''Wild turkey crossing the road.'' In fact, we counted thirteen in all.

''Fancy,'' exclaimed Emily, ''and 'the boys' saw only one!''

Next to cross the road was an alligator, his armored back covered with duckweed, making him look like some green monster. And then a turtle, a yellow-bellied slider, followed by a Blanding's turtle. ''There's a soft-shelled turtle on the road,'' called Gus quickly. ''I've never seen one out of water.''

His keen eyes picked up a dead great-crested flycatcher on the road and a live one perched on a nearby post. And then a dead chuck-will's-widow, a nighthawk, or goatsucker, killed on the previous evening's foray. We had scarcely driven off again when Gus called, ''Snake crossing, but I don't know what it is.'' It slithered by before we could identify it, but we still scurried to our mobile library in the van to try. It was certainly the day to keep our eyes on the road. We were buried in our snake pages when Gus called, ''Black rat snake.'' As we watched it squiggle over the bank, we read that it was a declining species. A few minutes later, we picked up two dead armadillos, prehistoric mammals that look like iron tanks and are not declining. They have spread north to Texas and Louisiana from Mexico, on their own, but came to Florida in settlers' luggage.

Standing at a single point near the lighthouse where the St. Marks and East rivers meet the Gulf of Mexico, I could see double-crested cormorants (each with its own post) perched on an old boat dock, snowy egrets and green herons stalking in the mud behind a fluttering pool of willets, American avocets sweeping their upturned bills like scythes through the lagoon, least terns dipping and dunlins stitching along the shoreline, and a mullet jumping in and out of the sea like a child skipping stones. And nesting on the door latch of the lighthouse was a pair of Carolina wrens, a species which some ornithologists believe is declining in northwest Florida.

The climax of our day came as we were driving away from the refuge. ''Swallow-tailed kites, hurry!''called Gus with unusual vigor as he skidded to a halt. Tess leapt out first. "What a graceful creature! Look at the way it opens and closes that long forked tail like a pair of scissors," she said, as if in a trance.

From now on, we would be seeing the natural and the unnatural worlds side by side: managed sanctuaries and remaining pockets of wilderness in the mornings; the commercialized wild in the afternoons. It seemed appropriate to begin our exploration of the civilized world's interaction with the natural world in St. Augustine, the first permanent European settlement in the United States. It was near here that Juan Ponce de Leon, the Spanish Governor of Puerto Rico, landed on April 2, 1513, to claim the land for Spain and name it La Florida.

"Marineland in five minutes," announced Gus as we drove down the coast. "Just in time for the last show."

When Roger Tory Peterson took James Fisher to Marineland in 1953, it was the only exhibit in North America (and perhaps in the world) to star a marine mammal performing acts like leaping out of the water to take fish from a human hand. It was the only oceanarium to house hundreds of fish, sharks, and turtles all in the one tank. Since then, dozens of cities in North America (and the rest of the world) have opened marinelands, so many that now the name is generic. Fisher was fascinated by the aerial gymnastics of one species, dolphins, or as they are known commonly, porpoises. Since then, seals, sealions, otters, walrus, manatees, and all kinds of whales have been made captive to entertain man — and they are taught to do such tricks as raise flags, put out fires, throw balls, and give handshakes. Once, an hour might have sufficed to see the show. Now it takes a whole day. Visitors hurry through landscaped pools and gardens, shell museums, "nature walks," and "jungles," past drink stands, snack bars, restaurants, fudge shops, cocktail lounges, souvenir stores, and teahouses, to be on time for penguin shows, tropical bird shows, manatee exhibits, electric eel demonstrations, and mood films of undersea life projected in Spacevision.

Although as Gus would say — often — "this is not the real world," marinelands have served some useful functions. They have funded research into the natural history of the sea, demonstrated the intelligence of marine mammals, bred them in captivity, and changed people's attitudes to once-maligned predators such as orcas, who are more likely now to be known as lovable circus clowns rather than killer whales. Some marinelands concentrate more on entertainment than on education and research, but happily, there has been a shift recently for all marinelands to dramatize the natural behavior of the captive animals rather than teach them human tricks. St. Augustine's Marineland had established a model for other marine attractions and was still in the forefront of research, but its current physical condition was very much betraying its age.

We were now back to the Atlantic Ocean, driving along Daytona Beach for part of its twenty-three miles of hard-packed sand, along the famous track where at low tide motorists outnumber swimmers. Now in the off-season, when the tourists had gone home and the hotels and restaurants along the promenade were deserted, we barreled down the sand with brown pelicans for companions. Long strings of pelicans undulated above the surf zone, arching and dipping over the waves. "I read that some sadist is cutting off their beaks to stop them fishing," said Gus as he drove. "Vets are putting on fiberglass beaks, but the sadist is cutting the birds' beaks back farther, so even the plastic beaks are no good. Many pelicans die too when fishermen snag their pouches."

Fishermen, however, were not the cause of the brown pelicans' demise in the early 1960s. In Florida the population was stable, but there was a severe decline in the Carolinas, two nests only in Texas, and total extinction in Louisiana where, ironically, it is the state's official bird. Like those of hawks, eagles, and falcons, the brown pelicans' eggs were contaminated by the pesticide DDE (a residue of DDT), passed on in their food, which in the pelicans' case was contaminated fish. This chemical poisoning was heaviest in the highly industrialized Mississippi River region. Since then, DDT has been banned, Florida birds have been re-introduced to Louisiana and Texas, and the brown pelican has its own recovery team and the "Brown Pelican Newsletter" to monitor its progress. Another bird makes a comeback.

"You'll want the Kennedy Space Centre," said the five-starred officer as Gus dutifully came to a stop next day by the sign that said "Cape Canaveral Air Force Station."

"No, we want the Merritt Island National Wildlife Refuge," Gus replied patiently.

Both attractions would have been new to Peterson and Fisher. Both share Merritt Island, a twenty-five-mile-long barrier island that protects Florida's east coast from some of the ravages of the Atlantic Ocean.

Ironically and uniquely, the refuge was not set up to protect migrating or wintering birds, like others along the Atlantic seaboard. Merritt Island Wildlife Refuge was a gift from NASA, which preferred birds as neighbors and offered its acquired land to the U.S. Fish and Wildlife Service.

More birds come now to the Merritt Island marshes than they did in the 1960s, when NASA began launching man into space. Its salt-water estuaries, brackish marshes, hardwood hammocks, and pine-woods provide diverse habitats for more than 285 species of birds, 25 mammals, 117 fishes, and 65 amphibians and reptiles. The refuge supports about 19 species listed as either endangered or threatened — more than any other refuge in the United States.

Despite the scowling clouds that turned into pelting rain and the "wrong" season for birding ("In November, these ponds would be black with birds," said Gus), despite the use of the refuge for hunting and fishing, despite its proximity to an attraction for millions of people, Merritt Island for us was a bonanza indeed. All the wading birds were there — herons, egrets, bitterns, ibises, stilts, several plovers, and one wood stork, a species whose numbers are very low in Florida.

It was a day for sandpipers — spotted, semipalmated, western, pec-toral, and, to Gus's delight, eighteen solitary. "This has got to be a world convention of solitary sandpipers," he enthused. "I've never seen so many of them at one spot. They're still migrating north. They may have wintered here, in the Bahamas, or as far away as central Argentina."

My thrill for the day was photographing black skimmers at a convention of their own, hundreds of them standing by a creek, facing the wind. When I moved toward them, they fluttered up a few feet, then landed again as if loath to leave. Skimmers get their name from their habit of flying low over the water, cleaving their knifelike lower mandibles through the water to skim off fish. They have several bizarre features: they are the only bird whose upper beak is shorter than the lower one (by one third); their short, stocky legs contrast with their extremely long wings; and they make short, barking sounds, some-thing like a puppy. But I find color is their most fascinating feature — their bright red beak tipped black at the end, and their black head cut off at eyeline by white. Skimmers look as if they have no eyes.

Another outstandingly colorful bird, a favorite with Emily, was the roseate spoonbill, a southern specialty. It was the next best thing to seeing the wild American flamingo. Flamingos are common in commercial establishments in Florida; since these birds are not native to the United States, I am never sure if a wild flamingo is an escape. Our roseate spoonbill with its greenish gray head, white neck, pink wings, red legs, and bizarre rich pink on its white chest looked to Emily as if it had been dipped, like an Easter chick, into a succession of paint bottles. Its pinkish red feathers glowed like fire in the spasmodic sunshine.

"Well, at least if we see a seaside sparrow on Merritt Island or over on the St. John's River, it'll be a dusky," I commented as we got back in the van. "They can't be found anywhere else." The dusky seaside sparrow is the rarest creature on earth. The last one that was seen in the wild, on June 20, 1980, was on a marsh by the St. John's River close to Merritt Island. Since duskies have a life expectancy of nine years, it is doubtful if any of them are alive today in the wild. There were five birds alive in captivity, all males. All except one have died. When it goes, the last of its kind will have left this earth forever.

In 1953, when Peterson and Fisher saw one on Merritt Island, there were perhaps 4000 of them in the vicinity. Their numbers declined drastically when their natural salt marshes on Merritt Island were diked to control mosquitoes, when a four-lane expressway was pushed through the St. John's River marsh, and when housing developments, pasture improvement, uncontrolled fires, and drainage ditches destroyed even more of their already restricted habitat. By 1968 only 900 pairs remained. By 1979 only thirteen males were left. No females have been seen since 1975.

Although it is impossible to save the subspecies, scientists have crossed the male duskies with females of the closely related Scott's seaside sparrow and have produced several hybrids. It is mathematically possible after six generations to get a 98.4 percent dusky hybrid, enough of them to be reintroduced into the St. John's marshes and Merritt Island — that is, if the aging male dusky stays alive.

Sign number nine on Merritt Island's Black Point Wildlife Drive looked onto the NASA building where rockets are assembled prior to launching. As we left the island and headed inland toward Orlando on a four-lane highway, I could not help wondering why man was spending so many billions to explore the barrenlands of space when the real treasures were here on Earth. Simplistic, maybe, but it seems to me that the money should be spent on maintaining the treasures we already have.

Perhaps the animals will have their way. In 1983 the estimated 5,000 wild pigs that roam NASA's land threatened its network of underground cables and communication lines by rooting for bugs, worms, and grass shoots. Trappers could not keep up with the pigs' breeding success. Space center officials still routinely clear runways of pigs — and alligators — to prevent damage to shuttle craft during landings.

The Big Top and the Big Dipper of Circus World rose above the citrus groves that edged the highway as Gus educated us. "Do you realize the scrub jays disappeared from here when man took over the pinelands to grow oranges? Scrub jays are now found only in a few localized areas. The species is in trouble."

James Fisher was enchanted by Cypress Gardens, both by its aquaballerinas and its butterflies. Since his visit, the original tropical gardens and water-ski revue has expanded in typical Florida fashion to include a southern town, a three-story-high film representation of such natural wonders as Mount St. Helen's volcano and the Grand Canyon, a computerized multimedia presentation of the South's legendary heroes, a children's funland, and an exotic bird revue where macaws water-ski.

Still, we were able to make close contact with several hundred birds, most of them rare, some nesting, living a more natural life in Cypress Gardens' huge forty-foot high, 15,000-square-foot, walk-in aviary. Emily, Tess, and I enjoyed the stunts of barefoot ballerinas on swiveling water-skis and four-tiered pyramids of tuxedoed skiers, pulled through the air behind motorboats shooting across Lake Eloise. But Gus lifted his binoculars above the bikinied maidens and concentrated on the wildlife overhead. "There's an osprey nest over there in the bald cypresses, and a great blue heron sitting above," he murmured.

Guiltily, we looked away from Corky the ski clown soaring in free flight in front of us and joined Gus in watching nature's spectacle. An osprey folded its wings, plunged into the lake, snatched up a fish in its talons, and, screaming continually, offered it to its mate. Even closer to us, a rock dove nested on the loudspeaker, a wood duck landed near the stage, a boat-tailed grackle fed on a dead fish, and there were double-crested cormorants, red-winged blackbirds, blue jays, starlings, fish crows, and ospreys doing a courtship flight. We were probably the only ones in the audience to notice.

As we strolled along the lake and through the various gardens, Emily recorded plants assiduously: a 1,600-year-old cypress tree, a magnificent bougainvillea capable of producing a million blooms a season — it was then producing a crop of nesting mourning doves — and a gigantic banyan tree. Perhaps Cypress Gardens did not have the same native diversity as when it was a swamp, but to my way of thinking, it was still full of life. I felt that James Fisher would have agreed. Gus was of a different mind.

"If this country hadn't been taken over by resorts and commercial attractions," he said as we drove south across the lake-studded Kissimmee Prairie, "we'd be seeing sandhill cranes, burrowing owls, and crested caracaras by now. Probably scrub jays too."

Suddenly a raptor with something dangling from its talons, perhaps a rat, flew low across the hood of the van and flapped into the sunset as a silhouette. Our first bald eagle. The Kissimmee Prairie is one of the better places in Florida to see bald eagles.

Despite its status as the national bird of the United States, the southern bald eagle is an endangered species. Little more than 1,700 pairs of birds breed in the contiguous forty-eight states, and only ten of these states have more than twenty-five nests. However, with recent management techniques — such as breeding eagles in captivity and releasing them into the wild through hacking stations, particularly in the East, and also relocating eagles from British Columbia to Santa Catalina Island in California, and establishing breeding pairs on reservoirs in Florida — they are increasing slowly everywhere in the United States, where once they were virtually decimated. There are reported to be sixty nesting pairs in Florida.

Next day was a relaxing one driving below a dike around Lake Okeechobee — the lake that nobody can see. This large freshwater lake connects on either side to the canal known as the Intracoastal Waterway, effectively making south Florida an island. Its waters are so shallow that wading birds may be seen a mile offshore. Our objective this day in cattle country was to find cattle egrets, as well as the sandhill cranes and crested caracaras we had missed the day before. We also wanted to see a short-tailed hawk, a bird that in its North American range is unique to Florida and probably is the state's rarest raptor. It is a crow-sized black or black-and-white bird so inconspicuous that it was not until 1977 that a photograph of it was published.

We kept glancing up at the sky for soaring hawks, but it was the ground that was more engrossing: on one side, palm-girt paddocks where retinues of cattle egrets followed grazing cows and where several pairs of sandhill cranes with reddish young walked like stately periscopes; on the other side, Australian casuarina trees full of elegant butterflies and dragonflies, and beyond that the marshy lake with limpkins calling. There were so many alligators in the canal among the water lettuce that I wondered why alligators were still considered an endangered species. Turtles splashed into the water and vulture-like, red-faced caracaras perched on fence posts as we passed. Even our windscreen had wildlife — it was plastered with thousands of mating lovebugs.

According to our original itinerary, Sam Grimes, one of the two ornithologists who in 1953 found and photographed the first cattle egret nest in North America, was to take us to the Kings Bar rookery in Lake Okeechobee, as he had taken Peterson and Fisher the day after his momentous discovery. When our schedules conflicted, we phoned him instead. He was rather pessimistic about changes he had noticed in the environment during the past thirty years, citing birds that he rarely saw now, like the hairy and red-cockaded woodpeckers, the loggerhead shrike, and some of the warblers. He blamed it on too many people and too little virgin timber. Like Gus, he agreed that the "weedy" species — the opportunists, the colonizers — were increasing, birds that moved into new areas and learned to adapt to a life with people, birds like house sparrows, starlings, mockingbirds, and cattle egrets.

We did not need Sam to show us cattle egrets. Dozens of these white birds decorated black olive trees like gold-tipped candles, strode like gods over the blooming water hyacinths, caught frogs, or pecked insects from the grass disturbed by grazing cattle. The cattle egret is a heron, but it does not compete with other herons for food. It fills a different ecological niche, primarily feeding on insects disturbed by grazing cattle or working tractors. And it has been remarkably suc- cessful — the species has increased worldwide. In North America cattle egrets have expanded their range as far north as Oregon and have even been sighted farther north, near my home in British Columbia.

I was just thinking optimistically about the cattle egret when I glanced out the van window to see and hear a subdivision-in-progress. The signs read "Real Life Ranch" and "Ancient Oaks RV Sales." Beside them construction machines were ripping out the soil, most of the cabbage palms, and all the ancient oaks except one, and were planting concrete instead. Gus grimaced.

We looked for Wild America in back yards between Clewiston and Belle Glade on the southern edge of Lake Okeechobee. Tess saw her first smooth-billed ani, the clown of the cuckoo world, flopping about on a private lawn. Anis, either the smooth-billed ani or the groove- billed ani, are unforgettable. "They look so unkempt, as if they just got out of bed," she laughed, "and their long tails look so awkward. They're an extraordinary bird, so primitive, even more so than our currawongs back home."

"I think they look like pterodactyls with that big black Roman nose," I added. "At least their feet are zygodactyl — two toes forward, two aft. Look at the way they clamber around the trees."

"Look in the next garden," called Gus. "You've got both members of the cuckoo family together, smooth-billed anis and yellow-billed cuckoos, and right beside them common and boat-tailed grackles. Good opportunity to compare them."

Anis and cuckoos and grackles have a lot in common: looks, behavior, and an ability to get along with people. Like the cattle egret, they are all expanding their range northward. A flock of smooth-billed anis blew in from the West Indies in 1937, and later, many anis began to nest in Clewiston. One particular ani, an abandoned fledgling raised as a pet, became famous. Not surprisingly, it was called Little Orphan Ani. Anis work together to build a communal nest, then the females lay their eggs inside in regular layers with leaves between. The birds sit on the nest together to hatch their eggs. When the top layer of eggs is hatched and the young fledged, the leaves are scraped away and incubation continues with each succeeding layer till all the eggs are hatched. A curious bird.

Anis and cattle egrets are recent arrivals in Florida. So are many others: insects, molluscs, crustaceans, more than fifty foreign birds, amphibians, reptiles, fish, and mammals, and innumerable exotic plants. They have walked in, flown in, swum in, boated in, hitchhiked in. They have come in both accidentally and purposely. Walking catfish escaped from a fish farm after a heavy rain and since the mid-1960s have proliferated through the canals of southern Florida and are heading north. Nine-banded armadillos that escaped from a zoo in 1924 and a circus in 1936 have now spread north to the Carolinas. Brazilian water hyacinths planted in a private pool in the 1880s and Asian hydrillas that escaped from aquariums in the 1950s have choked Florida waterways, and biologists expect them to spread throughout the country. Australian pines (casuarinas) and bottlebrush (*melaleucas*) are spreading through the Everglades. Despite more stringent controls, the list of alien creatures living in Florida grows longer, crowding out native species, changing original landscapes so that Florida looks more like India, Africa, Southeast Asia, South America, than it does native North America.

At the top of the list of aliens in Florida is *Homo sapiens*. Many of them think that manicured lawns, ornamental ponds, orderly canals, and carefully structured gardens are an improvement on the impenetrable swamps, forests, and palmetto thickets seen by Ponce de Leon. Millions of tourists a year and 4000 would-be residents *a week* come to Florida. The coast between West Palm Beach and Miami is crammed wall-to-wall with housing developments. Fortunately, there are still islands of original wilderness in southern Florida, and people who are working assiduously to maintain them. Turning our backs on the strip of artificial wonders along the east coast, we drove to the Loxahatchee National Wildlife Refuge on the eastern edge of the Everglades.

Loxahatchee was established in 1951 as a sanctuary for endangered species, especially the Florida subspecies of the snail kite, the Everglades kite. While my companions walked the boardwalk through the cypress swamp and the footpath over the marsh, I called in at the visitor center to talk to wildlife biologist Jean Takekawa about the most recent research into the biology of the Everglades kite, a bird whose habit of living almost entirely on apple snails is causing it problems.

"You probably won't see one here today," Jean said. "This kite is very erratic. It flies to where the water and apple snails are. We run a Kite Hot Line to monitor the population, and at the moment, most kites are not at Loxahatchee but at Lake Okeechobee and the Tamiami Trail. You should go and talk to Steve Beissinger at Shark Valley. He's winding up a five-year study on them there."

Prior to the 1950s the Everglades kite used to be common on freshwater marshes throughout Florida, but when "the boys" saw one quartering the reeds for snails in 1953, Peterson estimated "probably no more than twenty-five remaining." By 1964 the U.S. Fish and Wildlife Service believed that the kite population had declined to fifteen, fewer than either the California condor or the whooping crane, and that the surviving kites all lived in the Loxahatchee refuge.

Since then kite numbers have increased. "Prior to the drought in 1981 we had about 600 kites, although our latest figures for 1983 show about 250," Jean continued. Like many wildlife managers in Florida's refuges and national parks, she was fearful that in the ongoing battle for water between man and wildlife, man always wins and wildlife always loses.

Emily had sponsored Gus in the Long Point Birdathon. For one twenty-four-hour period he had to become a bird twitcher to raise money for the Long Point Bird Observatory on Lake Erie in Canada, the place where birdathons began and where more birds are banded for study than anywhere else in North America. Roger Tory Peterson and Robert Bateman had been the featured birders in previous birdathons, and today Gus was the invited guest. He decided his best bet to see the most species in the shortest time was the day we drove from Miami to Everglades National Park.

Miami, a port city with most of its native vegetation replaced by exotic vegetation, is a haven for exotic birds. Some birds are so localized that they have addresses — right down to street and house numbers. If an alien bird has nested successfully for ten years, the American Birding Association allows it to be counted as an official North American species. We just had to go to its address and count the bird at home.

"Look out for the spot-breasted oriole," said Gus as freeways like concrete snakes spewed us into the sky then dropped us down in coils to the ground.

"That was the bird 'the boys' found," said Emily. "It was first seen in Miami in 1949 and, to our knowledge, first nested there in 1953."

We reached Greynolds Park in north Miami at about four o'clock. It is truly an oasis of wildlife within a city. We saw thirty-two species in an hour.

It was prime time, just before sunset, to see birds pouring into the park to roost for the night: white ibises, tri-colored or Louisiana herons, great blue and little blue herons, black-crowned and yellow-crowned herons, cattle, great, and snowy egrets, and anhingas and double-crested cormorants. They lit up the mangrove trees with noise and color and movement. Their squawking and squabbling outdid the noise of traffic that hummed in the background.

Birders come to Greynolds Park to see the scarlet ibis, a long-billed wading bird known for its intense, almost painted-on colors. However, some of the scarlet ibises here were pink, some were white, and others were rather an indeterminate in-between. "In the early 1960s some eggs of the scarlet ibis from Trinidad were put in the nests of white ibis in this park," Gus explained. "Over the years the offspring have mated with the white ibis, and now some of the remaining offspring are pink."

Next day we were up early — with the birds — to continue the count, this time in the company of one of Miami's best birders, Morton Cooper. A tall, sun-tanned commercial artist with a white sculptured goatee beard, Morton takes his bird watching seriously. The licence plate on his Volkswagen read BULBUL, standing for the red-whiskered bulbul, a Southeast Asian bird that escaped from captivity in the 1960s. A handful of escapes has now grown to several hundred.

"Eighty-seventh Avenue used to be the western extension of the bulbul's range," he told us, "but now it's spread to 97th Avenue where I live. I saw one there last week." After considering birds like the cattle egret, whose range spanned a continent in a decade, I was intrigued with a bird whose range spanned a few streets. With Morton leading in his BULBUL car, we headed to his house to check his bird feeder. No bulbuls, but in a fig tree outside his house we did see a monk parakeet tearing away at a ball of Spanish moss to make a nest. This gray-green bird comes from Argentina and has tried to nest in a number of states from Massachusetts to Florida and west to Oklahoma, but according to our Peterson field guide, it is not expected to be successful.

Florida did have a native member of the parrot family, the Carolina parakeet, but it was extinct by 1920. At least two exotic members, the South American canary-winged parakeet and the Australian budgerigar, are well established in Florida. Perhaps the monk parakeet nesting at Morton's will be the next.

We continued our search for bulbuls up and down the streets, along wires, through the hedges of tennis clubs, into strangers' gardens.

"Let's try Ruth Gallagher's on SW 104th Street," suggested Gus. "She built bird feeders especially to entice bulbuls. And I've often got thirty other species in a few minutes in her garden."

There were no bulbuls there, however, and we followed Morton to other oases of wildlife in the city. We never did see the elusive bulbul, or the spot-breasted oriole, but Gus got excited at Key Biscayne sewage lagoon when he saw thirty bobolinks migrating along the east coast, when they usually used the west. I got excited at the airport to find tough little burrowing owls digging their own homes out of hard Miami oolite (sedimentry limestone rock), when in the West they take over burrows abandoned by badgers or ground squirrels. Andy Beck from the University of Florida told me he had found frogs down owl holes, although the owl's chief prey are insects and rodents.

By mid-afternoon we had only a few hours left to increase our tally. "We'd better get to the Everglades," said Gus when we parted from Morton. "On the way we can pick up a white-winged dove at the Redlands Fruit and Spice Park."

We were certainly bird twitchers at Redlands. No sooner had we clambered out of the van than Gus yelled, "There's the white-winged dove cooing in that coconut palm! We've got him. Back in the van."

All the way to the Everglades we were followed by common nighthawks — the bird with the outsize gape — sitting on posts, cruising low over the fields, hunching like dead leaves on the ground — fifty of them in all. Gus was amazed that there were so many, but it was species we needed now, not numbers.

"You've got forty-five minutes left, Gus," said Emily, the timekeeper.

Our best bet was to skip the Royal Palm Visitor Center and walk the boardwalk of the Anhinga Trail across Taylor Slough, which is where many of the Everglades' wildlife pictures are taken. We had come to the Everglades at the onset of the summer rainy season and had to expect wildlife to be scattered, but there were still a lot of animals along the Anhinga Trail: plops and ripples and splashes in the water beneath us testified to fish, frogs, snakes, turtles, alligators, and anhingas. But for the Birdathon we needed birds, and time was fast running out to find them. Gus photographed a great white heron, but because some ornithologists consider it only a different color phase of the great blue heron, he knew he would be unable to count it as a separate species.

A real find for the Birdathon would be a Cape Sable seaside sparrow, which like the dusky is a race of the seaside sparrow *Ammodramus maritimus*. Also like the dusky, it is an endangered species. Fisher had commented that the Cape Sable seaside sparrow was so rare that "not even Roger had seen it." It is a very secretive bird that shares its range with look-alikes such as swamp, savannah, and grasshopper sparrows. But if anybody could find it, we knew that Gus would.

Like the dusky seaside sparrow, it has a very restricted range: just a few square miles of freshwater prairie between Cape Sable, the southwest corner of the park, to Everglades City, the northwest corner. Nonmigratory and living in such a narrow habitat, its numbers have been devastated by hurricanes, fires, and encroaching mangroves. In 1953 "a few score" lived in the marshes south of the Tamiami Trail near Ochopee, but in 1975 only two singing males could be found there. Then in 1971 a new population of about a thousand was found at the Taylor Slough.

Suddenly Tess pointed upward and shouted, "Look, Gus, a swallow-tailed kitc! It's got a ball of Spanish moss in its beak . . . Oh, my! Did you see that? It's playing with it, dropping it, turning absolutely upside-down, catching it again, dropping it . . . Can you believe what you're looking at? Now that I've seen anis and swallow-tailed kites, I can die happy."

The kites were hard to leave, but with ten minutes to go for the Birdathon, we went looking for small birds through the junglelike hardwood hammock of the nearby Gumbo Limbo Trail. Immediately, we picked up a white-eyed vireo, a rose-breasted grosbeak, a cardinal, and a Carolina wren — four birds in about four minutes.

At the end of the twenty-four-hour period, Gus had sighted eighty-two species. It was almost dusk, but with the rest of the Everglades waiting, he had no intention of stopping just because the Birdathon had finished. There were many more trails, many more ponds to explore before we arrived at our destination thirty-five miles farther on at Flamingo on Florida Bay. I forgot I was tired when a naturalist at the Royal Palm Visitor Center told me that a Florida panther with young had been seen the week before on the service road leading to the research center, and another adult near Eco Pond. Gus drove down the Research Road (once a cornfield), but I did not see a panther. Now, if *I* saw a panther, *I* could die happy!

With the Birdathon finished, we could be more aware of plants, especially for Emily's sake. Florida has more tree species than any other state in the Union. Driving through Florida cities and suburbs was like driving through one big botanic garden. But in the Everglades we could appreciate more of the native vegetation — what was left of it.

Except for our jaunt along the coast at Miami, we had actually been in the Everglades ever since Lake Okeechobee. It is hard to believe, but the Everglades is really a river — six inches deep and fifty miles wide — oozing out of Lake Okeechobee.

Here and there, on slightly higher land where the limestone comes to the surface, the wetland prairie is dotted with islands: smaller tree islands and larger jungly hammocks of hardwood trees, palms and ferns, airplants and orchids; slash pine forests with an understory of saw-palmetto and strangler figs. And as the grassy river creeps south to meet the sea, it merges with the mangrove thickets, mangrove keys, and coral reefs of the Gulf of Mexico and the Atlantic Ocean.

Here in the basement of the Appalachians, the ancient rocks have been worn level, and the sea has flowed over them many times, leaving a layer cake of lime and sand. Muck — yes, an apt and allowable word for sticky black Everglades soil — forms on the oolitic limestone from the hard-packed sawgrass and other plants that have decomposed over the centuries. Plants grow from the precious muck and limestone waterholes.

Boardwalks allowed us to penetrate the mangrove swamps. It was like entering a labyrinth. The branches of trees formed a jungly tunnel cutting off the light; their waterlogged roots closed around us like spreading skirts. A myriad of insect bites inflamed my fingers to twice their normal size, and a smell like rotten eggs was all-pervasive. Everything looked brackish, dead. Considering the beer cans and other garbage dropped into the water below our feet, others must have thought so too.

Yet Gus was saying, ''A mangrove swamp is the richest biomass in the world. Notice the three different types of mangrove trees: growing farthest out in the water is the red mangrove with its skirt of proplike roots; inshore of that you have the bigger black mangrove with fingerlike aerial roots called breathing tubes, or pneumatophores. And closest in at the high tide line is the white mangrove, which doesn't have aerial roots.'' Peterson compares the fingerlike roots of the black mangrove thrusting up through the mud to a bed of nails. I thought the roots of the red mangrove were like the spokes of an opened umbrella that had lost its covering.

As you look down into the murky primeval-looking water, it is hard to realize that this is a luxuriant and productive environment. Yet the leaves of the mangroves drop into the water to become the foundation for complex food chains. They are broken down by one-celled organisms such as fungi and bacteria; they are consumed by such creatures as worms, shrimps, snails, and crabs, which in turn provide food for minnows and small fish and then, in their turn, food for large fish and fish-eating creatures such as herons, storks, ibises and people. The roots of the mangroves block tidal currents, causing them to drop their load of organic debris, which with the falling leaves and bird droppings gradually builds up soil to high-tide level. Mangroves act as nurseries, providing shelter for birds and many marine creatures.

The Everglades, originally extending from central Florida to Florida Bay, depends on water — the right quality of water in the right quantities at the right season. But mankind has blocked its free flow through Florida: by making a pipe (Canal 38) out of the Kissimmee River, thereby reducing the natural marshland by a sixth and making the stream flow so fast that waters polluted by fertilizers and various wastes rush directly into Lake Okeechobee and thence into Miami, and by making a latticework of canals across south Florida to drain even more marshland to provide dry land and water for farms, ranches, citrus groves, sugarcane fields, and real estate developments.

Mankind now plays God in the Everglades, shunting water around for its own purposes. When too little water is diverted to the Everglades at the southernmost tip of the system, the natural areas suffer drought; the muck layer, reduced by drainage in some places from thirteen feet to seven, becomes depleted further; fires burn deeply into the unprotected peaty soil; and without freshwater pressure to keep it back, heavier salt water intrudes. When too much water is diverted into the park — and at the wrong time — the ecological consequences can be equally devastating. For example, the wood stork needs a natural rhythm of high water between June through October to stimulate production of fish, and low water during nesting season at the right depth to concentrate fish for the wood storks to feed their young. If mankind does not play God correctly, then wood storks have to go too far from the nesting area to find food for their chicks — and they die. When Peterson and Fisher visited the East River rookery in 1953, they were overwhelmed by hundreds of thousands of birds, particularly wood storks. Now that the timing of water delivery to the Everglades is in human hands, the wood storks have abandoned this rookery.

The problems of the Everglades have increased since Peterson and Fisher made their trip. But there is hope now that the Everglades might be saved. In 1982 the park was dedicated as an International Biosphere Reserve and a World Heritage Site, recognized around the world for its outstanding natural resources. And in 1983 Bob Graham, the Governor of Florida, took on the Everglades as a personal crusade and announced a Save Our Everglades campaign. He promised to undo past mistakes and turn back the clock a hundred years. ''By the year 2000 the Everglades will look and function more like they did at the turn of the century,'' he said in a 1986 speech. Now lands cleared for housing and agriculture are being restored to their natural state. New laws are being enacted to improve air and water quality. Thousands of acres of drained marshland are being reflooded. The Tamiami Trail which cuts straight across the heart of the Everglades is to be replaced with a highway that allows freer passage of water to the Everglades National Park and Big Cypress National Preserve, a road which has thirty-six underpasses so fewer Florida panthers will be run over by traffic. Even the Kissimmee River is having its kinks put back. Ways are finally being found for Disney World and the Everglades to live side by side.

Since the national park was only six years old when Peterson and Fisher did their trip, they would not have been able to do any birding from a swimming pool with a poolside bar, or dine at the luxurious Flamingo Inn overlooking the bay (they went back at night to Miami) as we did. Nor could they have taken in any of the many interpretive programs conducted by park naturalists at the well-equipped visitor centers. In 1953 it was largely do-it-yourself. Since then there has been a growing movement, especially in national parks, to please people. As the planet is now largely managed by people, not nature, that makes sense.

The flipside, however, is that the more advantages there are for people, the fewer there often are for wilderness and wildlife. Peter

Allen, the park naturalist at Flamingo, like Jean Takekawa, the wildlife refuge biologist at Loxahatchee, was pessimistic. "Even in national parks, business interests predominate. We give greater priority to people by allowing commercial boat traffic, marinas, and concessions, but in so doing, we destroy our estuaries for shrimps and birds. Over the past ten years there has been a diminishing number of birds in the Everglades, yet our research budget is barely enough to work on helping endangered species." Steve Robinson, park naturalist at Royal Palms, concurred. "In recent years there's been a 90 percent decline in wading birds and a 75 percent decline in great and snowy egrets. We need at least five stable years to have a comeback." Other specialists point out that the Florida Bay population of reddish egrets, great white herons, and spoonbills has increased since Peterson and Fisher visited.

Although opinions and statistics vary, it seems a lot more people are still needed to love the Everglades in order to keep the scales loaded in its favor. Governor Bob Graham and the seventeen major conservation groups supporting his current Save Our Everglades campaign may make that difference. The Everglades needs this broad base of support.

Once the haunt of pirates, wreckers (people who salvaged shipwrecks on the reefs of the Spanish Main), fishermen, cigarmakers, and soldiers, the Florida Keys, a long necklace of islands stretching for 180 miles from Biscayne Bay south of Miami to the remote Dry Tortugas, are now a mecca for tourists, particularly bird watchers. The boom was clearly evident as we drove along the highway: construction-in-progress, time-sharing condos, crowded resorts, marinas, restaurants, motels, camping areas, shops.

It is intriguing to realize that though these coral reef and limestone islands overlay submerged foothills of the Appalachians, some are within a hundred miles of Cuba and thus attract many strange West Indian birds as well as the normal nesting residents like the magnificent frigatebird, the great white heron, the reddish egret, sooty tern, brown noddy, mangrove cuckoo, Antillean nighthawk, gray kingbird, black-whiskered vireo, and white-crowned pigeon.

We found birds in abundance. Gus was continually braking, swerving, stopping, and identifying some avian specialty before he even stopped his motor. Sometimes he called two things at once, "Frigatebird flying and century plant blooming." We all decided to rename the Overseas Highway the Osprey Highway, for the number of osprey nests (sixteen) that sat atop the telephone poles.

Long Key produced a real bonanza, including the black-necked stilt with its freakishly long red legs and the lovely roseate spoonbill. On Grassy Key shaggily plumed reddish egrets, looking like clowns in tutus, twirled, pirouetted, flapped their wings, and did their drunken dances. Gus thought that perhaps they did this to cast their shadows and provide shade to see underwater prey better. All the activity may also help to stir up bottom-dwelling food organisms.

At Marathon on Key Vaca, burrowing owls popped out of holes on the golf course. One was sitting in an Australian casuarina tree — and of course had two Aussies watching it.

There were thousands of shorebirds on Sunshine Key, but the one that intrigued us was a Würdemann's heron, which is like a great blue heron but without black head plumes. This heron is unique to the Florida Keys. Also unique were the least terns nesting by the roadside verge on the white oolitic limestone of Summerland Key. "Least terns are threatened because the beach colonies where they normally nest are being wiped out," said Gus as we got out to photograph the eggs sitting in little hollows by the busy highway. "Probably nowhere else in its range is the least tern doing this — nesting on the steep verge where cars and people can't reach them."

We stopped at Big Pine Key to look for Florida Key white-tailed deer, a small race of the Virginia white-tailed deer, which once were common throughout the Keys but almost became extinct through overhunting and loss of habitat to residential development. Less than fifty animals survived in 1947. Wildlife enthusiasts throughout the United States undertook to save the species. The Key Deer National Wildlife Refuge was established in 1954, and by 1978 the population exceeded 400 animals.

Marge Brown, one of Gus's buddies, met us at Big Pine Key. Like Morton Cooper with his BULBUL, Marge had a distinctive sign on her car — BIRDWATCHER — BEWARE — BE CAREFUL. We tramped through the flowering mangroves over arching, stiltlike roots, looking for the mangrove cuckoo. Marge played a tape recording of its call; I recorded hers on my machine, and we did a duet throughout the woods. Surely no mangrove cuckoo could resist? Half an hour later, I turned around to get another view of yet another splotch on a branch above, and this time — do I dare identify it? — it *was* the white-spotted undertail of a mangrove cuckoo.

We went birding with more of Gus's friends in Key West. Many visiting birders look up Frances Hames, who has lived in Key West for over forty-five years. Frances, a tiny, gracious woman, was the first person to record the nests of Antillean nighthawks, Antillean palm swifts, and Baltimore, or northern, orioles, in Key West. She mourns the changes that have come to this historic seacoast town with its typical Bahamian architecture of white clapboard two- and three-story houses clothed in lush tropical vegetation. "Monstrosities," she complained as we passed new motels being built on Atlantic Avenue.

Her current project was to stall the demolition of Buildings 137 and 142, two cement hangars down by the Navy and Coastguard stations. "I would be much obliged, Gus, if you could officially record the least and roseate terns nesting on the roofs there to help our campaign to protect them at least till the nesting season is over," she said, then sighed. "So fast these buildings come down, and yet both terns are threatened because they just do not have enough places to nest any more."

It took "the boys" six hours by boat to get to the Dry Tortugas. We went by Cessna floatplane in thirty-five minutes. "I'm Russ Sprague," said the pilot with a smile and a hearty handshake at Murray's Marina. "And this is my Russ's Goose. We'll do a bit of sightseeing on the way."

Russ kept up a constant commentary as he flew west to one of the most isolated and overlooked spots in the United States. "Tons of sharks yesterday," he said, skimming low over the sheetlike sea. "May see some turtles today — hawksbill, green, loggerhead — they were pretty well wiped out, but young ones have been released in the Tortugas and beaches of the Everglades, so they nest on all these islands now. They nest end of May and June, so we should see them start moving around. . . . The Keys below are the Marquesas, the only place in the States where the magnificent frigatebird nests."

The sea seemed so shallow, I felt sure we could have waded to the Dry Tortugas. The colors were incredible and ever-changing: jade, emerald, and milkshake lime; blue, turquoise, and aquamarine; splotched here and there with reefs in brown and yellow.

Russ pointed out shrimp boats, a sunken naval destroyer now used for target practice, a ferry sunk by a hurricane, the site of a sunken Spanish galleon where for more than a decade wreckers have been searching for $60 million in treasure, underwater quicksands, private islands, and then the most fantastic sight of all, a fort that grew out of the sea, the Fort Jefferson National Monument on Garden Key. It was a total shock to fly over those sixty-eight miles of water and find a hexagonal, two-tiered, moated, medieval-looking fort that covered the entire island.

In 1908 the sooty tern rookery on neighboring Bird Key was declared a wildlife refuge to protect the birds from egg collectors. (John James Audubon had found one party of eggers alone removing eight tons of eggs, which meant the destruction of a quarter of a million eggs.) Bird Key was demolished in a hurricane, but the terns began nesting on Bush Key, within a hundred feet of the fort on Garden Key. Although these terns have at one time nested in Louisiana and Texas, the Dry Tortugas site is currently the only place in the United States where they nest. They are at the northern limit of their range.

The fort, with its native and ornamental trees, is an ideal spot for birds migrating north from the West Indies or South America. Migrants that normally use more western flyways may be blown off course in a sudden storm and can find shelter at the fort.

It was like walking on water as we strolled around the moat. There were no sharks that legend says were enticed into the moat to deter escaping prisoners, but reef fishes in red, blue, green, and yellow darted beneath our feet. Galleons of dark, magnificent frigatebirds glided overhead. Arthur Cleveland Bent, who wrote the classic *Life Histories of North American Birds*, said that words are powerless to describe the flight of this wondrous airplane, "the most marvelous and most perfect flying machine that has ever been produced."

I nearly fell into the lagoon looking upward in the attempt. Frigatebirds are large black seabirds with sharply angled wings and a long, pointed tail. They can float in the sky with scarcely a movement, as Bent says, "painted birds against a painted sky." But when pirating food, chasing prey, fighting, or playing, this man-o'-war bird can dance in the air like a ballet star, opening and closing its tail like a pair of scissors to get the utmost in speed and direction from the air.

"There's a white-tailed tropicbird," called Gus, "One of the accidentals from the West Indies, it breeds in Bermuda on shoreline rockfaces . . . no, there's three more . . . four of them. They weren't here on Peterson and Fisher's trip. I wonder if they are inspecting the fort for potential nest sites." During the last decade, about ten birds a year routinely do courtship flights over the fort, but they have not yet nested there. The white-tailed tropicbirds were as expert fliers as the frigatebirds but even more beautiful. Their long creamy-white tail feathers streamed behind them gracefully like a bridal train.

Some birds visit Fort Jefferson in transit, some visit on short foraging holidays, others call it home. The most famous occupants are the sooty and brown noddy terns that come by the thousands from the Caribbean Sea and the west-central Atlantic Ocean to nest on Bush Key. As early as mid-January, terns make nocturnal maneuvers over the Tortugas, perhaps mating at that time in readiness for the egg-laying season, which begins in March. "The boys" rowed over to Bush Key, then picked their way through the colony to sit among them. You cannot do that now between March and September, when the terns are raising their young. When Peterson visited again, he had to walk around the island in the water. We, however, without a boat, had to look from the fort.

The top tier of the fort is the best place to see the birds of Bush Key. We waited until the sun had passed its zenith to have it behind us and thus reduce the glare through our lenses, then we spiraled under the brick arches and through the stone galleries past damp wet cells till we reached the roof. Barn and cliff swallows darted in and out of the portals, and down in the courtyard various birds — warblers, indigo buntings, yellow-billed cuckoos — flitted through introduced Brazilian pepper and Australian casuarina trees. Outside the fort other birds were moving around the buttonwood trees, candelabra cacti, and a flowering Geiger-tree. The din of terns erupting in black clouds from the colony, skimming the surface of the lagoon for minnows, or hanging in the air above their nests, was deafening and all-encompassing.

In 1875 Bush Key was just a narrow sandbar. Except for a small spit at its eastern end, it is now covered with vegetation — grasses, cacti, and bushes. Sooty terns (the black-backed ones with the whitish underparts) merely scratch hollows in the sand to lay their eggs, but the noddy terns (the smoky brown ones with the whitish cap), the only terns in North America that nest above ground, lay their eggs in bay-cedar bushes or prickly pear cacti. Noddy nests are loosely constructed from twigs and seaweed, even shells and coral.

When John James Audubon visited in 1832, the terns were so thick that he felt "as if the birds would raise me from the ground." He was probably exaggerating, but it does seem clear that numbers fell drastically by 1903, when the first reliable counts were made. Researchers found 7,000 sooty nests and 200 noddy nests. Numbers fluctuated throughout the 1900s, but by 1986, research biologist Bill Robertson estimated an increase to 40,000 sooty nests and about 4,000 noddy nests. The populations are stable and increasing, especially the noddies'.

From our blind in the sky we saw royal terns, least terns, Forster's terns, and roseate terns. (The last species nests on three of the Tortugas islands — Bush, Hospital, and Long Keys.) We picked out three merlins, a kestrel, and a sharp-shinned hawk. Gus counted forty cattle egrets, including three dead ones. Some of the prey the egrets were taking were probably just-hatched tern chicks. Catttle egrets use the fort as a stopover on migration, but probably only the sick ones stay. Resting on the sandspit by the terns were ruddy turnstones, sanderlings, semipalmated and spotted sandpipers, and a golden plover.

I could bear it no longer. The limpid green waters of the lagoon had been beckoning relentlessly, and Russ would soon be readying the plane for our return. Leaving the others huddled around Gus's telescope, I sneaked away for a swim. I wanted to feel Wild America as well as just see it. I headed for the cell with the do-it-yourself slide show and, taking a chance that I was the only audience, watched it while changing into a swimsuit. Oh, that tropical water, encasing my sunburn as I floated beside the seawall! A bright yellow palm warbler flitted between cracks, and swallows dipped beside me. Gus, you'd be pleased.

So far, the Dry Tortugas was the highlight of Wild America. Next, hopefully, would be a Florida panther. And, of course for Emily, a Florida yew, whose habitat we were approaching.

West from Miami, the Tamiami Trail (Miami to Tampa) forms the northern boundary of Everglades National Park. At 13 Mile Bend, half a dozen snail kites flew over the canal, the bright sun glinting on their feathers, red legs, and red-based, long, hooked beaks. "These are endangered?" Emily said in surprise.

"Well, we've obviously come to the right place," I replied. "I'll check it out with Steve Beissinger. He's winding up a five-year study of them."

We found Steve in a trailer at the research station near the park entrance. He was charming and knowledgeable and took us to see a nest in the reeds about three hundred yards north of the highway, where the chicks had just been hatched the week before. Steve was thrilled because he had located sixty nests in the past season in his study area. He was even more thrilled that the one he had shown us was the first one officially recorded in the park.

He had been making several intriguing discoveries. Snail kites are prepared to move more than three hundred miles in drought periods, when snails are scarce. Kites forsake their usual haunts in fall and may even fly to Cuba. But Steve's most fascinating discovery was the kite's mating system, probably unique in the bird world.

"About halfway through the rearing period, one of the parents will desert the nest and leave its mate to take care of the young till they fledge and become independent, which could take another three to five weeks,'' he told me. ''This could be a good thing, because the kite's breeding season is as long as nine or ten months. So if conditions are right, a mate can go off and remate, build a new nest, and have a second brood. The deserted mate seems able to take care of the young alone.'' By the end of the season, Steve would have documented mate desertion in twenty-eight out of thirty-six snail kite nests. He discovered that small broods were deserted earlier than large ones, and more frequently by females than males.

Mate desertion makes sense for these kites. Normally they have a very high nest-failure rate because of predators and unstable nest sites. Their population fluctuates according to water level, and their long nesting season permits mate desertion. Kites often lay double clutches (two batches of eggs) anyway.

''Lyn, wake up, you're in panther — '' Tess poked me. At that magic word I shot upright.

''Panthers? Where?'' I yelled, grabbing my cameras and reaching for the door.

Gus, with an automatic glance behind, lurched to a stop and I took a picture, not of panthers, but of the new signs that had just been erected on the Tamiami Trail warning motorists to watch out for panthers. The billboards were staggered: ENTERING PANTHER HABITAT . . . LESS THAN 30 REMAINING . . . PLEASE DRIVE CAREFULLY. The animals on the billboards were painted in black, even though black panthers are not indigenous to America (many people confuse American panthers with the black panthers of India). My companions were far less interested in panthers than I was, but even Gus and Tess got out of the van and took a picture of me standing by the painted panther — probably the closest I would ever get to the real thing.

The signs are too true, even optimistic. Since 1981 nine panthers have been killed by cars along the busy Tamiami Trail. At the time of our trip, a night speed limit of 30 mph was imposed, and plans were afoot to widen the road to four lanes. Governor Bob Graham's Save Our Everglades campaign also included thirty-six panther underpasses, so Florida's official state animal may yet be saved from extinction after years of persecution.

The Florida panther differs from other subspecies by having a tail with a distinctive kink at the end, a cowlick, or whorl of hair, in the middle of its back, and a particularly pronounced white flecking on its head, neck, and shoulders. In Florida the panther has adapted to high water; in contrast to most cats' finickiness, it splashes through canals and sloughs and swamps.

Once, this subspecies ranged over the entire southeast United States. Now a pitiful twenty-two individuals are isolated in the wildest parts of Florida: the Fakahatchee Strand State Preserve, west of the Big Cypress Swamp, Raccoon Point in Big Cypress, and the section of Everglades National Park near the research center known as The Hole in the Doughnut. Buying land for panthers and restricting human access to that land are essential if the panther is to survive in Florida. At the time of writing, plans were being made to buy the last important area of panther habitat not in public ownership to create a Florida Panther National Wildlife Refuge.

We headed now along Highway 29 through the Big Cypress Swamp — panther country. Much of this area has resisted development and access by mankind even in his airboats and swamp buggies. Its comparative inaccessibility is probably the reason why there are any panthers left in Florida today. To the west of the road is the Fakahatchee Strand State Preserve, and to the east the Big Cypress National Preserve. Since 1974 these lands have been bought by governments to preserve the wilderness — and thus panthers. And it is in this area that Chris Belden, a biologist with the U.S. Fish and Wildlife Service and leader of the Florida Panther Recovery Team, has been working since 1976 to prevent the extinction of the panther by finding out where the cats are and what they do, breeding them in captivity, and planning where and how to release them in the wild. Panthers are elusive, secretive animals, and Chris had worked for four years in panther country without ever seeing one, although he found signs of them.

He talked to me about the threats to panther habitat. ''Oil has been found in the Big Cypress. Twenty-five oil wells are there right now, with more planned. But it is the access roads to them that cause the greater danger. Subdivisions are also a threat. Some people are lobbying to allow different developments in both the park and the preserve.

For an intimate look at life in panther habitat, we stopped near Immokalee to walk the boardwalk of the National Audubon Society's Corkscrew Swamp Sanctuary. These eleven thousand acres contain the country's largest remaining stand of virgin bald cypress, the oldest trees in eastern North America (perhaps seven hundred years old) and the only trees in south Florida to drop their leaves (in this case, needles) in winter, hence their name.

Cypress trees perhaps 125 feet tall reared above the boardwalk, their trunks flared at the bottom like spreading buttresses to anchor their shallow roots in the muck, their woody "knees" sticking vertically out of the water. Many were shrouded with several varieties of *Tillandsias*, airplants that grow upon other plants, not parasitically for food but using the host plant for physical support. Spanish moss *Tillandsias* draped the trees like gray beards to give the swamp an eerie appearance.

We emerged from the darkness of the canopied swamp into blue skies and sunlight and walked to an open area at the end of the observation platform in the central marsh. Wood storks were flying over empty nests. They had probably raised a brood between November and April, and the young were either now a-wing or they had failed and were now dispersing.

Wood storks, large white wading birds with vulturelike naked heads and black-edged wings, are Corkscrew's most celebrated residents. The National Audubon Society has been studying them here and elsewhere since 1957. Historically, wood storks bred in all the coastal states between Texas and South Carolina, but by the early 1980s they were entering their fifth consecutive decade of decline. There were about 10,000 nesting pairs of wood storks in Florida in 1960 and only about 4,500 in 1981. The National Audubon Society believed that they would be close to extinction by the end of the twentieth century. However, in 1986 there were glimmers of hope. Sandy Sprunt, the society's research director, found that the population had stabilized, even slightly increased, and that the main wood stork breeding area had been moved from Florida to areas farther north. Wood storks had even moved back to Georgia and North Carolina.

During the drive north through the cattle lands and citrus groves of Florida, we talked as usual of species endangered—or extinct—through loss of habitat. In 1953 Peterson and Fisher drove this same route through mile after mile of longleaf pinewoods, and anticipated finding an ivory-billed woodpecker at its last known roosting place in a cypress tree by the Chipola River. "But look," said Gus at the wheel, "this land is no longer wild. Trees are not allowed to grow to their climax. They don't have the same diversity, so there's not the same diversity in woodpeckers. The ivory-billed was the largest of the woodpeckers and needed the biggest, oldest trees with the most insects. When those trees went, the ivory-billed went too."

The ivory-billed woodpecker with its almost-white bill, its flaming red crest, and dramatic black and white wings is a well-known symbol of extinction. Even a person not remotely interested in birds knows what it looks like. Yet it was almost extinct before anyone had learned much about it. John James Audubon noted that ivory-bills abandoned nests even when watched from a distance. It was not able to adapt to living in proximity with mankind. But the main reason for its demise was loss of habitat. When the large trees were logged and the forests were destroyed in the Deep South after 1885, the local ivory-bills did not move away to find new areas. They died.

Roger Tory Peterson is one of very few living naturalists to have seen ivory-billed woodpeckers — two females in 1941 in the Singer Forest in Louisiana. He still had a chance in 1953 to show one to Fisher in the swamps of the Chipola and Apalachicola rivers in northwestern Florida, as one had been seen there the year before. "The boys" drifted downstream listening intently for the bird's distinctive nasal tooting, and they visited its last nesting hole, but they found a coral snake instead.

Since then, there have been unconfirmed sightings in northwestern Florida and South Carolina (1963), in Texas (1966), and in Louisiana (1971). In spite of the rumors, most ornithologists believed that the ivory-billed woodpecker was extinct, that soon it would be only a mechanical memory as they played a tape recording of its voice. Until 1986. Two biologists spotted one male and possibly two female ivory-bills near a lumber camp in Cuba, and announced the news to a startled world. Lumbering was immediately stopped within four miles of the sighting — showing how much attitudes to wildlife have changed.

Near Blountstown and Scotts Ferry between the Chipola and the Apalachicola rivers, we looked at what was once prime ivory-billed woodpecker habitat. It seemed a sad land still, apart from the demise of a species. Tired-looking houses. Many For Sale signs. A recreation area called Dead Lakes. Ghostly trees with their feet drowned, their arms hoar-hung with lichen. It seemed that more than a bird had died.

We may not have found *Campephilus principalis* — the ivory-billed woodpecker — but we did succeed in tracking down *Torreya taxifolia* and capturing *Croomia pauciflora*. "The boys" looked for the ivory-billed and found snakes; we looked for the ivory-billed and found plants. As we walked along the steep forested banks of the Apalachicola River in Torreya State Park, Gus was fascinated by new plants he had not seen before, plants that are not found anywhere else. Emily was overjoyed, on this the second-last day of her trip, to find the rare Florida species she had made this journey for.

We hit the Gulf Coast — the beach and the bedlam — at Biloxi, Mississippi. Buildings, bodies, and bright lights. Hotels, restaurants, boutiques. Dense traffic swept us along the boulevard to Gulfport.

On our north side were beautifully columned white antebellum houses draped in flowering magnolias; on our south side, miles of scintillating white sand beaches, deserted except for birds. Incredibly, least terns were nesting beside a four-lane highway that was busier than the Overseas Highway across the Florida Keys. The sign said, ''LEAST TERN NESTING COLONY — THE LARGEST PROTECTED NESTING COLONY ON THE UNITED STATES MAINLAND — THOUSANDS OF BIRDS.'' Gus could not stop to read the rest. It was late afternoon and we had many miles to go to reach New Orleans.

Fortunately, I had visited this colony before and knew the remarkable story of the individuals who persuaded a whole town to save more than a mile of commercially valuable, prime waterfront for birds.

Least terns were almost decimated in the first part of this century by gunners who were after their plumage. Because of its small size, the entire bird was sewn onto women's hats. Following World War Two, developers and tourists discovered the Riviera of the Gulf Coast, and the remaining terns there had little chance for survival. By the spring of 1982, about two dozen pairs finally succeeded in forming a little nesting colony, but were cleaned up with the garbage by big machines, crushed by human feet, and attacked by dogs. They too had little chance for survival.

Then in 1972 local birders from the newly formed Mississippi Coast Audubon Society, led by two indomitable women, Ethel Floyd and Judith Toups, started a campaign to protect the fledgling colony. Judith told me that for several years there were numerous confrontations between conservationists and the political-business-tourism bloc (''We defended the birds with our bodies if we had to''), but progress was made and the colony grew from twenty-four pairs in 1972 to an incredible five thousand pairs in 1983.

Jerome Jackson of the Mississippi State University was very impressed with the strong protective attitude Gulfport residents show toward their terns. ''Every fifteen minutes or so of the five hours we worked in the colony,'' he said, ''someone would shout from one of the speeding cars on the highway for us to get the hell away from the birds.''

A couple of weeks after we whizzed through Gulfport, members of the Mississippi Coast Audubon Society, as well as volunteers from Biloxi, put out 3,150 orange-topped stakes to mark the nests of the terns and four new signs that said, ''LITTLE LEAST TERN AREA . . . PLEASE KEEP OUT . . . NEST IN PEACE.'' The next day, Peterson saw and photographed the colony for the first time. He too was impressed and congratulated Gulfport on being the Little Tern Capital of the World. He said it was the most amazing example of intelligent management he had seen.

But vigilance must be maintained. Signs and laws are in place, but sometimes terns are disturbed, though no one yet has been prosecuted for breaking the law, not even when a person collected 150 eggs and left them on the seawall to bake in the sun, or when two boys clubbed at least twenty-eight black skimmers sharing space with the terns, or when a tourist and his two sons tore the wings off chicks to take home as souvenirs, or when fireworks were set off in the midst of the colony.

Least terns who choose to nest on beaches that attract holidaymakers are bound to come into conflict with some people. However, after declining generally since the 1960s, they are now increasing as a result of public pressure to protect their nesting sites. It is happening in California, in Australia, in England, but nowhere is the choice for the birds — and people — more apparent than between Biloxi and Gulfport.

Whooping Crane
Grus americana

Chapter Four
The Middle South
May 15–31

"Louisiana has more marshland than all the other forty-nine states combined," said Gus as we drove west along the Mississippi River, west for miles upon miles of elevated concrete built over the state's vast complex of lakes, deltas, ponds, bays, and bayous. The rain had stopped, but water was the predominant feature of the landscape. We were crossing the massive Mississippi Delta.

"Like the coast of Texas, it is one of America's best birding areas," Gus continued. "It's right in the middle of the Mississippi Flyway and on the edge of the Central Flyway, so it attracts wintering birds as well as spring and fall migrants. It also gets some western species that move eastward along the coast.

"The birds you should expect to see breeding in these marshes are *Rallus limicola*, *Rallus elegans*, *Rallus longirostris*, but *Coturnicops noveboracensis* has probably left by now for . . ."

"Heavens!" whispered Marie Gillespie, a librarian and naturalist from Saskatoon who replaced Emily in New Orleans. "Five weeks of this? Does he use Latin names for plants too? I'm going to have to spend my nights studying."

"And then with the other rails you should see fence rails . . ." Gus continued impassively, testing whether or not we were listening. Gus is sorely tried by us lesser mortals, but he never loses his enthusiasm for teaching or his sense of humor.

At the first rest stop an unmistakable *whee-whee, whee-whee, whee-whee, whee* sang out from the tangle. A Swainson's warbler! In a flurry of excited anticipation, we piled out of the mini-bus and lined up along the road, training our binoculars on a barrage of bushes. Quickly, Gus set up his high-powered Questar telescope.

All morning, we had been searching for the elusive Swainson's warbler in the rain-swollen swamps of Louisiana. For hours we had tramped through puddles, stared into impenetrable tangles, tried such enticements as "pssh! pssh! pssh!-ing" into the bushes and playing its tape-recorded call. We had attracted the great-crested flycatcher, the Acadian flycatcher, the blue-gray gnatcatcher, we'd successfully pursued the prothonotary warbler and had heard the yellow-breasted chat mimicking the Swainson's — but this seldom seen skulker of the southeastern states lived up to its reputation and eluded us.

Then, Gus heard its call, which A.C. Bent describes as "one of the most outstanding warbler songs . . . (it) leaves a lasting impression on the listener." From somewhere in that thicket of vines, greenbrier and honeysuckle now came the slurred "whee-ee whee-ee, whee whee, whee." But the Swainson's warbler stayed hidden.

"Here he is, twenty feet in front of me," Gus said calmly, gazing into the greenery while we slowly swung our binoculars at his direction. "No, there he goes across the road. Don't move. He'll come back . . . Yes, here he comes. There, on the bare branch. Do you see him?"

We stood in line on the verge, motionless, trying to see what Gus was seeing. A car and then a truck slowed to a stop beside us. We didn't move. I couldn't help wondering what they were thinking. That we were having a restroom stop? "Looking for 'gators?" they asked eventually. Two boys on bikes pulled up behind them. "There's snakes in there, you know," one warned darkly. Horrified, they watched while indomitable Gus slogged into the head-high tangle to flush the warbler out.

Our onlookers were amazed that we could spend hours in the hot sun hoping for a glimpse of a tiny olive-brown bird that Bent calls "plain, of neutral colour with no conspicuous field marks," but we were delighted. "Not many people get a good view of this shy bird," Gus told us. We were possibly the first people from Canada to see one so clearly.

(The following day Tess Kloot, presented Gus with the Limnothlypis Swainsonii Award for his "patience, perseverance and perspicacity" in stalking the Swainson's warbler.)

Later we drove into Baton Rouge, the gracious capital of Louisiana, under a glide of chimney swifts. Our destination was Avery Island, the home of Tabasco sauce and the McIlhenny family that manufactures it.

I had been corresponding with one member of the McIlhenny family, for a number of years, ever since we had met over my pet raccoon. An orphan raccoon was given to me after her mother was killed for raising her family in the attic of a suburban home in Vancouver. At that time, a local radio station was soliciting solutions to the problem of raccoons damaging roofs in the city. The winner suggested fending them off by painting the roofs with Tabasco sauce. Thus my raccoon got her name. I was asked often over the next few years to tell how

Tabasco was named and whenever it was reported, headlines played on the theme "SAUCY RACCOON VISITS STUDIO" or "TABASCO RACCOON ADDS SPICE TO EVERY CONVERSATION." Mr. Walter McIlhenny, on a visit to Montreal, read such a headline in the local paper and wrote to ask me if I had named my raccoon after his sauce. When I replied that I had, he sent me a dozen miniature bottles of Tabasco sauce. However it was the reputation of the family as conservationists that caused us to visit.

We roller-coastered west over the Atchafalaya River, America's last great undrained river-basin swamp. About six miles south of New Iberia, we crossed the canal and passed through the tollgates onto Avery Island. Although surrounded by marshland and bayous, it is not really an island, but one of five salt domes rising above the flat wet Louisiana coast. Avery Island is a mountain of rock salt eight miles deep underground and six miles round at its top. The ground is clothed in woods and meadows and fields. And in these fields grows the Latin American weed *Capsicum frutescens*, the hot red pepper in Tabasco sauce. The McIlhenny family built its fortune on salt and pepper, then added oil.

Edward Avery McIlhenny, who died in 1942, was a pioneer conservationist who spurred the American Congress to end the trade in wild bird feathers. Known affectionately as Uncle Ned or Mr. Ned, he made Avery Island what Arthur Cleveland Bent calls "one of the most remarkable and successful experiments in conservation of which we have any record." McIlhenny was a naturalist who imported and bred hundreds of species of plants from around the world and displayed them in what is now 250 acres of jungle gardens that Fisher called "a Garden of Eden." Uncle Ned banded more than 200,000 birds to study their migration patterns, wrote books on alligators and egrets, engineered the preservation of many thousands of acres of Louisiana as wildlife refuges, supported the Louisiana State University Museum of Natural Science, and brought back from near extinction the snowy egret.

The snowy egret, according to Arthur Bent, is "one of nature's daintiest and most exquisite creatures, the most charming of all our marsh birds. The spotless purity of its snowy plumage, adorned with airy, waving plumes, and its gentle, graceful manners, make it the center of attraction wherever it is seen." And it was equally attractive to the plume hunters who slaughtered it in much greater numbers than similar herons with plumes not as delicate.

In the spring of 1895, after much searching, Uncle Ned found two nests of snowy egrets and put eight young birds in a large wire cage on the edge of a two-acre pond near his home. He raised them by hand, left the doors of their cage open after November, and they finally flew away. The following March six of them returned, two pairs nested, and the colony grew to thirteen. Roger reported 100,000 egrets in 1912. Today the McIlhennys estimate that 20,000 heron families raise their young each year in Avery Island's famous Bird City — a garden of several thousand birds that look like myriad white magnolias blossoming from the buttonwoods, or rising out of the duckweed-covered lake.

So numerous are the birds now — not just snowy egrets but great egrets, cattle egrets, little blue herons, Louisiana herons, green-backed herons, and anhingas as well — that the McIlhennys must dump more than thirty truckloads of twigs for nesting material into the area and supplement the natural fringe of buttonwood bushes around the lake with double-decked nesting platforms of bamboo floored with brush.

Visitors are welcome at Avery Island to see Bird City and the Jungle Gardens. Several hundred workers come and go each day to work in the salt mines, the oil wells, the pepper fields, and the factory. With Paul McIlhenny as our personal guide, we birded from the van as we drove along the canals, over the levees, around the ponds, and through the woods. In between spotting birds (and alligators, raccoons, nutrias, muskrats, marsh rabbits, white-tailed deer, slider turtles, and bullfrogs), trading ornithological jokes, inspecting beehives, pepper fields, and a new oil well, we tried to solve the conservation problems of the world.

The McIlhenny family are certainly conservation-conscious. They terrace their fields and edge them with white pine trees to prevent erosion, freshen saltwater marshes to grow bald cypresses again, bury pipelines, and fill and revegetate mud pits. "We'd sacrifice a pepper tree but never a live oak," Paul drawled to illustrate his point. "If we don't manage the environment, we won't have it. And I think here on Avery Island we're showing that industry can work cooperatively with conservation, that they are not economically exclusive."

We went west toward Texas on back roads, past rice paddies, sugar-cane fields, and pumping oil wells, looking for the black francolin. This chickenlike bird from Pakistan was introduced as a game bird in 1961 on the Moore-Odom Ranch at Gum Cove, Louisiana, near the Sabine Wildlife Reserve. It is well established in Louisiana (as well as Florida) and we hoped to find it in the pasturelands south of Vinton.

"The black francolin is very wary and is usually hidden in the grass, but look for it on fence posts," advised Gus. "We'll drive along Farm

Road 108 and Gum Cove Road till we hear its call. It makes a *beep-beep, beep-beep-beep* sound that some people say is like Morse code.''

We had not seen or heard any francolins by the time we had reached the Intracoastal Waterway, so while we were waiting at the ferry for the barges and freighters to pass, I got out of the van to see if some of the locals knew where francolins were.

"Come to see the alligators?" asked a friendly oil rigger a couple of vehicles behind.

"No, I've seen enough 'gators," I shrugged.

"The deer then?" Without waiting for an answer he went on. "Lots of deer around here, they come up to you. And a motherlode of 'gators. A millionaire owns the land up the road apiece. You'll know when you get there. Armed guards all over the place. Man called Odum owns it. He owns half of Louisiana, but he goes around in his gardening clothes. He sure protects the wildlife. Loves the deers, feeds them.''

We found no francolins, but we left Louisiana elated. In a very short time as we approached the Texas border, we saw a red fox, a skunk scrabbling up the bank sending the dirt flying, mottled ducks, black terns, Canada geese with young (having too good a time down south, I guess, to go home), several loggerhead shrikes (a species threatened in the northern part of its range, but more stable in the south), two dozen fulvous whistling-ducks in a flooded rice field (these ducks have declined rapidly since farmers started treating their seed rice with pesticides), a red knot that went *kloot, kloot, kloot* (much to Tess's delight), and the bird that became Tess's favorite bird in North America — scissor-tailed flycatchers.

I agreed with Arthur Bent, who said that there is no excuse for not recognizing this largest of the flycatchers, with its extremely long, scissor-like tail, pearly gray back, and salmon-pink sides, offset with a dash of scarlet under the wing. It is Texas's bird of paradise.

"The absolute delight of the entire day, the entire trip, was seeing scissor-tailed flycatchers," Tess wrote in her journal. "They are exquisite birds, graceful and elegant. We have nothing to match them in Australia.''

We entered Texas in a rainstorm. Texas, Miss Smith had said, was the best state to see birds in. With its large area, altitudes from sea level to over eight thousand feet, rainfall from less than ten inches annually to more than fifty-five inches, varied vegetation, and a strategic position on the Central Flyway, Texas has three-fourths of all known American birds. I had to buy two of James Lane's birding guides to cover this state.

We were lucky to run into an incredible bird bonanza at the Anahuac National Wildlife Refuge. Usually, migrants boosted by prevailing southeast winds over the Gulf of Mexico pass over the coast almost unseen and land farther inland. But when forced down by thunderstorms or a change in the wind, they land on the first perches available — the few trees of the Gulf Coast — and it rains birds.

We were inundated with birds as soon as we turned off Farm Road 1985 to the Anahuac National Wildlife Refuge beside East Galveston Bay. This marshland was established in 1963 as a sanctuary for wintering ducks and geese of the Central Flyway and for the protection of the endangered red wolf and alligator. It was greatly expanded in 1982 by the addition of an adjacent ranch. Wildlife refuges have increased in numbers and acreages all over North America since Peterson and Fisher's trip, but demands upon them have increased too. They are now managed for such activities as hunting, fishing, boating, trapping, grazing, and oil drilling. The federal duck stamp bought by each waterfowl hunter before the fall hunting season gives the refuges much-needed money to acquire habitat for wildlife, but there is a trade-off. According to a 1983 National Audubon Report, "the only animals that matter now are the ones you can shoot, hook, or trap. . . . In the seven-plus decades of its existence, the refuge system has been transformed from a single-purpose reservoir for the protection of wildlife into a multi-use circus in which anything goes." In 1983, the year we were traveling around the United States, the Reagan Administration was being panned everywhere for transferring vital habitat from preservation to consumptive uses, for refusing to buy more refuge lands, and for underbudgeting current management.

"Much of that was rhetoric and media hype," said Tom Wilson, spokesman for the National Wildlife Refuge System in Washington, D.C. "Admittedly, we slowed down in those years, but not one acre of protected land did we lose. Consumptive use had to be consistent with the original purpose of the refuge, the protection of particular species and habitats — it still must." He agreed that the problem now was not the quality of the refuges, but the quality of the buffer lands outside.

Since those controversial days, more than a billion dollars have been allocated to the parks system, millions of acres have been added to the wilderness system, and there are continuing additions to the wildlife refuge system. The question of whether or not this is enough remains controversial.

All that seemed very far away that day in Anahuac.

Dozens of small birds were flitting down the road, across the canal, around the trees: bay-breasted, Blackburnian, and common yellow-throated warblers, American redstarts, northern cardinals, orchard orioles, eastern kingbirds (we had not seen the western kingbirds yet). A soggy yellow-billed cuckoo held its wings out to dry like a brown raincoat. Mockingbirds, the state bird of Texas, played in the air around us, full of joie de vivre despite the drizzle.

Shoveller Pond was like a stage. Brightly costumed players lit up a drab backdrop of murky water and spartina grass with color and movement. We sat in the van entranced while each actor entered in turn: coots, herons, egrets, spoonbills, gallinules, six species of sandpiper, three of teal, four terns, three ibises, and three rails — this last a real treat, as rails are usually elusive.

Typically, we had the refuge to ourselves. Then, to our surprise, another van pulled up behind. A workman, trying to be helpful, got out to say enthusiastically, "Lots of alligators in that pond, you know. Have you seen any yet?"

To which Gus replied, "Yes, but have *you* seen the stilts, the bay-breasted and Blackburnian warblers?"

He looked quizzical. "Birds? Oh, you'll find some flamingos farther up the road."

"You mean roseate spoonbills," Gus said, more of a statement than a question.

"Is that what they are?" The man looked a little nonplussed when he returned to his van.

Rabbits, both cottontails and jackrabbits, were abundant. I also liked the armadillos that lumbered across the road into the shrubbery, and the beaverlike nutrias (introduced from South America) swimming in the canals. I did not like the mosquitoes.

Next day we ignored the rain and gloried in the birds of West Galveston Island. Galveston, Texas, is a birding mecca. Oil wells, storage tanks, skyscrapers, and the city of Houston were not far away, but we were more aware of a more natural Texas. Scissor-tailed flycatchers (we now saw them daily) continued to electrify Tess. She was also intrigued by another of her life birds, a sandwich tern ("The yellow tips on their beaks look as if they've been dipped in mustard"). An olivaceous cormorant sat on a piling beside a great egret. An Inca dove and a white-winged dove pecked grit together in a driveway. Black-throated green and Cape May warblers lingered in the tamarisks, late for their appointments in the north.

Some birds with aberrant markings had us confused for a while. A female cardinal looked like an eastbound female pyrrhuloxia until we saw its red beak. One of the many willets had unusual markings on its head like vermicelli. Large and lively boat-tailed and great-tailed grackles were obviously enjoying the mating season; one was even courting a piece of black plastic. But we were interested in their eyes: most of the great-tailed grackles along the Gulf of Mexico have brown eyes, but both our bird species had yellow eyes. And then we saw two phases of the reddish egret together, one with the usual gray back and rusty head, the other all white. I was checking the bicolored bills and bluish legs they had in common when I suddenly realized I should be taking their picture. Just as I raised the camera, they flew off together over the green marsh, as crazy-looking in the air with their legs dangling as they are on the ground.

On Sportsmen Road, which the locals call Rail Road for its numerous rail sightings, Marie spotted the highlight of our day. A little king rail chick came pattering all alone down the road in front of the van. Mother was swimming down the canal that ran beside the road, but she was going in the opposite direction to her offspring. I was tempted to get out and photograph it, but Gus warned of imprinting the chick to humans and pulled away.

Of course, we hoped the highlight of our day on Galveston Island would be finding an Eskimo curlew dallying a month late on spring migration. We turned onto Settegest Road, a likely spot, and saw a long-billed curlew, a closely related shorebird with similar markings, but no Eskimo curlew. Perhaps no one will ever see an Eskimo curlew again. As late as the 1830s its numbers were such that John James Audubon compared its vast flocks with the passenger pigeon's. Then they became the easy target of market gunners as they flew north from South America to their breeding grounds in the Arctic. John Mackenzie in his book *Birds in Peril* describes how often the numbers of birds shot far exceeded the capacity of the wagons brought by the hunters to carry the slaughtered flocks away: thousands of curlews were left to rot.

For several decades the species was considered extinct. Then between 1959 and 1965 an Eskimo curlew was seen every April on West Galveston Island. Since then, Peterson's field guide says there have been occasional sightings in several states (and two birds were seen in James Bay, Ontario, in 1976), but most observations still come from the Galveston area.

Another bird brought to the edge of extinction is the whooping crane: in 1945 there were only seventeen birds in Texas and two birds in

Louisiana. During the afternoon, we headed to its winter home at the Aransas National Wildlife Refuge north of Rockport. The seventy-five whooping cranes that wintered at Aransas in 1983 had left for their summer home in Canada the month before, so we did not expect to see any; probably for the same reason, "the boys" did not mention them in *Wild America*.

Ironically, the seemingly vast expanse of marsh seen from the observation tower is the territory of just one whooping crane family. The whole refuge covers some 55,000 acres, but only about 5,000 acres are suitable for feeding cranes, so only ten to fifteen pairs of birds can claim territory in this sanctuary. Others spend the winter on neighbouring marshlands.

A single pair of whooping cranes needs about a thousand acres of undisturbed marsh area in summer for nesting and 400 to 600 acres in winter for feeding. Their need for so much space led to their decline. Whoopers used to winter in suitable marshes from western Mexico to the Atlantic; they used to nest in Illinois, Iowa, Minnesota, North Dakota, Manitoba, Saskatchewan, and Alberta. But the prairies were settled, marshes were drained to grow crops and make pasture for livestock, birds were shot for food or for "the hell of it." The last nest was found in the United States in 1889; in Canada in 1922. A resident flock in Louisiana was decimated by a hurricane and became extinct by 1949.

Aransas National Wildlife Refuge was established in 1937 primarily to protect wintering habitat for the whooping crane. At that time there were perhaps eighteen birds left in Texas, eleven in Louisiana. In 1953, when "the boys" came by, there were twenty-four in Texas, none in Louisiana. The big news came a year later when a nesting area (the only one known) was discovered in the Northwest Territories, Canada, fortunately in Wood Buffalo National Park. Since then, with protection at both ends of their range, with propagation of captive cranes at the Patuxent Center for Endangered Wildlife in Maryland (starting in 1966), and with incubation of whooping crane eggs by specially selected greater sandhill cranes nesting in Gray's Lake National Wildlife Refuge in Idaho (starting in 1975), the three populations of whooping cranes have steadily increased.

In 1983 there were seventy-five birds in Aransas, thirty-two in the Rocky Mountains (these cranes winter on refuges in Colorado and New Mexico), and thirty-four at Patuxent. In 1985 there were ninety-four in Aransas, forty-four in the Rocky Mountains, and forty-one at Patuxent. More importantly, in 1984 and 1985 the number of young more than doubled. In 1986 sixteen chicks were hatched at Wood

Buffalo, a record year. The world population now stands at 176 (ninety-six at Aransas, forty in Idaho, and forty in captivity).

Whooping cranes are still threatened at both ends of their range. At Aransas, barges carrying oil and chemicals ply past the refuge daily, and it seems just a matter of time before a spill or a well blowout escapes man's best efforts to contain them. At Wood Buffalo in the Northwest Territories the nesting grounds are remote and off-limits to people, yet plans are regularly put forward to develop the hinterland, to build a railway line, a microwave tower, an electric transmission line, a hydroelectric dam.

Nevertheless, the whooping story is a success story. Oil and wildlife seem to mix, at least at Aransas, where whoopers share their refuge with wells. More birds are breeding, and the populations are increasing. More land for wintering habitat is being acquired. And such is the public image of the bird and its symbolism to the whole conservation movement that any threats to its continued existence are met with a barrage of opposition from its many supporters.

Aransas is reputed to have, with 350 species, the longest bird list of any national wildlife refuge and the largest list of birds ever tallied at a U.S. refuge in one day — 204 species. On this particular day I was more interested in mammals. By the time we had driven the refuge's Twelve-Mile Loop Road, we had seen eighty-eight white-tailed deer, many javelina, or collared peccaries, two armadillos, and a honey-colored raccoon.

There seems to be a lot of concern for wildlife along the Texas coast. When Gus stopped for gas in Tivoli, the gas station attendant wanted to know if we had seen an Attwater's prairie-chicken. We had not. "Used to see lots of them around here," he said while the tank was filling up. "Bobwhites and wild turkeys too. But they all ate spilled grain that had been treated with a fungicide and it killed them off. Can't raise many prairie-chickens round here anyway. It's mostly all farms."

About fifty or so Attwater's prairie-chickens find shelter in the Aransas refuge. A couple of hundred more live in the Attwater Prairie-Chicken National Wildlife Refuge at Eagle Lake, some fifty miles west of Houston. We could not visit this refuge because it is only open to the general public in February, March, and April, when guides take visitors to the breeding, or booming, grounds to watch the males challenge each other and display to the females. About 600 Attwater's prairie-chickens live outside the two refuges.

In the early days before settlement, when there were hundreds of thousands of these birds along the coast between Louisiana and the Rio Grande and up to a hundred miles inland, the old-timers complained that the males' continual booming pained their ears. It begins in late January, when groups of males congregate in open fields to fight for the best positions in the breeding area; it continues three weeks later, when the females appear and they intensify their display — strutting, circling, dancing, pecking at the ground, stomping their feet, inflating great orange air sacs at the sides of their necks, raising their neck tufts like jackrabbit ears, and all the time thundering the dawn air with *whur-zu-rr, whur-zu-rr* sounds that can be heard a mile away.

Prairie-chickens declined drastically when their wet grasslands were eliminated by drainage, rice farming, overgrazing, oil development, and urban spread, and they themselves were eliminated by shooting and introduced predators such as feral hogs, cats, and dogs. But there are always dedicated people, individuals and groups alike, who come forth to fight for a dying species. H. P. Attwater spent fifteen years trying to get hunting stopped (the bird was finally protected by law in 1937) and Val W. Lehmann spent more than forty years studying its biology and promoting its welfare. Unlike the whooping crane, this subspecies does not breed in captivity, so sanctuaries are vital to prevent its extinction.

We discovered several other examples of local conservation efforts. In Rockport, another birding mecca on the Texas coast, there is a least tern nesting colony in the middle of town. When we arrived, it had just recently been given protection, after years of effort by local citizens like Doris Winship and Chuck Kaigler. Rockport is also famous for Charlie, a heron who does his fishing from a bucket. Each day he flies in to stand beside Bo, one of Rockport's human fishermen. As soon as Bo catches what he calls "a speckled trout," Charlie spears it from his fishing line. Other great-blues sneak in to snatch any fish in the bucket, and great egrets stand shyly by, waiting. A pet skunk turned loose on nearby islands destroyed a colony of great blue herons, black skimmers, and gull-billed terns, and the birds never returned. But apart from that, birds and humans get along very well in Rockport.

Tess had anticipated a visit to Lydia Ann Island, where Roger Tory Peterson and James Fisher had enjoyed "a wonderful heron day." Lydia Ann is another National Audubon Society sanctuary, in Aransas Pass just north of Port Aransas, but the birding is not as good there now as it was when "the boys" visited. High tides and new spoil banks — waste material dumps — nearby have reduced the nesting colonies.

The Texas coast is a treasure trove, but whether for wildlife or for wild recreation is the question. We drove for about thirty miles along sand dunes awaiting development. Our way was lined with billboards promising trendy condominiums, beachfront motels, and restaurants. Once ranchland, these barrier islands are now recreation land. "Gateway to Excellence," said one sign. For whom, I wondered. Could there still be birds in these backyards not yet built? Fortunately, Padre Island had sixty-nine miles of wild seashore farther on. We turned our backs on the ocean and headed inland through the big city of Corpus Christi.

"Be prepared now," announced Gus at the wheel next morning, "to meet the kiskadee flycatcher, the green jay, the white-tailed hawk, the ferruginous pygmy-owl, the golden-fronted woodpecker, the black-chinned hummingbird, the tropical parula — and the King Ranch." It was to be our Big Day — ninety-seven species.

We were heading west toward the 100th meridian, an arbitrary line dividing western and eastern species. We were also going south toward the Rio Grande and Mexico. At such a crossroads, we expected to see many and varied species from the West and the East, the North and the South.

We had been in Texas four days. For me, the legendary Texas had only been hinted at in distant smudges of offshore oil drilling rigs and tall storage tanks. Now, as we drove through sleepy Kingsville and entered the King Ranch, we were in the center of Texas's other legend, Santa Gertrudis cattle developed here in the United States on almost a million acres of the mighty King Ranch. It had become a tourist attraction since that swelteringly hot day thirty years before when "the boys" came through what Peterson called "monotonous cow country." As we began the twelve-mile loop drive through the public-relations section of the ranch, Gus plugged in a self-guiding tape cassette, and I photographed the historical marker at the entrance.

Most tourists would be looking for cattle or quarter horses on the King Ranch, but even before we drew away from the gatehouse, Gus called out, "Curve-bill thrasher, golden-fronted woodpecker, grasshopper sparrow, and orange-crowned warbler." Four birds in less than four minutes among the ebony trees and date palms. (Henrietta King, the matriarch of the King Ranch between 1854 and 1925, probably planted them for shade and beauty, but the birds appreciated them for food.) The official brochure says that birds on the King Ranch are too numerous to list.

Most people would not think that doves and sparrows could be highlights. But the quiet cooing of the white-winged doves, mourning doves, Inca doves, and common ground-doves contrasted sharply with the buzzing of the grasshopper sparrow, the trills of the Cassin's sparrow, the churrs of the lark sparrow, and the bouncing pingpong ball chirps of the olive sparrow.

Red-eyed or bronzed, cowbirds put on a fascinating display for us. Both the males and females have inflatable ruffs on the backs of their necks, which look like lions' manes when they raise them. I was intrigued by one male that acted like a helicopter: fluffing out his feathers like wings, he quivered till momentum caused him to leap into the air. Besides the male were two females. Suddenly a second male dropped into the group, and the first male choppered into the air, with the second male winging after it into the bushes.

The headquarters of the ranch looming on the horizon looked like a grandiose Spanish castle. We gave it a quick glance, but Gus drew our attention to two nighthawks doing a courtship flight over a field of yellow grass. "The tourists that drive this road would never see those nighthawks," he commented dryly.

The King Ranch continues for almost fifty miles south of Kingsville and over fifty miles to the Mexican border. Farms and ranches cover 79 percent of all lands in Texas, so most of the original grassland is changed: irrigated cotton fields, rice farms, and citrus groves contrast sharply with vast, overgrazed sheep and cattle ranches. We were now in ranching country, dominated not by natural grasslands but by mesquite, a thorny Mexican tree, twenty to fifty feet high, from the legume family, whose long leaves with their small, perfectly even leaflets seemed, to me, unreal. Most people will drive through these flat, semiarid landscapes mesmerized by mile upon mile of mesquite scrub, broken intermittently by creosote bush and yucca, and beavertail and prickly pear cacti. In the warm winter and the scalding summer, they will think only of thirst-quenching drinks at the end of the road. They will probably fall asleep at the wheel. "The boys" nearly did.

We did not have a chance to sleep. Whereas others would probably cover this route in a couple of hours, we dawdled all day. As soon as Marie and I closed our eyes, Gus invariably stopped the van—at a rest area, a pond, or a fence post. Mottes of gnarled and twisted oaks in the middle of the divided highway were excellent places to find birds. We had passed out of eastern kingbird country, so now on the wires we found western, Cassin's, and Couch's kingbirds. We still saw the captivating scissor-tailed flycatcher, but now we also saw the brown-crested flycatcher. To our dove list we added the white-tipped dove, and to our raptor list Harris's hawk and the black-shouldered kite, formerly the white-tailed kite (a species that has increased its range since Fisher commented that it was very rare in Texas; he did not see it in 1953).

By Harlingen we had dawdled so much through King Ranch country that Gus decided against a detour to Laguna Atascosa ("Muddy Lagoon") National Wildlife Refuge. This southernmost waterfowl refuge of the Central Flyway is where Luther Goldman showed Fisher most of the birds on *his* record Big Day (132 species with 38 "lifers"). Eighty percent of the continent's redhead ducks winter here. Redhead Ridge used to be a famous hunting spot in the 1700s, when the ducks flew by in streams up to five miles long. Tens of thousands of redheads were killed solely for their fat deposits, which were rendered down for saddle ointment.

Thirty years ago "the boys" had spent several days in Mexico near the forest of Xilitla, and Fisher had counted fifty new species in three hours. However, Doris Winship of Rockport said that Xilitla birding was not as productive now. Since birds do not recognize political boundaries, we hoped to see many of the Mexican species along the Rio Grande border in Texas.

The Rio Grande begins in the mountains of Colorado and winds 1,885 miles through New Mexico and Texas to the Gulf of Mexico. Before its floodplain was cleared for agriculture, and dams such as the Falcon Dam of 1954 and the Amistad Dam of 1969 harnessed its waters, dense thickets and subtropical jungles a mile wide clad its banks. Now, little of the original woodland and brushland remain except in special reserves. Santa Ana National Wildlife Refuge and the Bentsen–Rio Grande Valley State Park are two such islands of original habitat and as such are the custodians of native creatures found nowhere else in the United States.

The noisiest of those greeted us at the entrance, and we were subjected to their raucous cacophony and their garrulous chatter all the time we were in the park. Not that we could see them. We just heard over and over again their incredible duet, tenor and bass in the same tree, as plain chachalacas sang their sunrise chorus. These little arboreal turkeys kept up a beat that remained constant, rhythmic, consistent. When the discordant squawks of the great-tailed grackles joined the band, the noise was overwhelming. Great-tailed grackles are spreading inland from the Gulf Coast, so the southern United States will be a livelier place for their presence. Meanwhile, five species of doves maintained a low, incessant humming, the perfect complement.

As usual we had the national wildlife refuge to ourselves. The visitor center was closed, but I flagged down an official in a truck. "You're the most people I've seen for months," he said. "Very few people come here in summer."

I was glad of that. Leaving my companions looking at a least grebe building a semifloating raft nest on Cattail Lake, I wandered alone through the subtropical jungle of the Owl and Mesquite trails. There was no sky overhead. I was totally enclosed by trees, the typical trees of these remaining riparian woodlands — cedar elm; Texas ebony; Rio Grande ash; granjeno, or spiny hackberry (whose tangerine-colored fruit is a special favorite of the green jay); anaqua, or the sandpaper tree; and the huisache, or sweet acacia. Many of them, especially the elms and ebonies, were draped in *Tillandsia usneoides*, the Spanish moss that is not a moss at all. Dark, dank, eerie, the place felt like a cemetery, except that the chachalacas above, unseen but not unheard, were scarcely quiet ghosts.

Nobody was at the van when I got back, so I raced along the wide open pathway to the Pintail Lakes to look for them — and ran right into a coyote. No time or opportunity to take its picture, but I thrilled at the glimpse before it disappeared into the brush. Perhaps I would see a jaguarundi, or maybe a mountain lion. The man in the truck had told me that an ocelot had been seen recently and that someone was trying to catch it to prove that it lived in the park.

Unlike Santa Ana, our next stop along the river was crowded. Bentsen–Rio Grande Valley State Park was popular with picnickers and campers on this hot Sunday afternoon. Ironically, Bentsen's public park attracts more birds than the more pristine Santa Ana wildlife refuge. Ornithologist James Lane calls it "the best birding spot in the Lower Rio Grande Valley." Many of the campers had hung up milk cartons filled with seeds to feed the birds.

"We haven't yet seen the ferruginous pygmy-owl, one of the Rio Grande specialties," said Gus as we left the throngs at the picnic area, "but this is a great place for owls, especially at night. I've seen barn, screech, short-eared, great-horned, and elf owls here. For years a pair of elf owls nested in this telephone pole. At dusk the pauraques come out, but we'll try to pick them up tonight in Rio Grande City." With a name like pauraque (which rhymes with Yaki), I looked forward to meeting it later that night.

Meanwhile, another Rio Grande specialty, the green jay, drew my attention, rather easily as the bird is almost as noisy as the chachalacas but much more brilliantly colored. A blur of green, blue, and yellow flitted through the willows, then landed. The jay was well named. It *was* green, a gaudy, emerald green on its back and upper tail. "Look at its black eyelashes and eyebrows, though," I said. "It's a real Groucho Marx."

"I haven't noticed those before," murmured Gus, who birds here in winter. "It must be the breeding plumage."

We were up with the chachalacas at dawn at Santa Ana and we went to bed at midnight with the pauraques in Rio Grande City. "I can sleep when I get home," said Tireless Tess gleefully when Gus told us to meet him at moonlight by the golf course next to our hotel. We were right beside the Rio Grande. The lights of Mexico were one short swim, or a bridge-length, away.

Creeping single file behind Gus, we followed the sounds to the trees, and Gus searched the grounds with his flashlight. But where were the birds? They seemed to be all around us. We heard their rustling, we heard their calls. Gus swept the torch to the trees, to the ground. Nothing. Perhaps the pauraques turned their heads to avoid the light or to see us better. We could hear them; we could not see them.

"Look, there on the ground," said Gus suddenly, swinging his light toward a pair of shining yellow jewels in the darkness. The nearly invisible bird was a little larger than the common nighthawk but with the same large flat head, enormous mouth, and hunched resting position. The pauraque sprang six feet or more into the air and closed its mouth around some flying insect, then dropped to the ground again, crouched, and fluffed out its feathers.

"Gee, I wonder how many insects it takes to fill that gargantuan mouth," I thought aloud.

"With the abundance around here, it won't take long," answered Gus. "The bird could get all it wants in an hour."

Actually, when caught flying in Gus's flashlight the birds looked like insects themselves, like glowworms, like lighted butterflies weaving across the night sky. Few let us close. We followed their light, but they kept ahead, drawing us on till dawn probably or back to the Bentsen or Santa Ana, if Gus had not finally called it a day — a pauraque's day, but the end of a long night for us.

Early next morning we continued northwest along the border to the Santa Margarita Ranch. "We could find more bird species, more rarities there than at the parks and refuges,'' Gus told us. ''The Gonzales family have owned it for several hundred years, but they let birders in for a dollar each.'' The Santa Margarita Ranch right on the Rio Grande became famous in 1974 when some birders discovered brown jays nesting there. Since then this Mexican species has increased in numbers and has spread to other parts of Texas.

Gus hoped to find other Rio Grande Valley specialties too, such as the rare ringed and green kingfishers. That was why he got us up at dawn again despite our previous midnight's pursuit of the pauraque. These kingfishers are more easily seen when fishing in shallow waters and isolated pools left when the river is low, and this usually happens early in the morning before water is released from the Falcon Dam.

The terrain was now changing, becoming hillier, bushier. Where the land was not farmed for fruits and vegetables, cattle roamed the chaparral. This habitat is sometimes called monte, or subtropical thorn woodland. Birds gave us plenty of opportunities to stop — often they were feeding on the road. Pyrrhuloxias were not as colorful as the more abundant, closely related cardinals till they flew, and then we clearly saw their pink underwings. A long-legged, crested caracara fed on a roadside kill, its chest splotched red with blood. A Chihuahuan raven flew up. Mockingbirds sang with such exuberance that they jumped up and down on telephone wires. Above them soared turkey vultures and Harris's hawks.

Several greater roadrunners did what their names suggested they do — they ran across the road (roadrunners have been clocked at fifteen miles an hour) and chased each other into the mesquite scrub. We had been seeing these shaggy-crested, long-tailed ground cuckoos all through Texas (recently they have been extending their range eastward).

Arthur Bent quotes J. L. Sloanaker as saying, ''Of all the birds on our list, the roadrunner is doubtless the most unique; indeed, he is queer, and would certainly take first prize in the freak class at the Arizona state fair . . . Try and think of a long striped snake on two legs, a feather duster on his head and another trailing behind; or a tall, slim tramp in a swallow-tailed coat, a black and a blue eye, and a head of hair standing straight on end!''

Gus parked the van by a herd of skinny cows on the Santa Margarita Ranch, and we walked along an old cattle trail through the chaparral down to the Rio Grande. On the way he pointed out the characteristic plants, the honey mesquite, coyotillo, Jerusalem-thorn, catclaw acacia, huisache acacia, spiny hackberry, desert olive, and several kinds of cacti including various *Opuntias* known locally as chollas, prickly pears and beavertail cacti. Most were in flower or fruit, perhaps as a result of the heavy rains over the past several days. But all had glochids, tiny barbed bristles that detach easily and can really work their way into your flesh. No wonder the traditional cowboy wears chaps when walking through the chaparral.

For the next two days it was Wild America on the run. We drove for hundreds of miles on flat lonely roads across one of the emptiest spaces on the map, from chaparral to mesquite grassland to Chihuahuan desert, from the Rio Grande to Laredo to Langtry and beyond. It was empty of people, empty of vegetation, but, with Gus at the wheel, not empty of birds. Even when it rained, and even in places where there were not supposed to be any, he was still calling birds, identifying specks and blobs and flickers on wires and poles and fence posts. "Verdin!" he would call. To the rest of us the wire would be bare, but within seconds, a tiny speck became a verdin, the yellow-faced relative of the chickadee, less than four inches long. People who drove sleepily, unseeingly, through this vast thorny desert would miss the joy of a verdin.

Lining the walls of culverts were the open mud-cup nests of swallows, each with chicks hunched down inside, their heads just creaming the edge. Three species — cave, barn, and cliff swallows — species that are not supposed to nest together, according to our knowledge, were twittering and swooping by culvert entrances, defending their nests. Cave swallows nesting in culverts with cliff swallows is a recent phenomenon in Texas, revealing an expansion of both range and niche — and the adaptability of wildlife.

"Is there anybody who can tell me about the cougars on the wall?" I asked our waitress at Sanderson's Kountry Kitchen Restaurant when she brought the enchiladas.

"Yes, I can," she replied with unexpected vehemence. "My brother's a rancher and he caught one of those cougars in a trap. But the trap was too loose and the cat was coming at him. The only thing between him and the cougar was his dog. You'll notice one of the pictures isn't as good as the others. Well, that's because the cat was coming at him and he got in a shot with his camera before he used his gun."

I tried not to look too critical, but I knew that traditional antipredator attitudes were strong in Texas, particularly among sheep farmers and cattlemen. There were estimated to be only between five hundred and a thousand cougars in the state in 1986. Some Texas counties still pay bounties on them, the only jurisdictions in North America to do so. Despite this, the cougar population trend is on the rise, probably because sheep farming has been so reduced in the last thirty years that fewer cougars have been killed as predators.

"We have thousands of cougars around here," the waitress told me. "The ranchers are losing all their animals to cougars. Cougars eat a goat and a sheep for breakfast and another goat and a sheep for dinner. If our men didn't kill every cougar they could, they'd have no stock left. They go and get them in helicopters, any way they can. We look after what is our own. That is the way it is around here."

She sounded grim, threatening. Others began to take an interest in our table. I remembered how "the boys" at Langtry had downed their drinks and departed, but with my enchiladas waiting, I put my appetite before principles, and contrary to character, just listened.

Not so Gus the Brave. "It's not the cougar that's the problem," he remonstrated. "It's overgrazing. You've got too many sheep and cattle on your land. They've picked it bare. It'd be a good thing if the cougar cleaned up on some of your sheep."

The waitress looked grimmer. I intervened. "When did you last kill a cougar?"

"Today," she replied swiftly. "We kill as many as we can — every day."

If I could believe the waitress at the restaurant and the manager at the motel, the road to our next destination, Big Bend National Park, would be paved with "thousands of mountain lions" and "so many pronghorns you'll hardly get around." Perhaps I will get to see a cougar in the wild yet, I thought as we loaded the bus for Big Bend and the Rio Grande again.

If Wild America is measured in vast distances devoid of people, then this was the Wildest America yet. The Chihuahuan Desert is "a harsh habitat," Tess wrote in her journal, "spiny, stony, waterless, hot, hot, hot, looking so inhospitable mile after mile after mile, but utterly fascinating. I found it gripping, quite overwhelming."

We were continuing west through Texas's Trans-Pecos region, west with the railroad, west for a while with the wheels of the train. For more than a mile, it seemed, the "Cotton Belt" rushed alongside us, echoing the same refrain, "We're going West, we're going West, we're going West."

Our road ran across a white stony desert, cleaved through amber-colored rock cuttings, rolled over dry arroyos — dry washes — and climbed gradually over an elevated plateau toward the western mountains. Smudges on the horizon around us were flat-topped mesas and buttes, or isolated mountain peaks. Clumps of vegetation beside us were the stiff-leaved thorny desert plants, the cacti and creosotes, the sotols and century plants, the yuccas and ocotillos, and the unique plant of the Chihuahuan Desert, the space-needle lechuguilla. It was a pimply, pockmarked, and pincushioned land. It looked barren and uninviting, uncared for except in places where yellow grasses grew once again on the overgrazed terrain.

It was wild, but there was life in the wild. About a dozen prong-horns saw us coming and stood watching us. We had plenty of time to take in their unique markings: their soft tan backs and white-striped chests, their black muzzles and pronged horns, even their large dark eyes and long eyelashes; and then when they ran, their startling white rump patches, rosettes of long white radiating hairs that spread when the animal is alarmed. Pronghorns are among the fastest animals in the world, clocked at sixty-one miles an hour. They are not as fast as a cheetah but they have more endurance. These long-legged bovids of the open plains need to be fast, for they have no other protection against their enemies like wolves and humans.

The story of the pronghorn is one of the success stories of wildlife management. Fencing of their range, and herding and slaughtering by both Indians and white settlers, severely depleted their numbers. Two subspecies are currently endangered — the Mexican pronghorn and the Sonoran pronghorn — but in Texas, Arizona, Utah, New Mexico, Colorado, California, Wyoming, North and South Dakota, Saskat-chewan, and Alberta, antelope have been protected by laws, preserved in special refuges, and translocated to vacant range. Their numbers in North America have increased to more than half a million. Only in Mexico, where poaching and habitat loss continue, is there still great cause for concern. We had only begun to explore the pronghorn's range. We would be seeing them again.

As well as pronghorn, we saw groups of tawny brown, jug-eared mule deer and those other large-eared animals, the desert jackrabbit and the fox squirrel. But it was the birds and flowers that made the desert come to life for us.

Gus started calling birds as soon as we left Sanderson. A Cassin's sparrow did a remarkable skylarking display. It fluttered up and down in the air, spreading its tiny wings, splaying its tail feathers like a parachute, and as it danced in the air it sang, beginning with two short openers, climaxing to a trill and ending on two distinctive notes again, a song which seemed disembodied from the bird.

Later, while we were watching a yellow-breasted chat doing a slower version of the Cassin's parachuting song-and-dance act, a breathtaking, unbelievable feast of birds flew into the same tamarisk tree: a cowbird, a pyrrhuloxia, a cardinal, a magnificent hummingbird, and several blue grosbeaks. The tree vibrated with a riot of sound and color.

Gus called another lineup of colorful birds in quick succession — the lesser goldfinch, orchard oriole, summer tanager, horned lark — but none could beat the blazing colors of the buntings, the varied bunting, lark bunting (really a sparrow), and so many painted buntings in their glorious patchwork coats that we began to call them our ho-hum birds.

The flowers too were dazzling: ditches full of yellow evening-primrose, sandy flats covered with yellow melon-loco, purple thistles, orange prickly poppies, stony plains spiked with creamy blue yucca, red ocotillo, and claret cup cactus. Like the birds, they seemed incongruous in these otherwise barren landscapes; they seemed more suited to lush tropical jungles. Instead, they made miniature tropical wonderlands in the desert. Brightly colored flowers are not only aesthetically pleasing, they are functional for plants having to attract insects when rain is irregular and blooming periods are brief, sometimes as short as a single night. The rich red cuplike petals of the poppy-mallow and the yellow petal-skirted Mexican hat (looking just like its namesake) were two of my favorites. Tess was drawn to the blue widow's-tears and wanted to press a specimen in her journal, but the flower was so fragile that it disintegrated in her fingers.

"Check out all the turkey vultures," advised Gus as we continued west to the mountains. "One might be a zone-tailed hawk. It breeds here in the Trans-Pecos, but it's rare. In flight it can be confused with the turkey vulture, which also has two-toned blackish wings. Ground squirrels can be confused too, feeding complacently by the roadside thinking that turkey vultures are overhead, then suddenly getting nabbed by a zone-tailed hawk."

We halted our westward climb at the tiny town of Marathon, the entry point for Big Bend National Park about eighty miles to the south. "Be prepared to see some of the most dramatic landscapes in the country," Gus said as an overture to our next few days' exploration of Texas's last great wilderness area.

James Fisher said that with the exception of Mount McKinley (Denali), Big Bend is "America's loneliest national park." Nestled in a 107-mile U-shaped bend of the Rio Grande, it is remote, isolated, and in its scenery and wildlife more like Mexico than the United States.

"Big Bend spans so many life zones that there are plants and animals here that are found nowhere else in the United States,'' Gus explained. ''It has the river, the desert, the mountains, and the forests. Four hundred species of birds have been seen here, more than in any other national park. We'll see a few more Mexican species, including our main objective, the Colima warbler. It was found nesting in the Chisos Mountains in 1932 and it's still the only place in the United States where you find it.''

Big Bend National Park was only nine years old when ''the boys'' sped through. At that time its landscapes had been devastated by mankind for centuries: by the Comanche Indians who swept through the same pass we were using to reach the heart of the park, driving slaves, livestock, and horses before them and setting grass fires to discourage the Mexicans from pursuing them; by the United States soldier-explorers who came with camels and built forts; by mercury (quicksilver) miners, by candelilla wax producers; by farmers and ranchers. Cattle, horses, sheep, and goats overgrazed what was once some of the best grassland in Texas, removing the protective covering, exposing the topsoil to erosion, and leaving little vegetation for the pronghorn; introduced plants dispossessed the native vegetation; humans exterminated the wolf, black bear, and bighorn sheep.

Big Bend National Park is a good example of Wild America Reclaimed. Since Roger Tory Peterson took James Fisher to Big Bend, the park has been improved for people. Roads have been paved, visitor centers built, trails signposted, villages and campsites organized. According to park naturalist Bob Huggins at the Persimmon Gap Ranger Station, it has been improved for land and wildlife too. For economic reasons (the bane of all national parks and wildlife refuges) Bob could not give me the background papers, but his conversation was free. ''In the last decades, with the last of the livestock gone, the vegetation has made a remarkable recovery except in some of the low areas. Predators have increased. We have panthers back. One killed a burro last week on the Mexican side, and we see them regularly around the Grapevine Hills and the Chisos Mountains. Peregrine falcons are increasing too. They're nesting in each of the canyons.''

It was at the river that we stopped to look through our binoculars. We could have walked into Mexico. The Rio Grande was a mere chocolate milk trickle fifty feet across the canyon. ''We're getting quite a Mexican bird list,'' smiled Tess as she picked out birds across the river. The few vacationers in the campground may have wondered what we were looking for as we wandered along the river, peering through the Carrizo cane, scanning the willows and cottonwoods. Unlike the desert we had roller-coastered through en route, the river was an oasis. Attracted to its shade, its water, or its wealth of blossoms were magnificent hummingbirds, yellow-billed cuckoos, cactus wrens, killdeer, Bell's vireos, black-tailed gnatcatchers, the colorful vermilion flycatchers, summer tanagers, cardinals, blue grosbeaks, pyrrhuloxias, and some new species, black-chinned hummingbirds, Say's and black phoebes, and a rock wren. The rock wren has the unique and curious habit of building a pebbled pathway to its nest in the crevice of a cliff. Sometimes it heaps up the stones so high in front of its nest that it must flatten itself to enter.

The heart of Big Bend is the Chisos Mountains in the center of the park. Their highest peaks rise like the walls of a castle, giving cool relief in summer from the burning desert below. Today in our search for the Colima warbler we were to climb these islands in the sky. Green Gulch Road hairpins for seven miles to The Basin, a large bowl-shaped valley or amphitheater in the center of the Chisos Mountains at about 5,500 feet elevation. From The Basin, hiking trails reach out through canyons, along ridges, around meadows, up to peaks. Emory Peak, at 7,835 feet, is the highest in the park.

As our altitude changed, so did the vegetation. Sparse desert plants gave way to thicker brushlands, low-growing shrubby junipers gave way to woodlands of taller junipers, oaks, and pinyon trees. Some, like the Chisos oak and the Chisos agave, are found nowhere else in the world; others, like the drooping juniper and the Mexican pinyon, reach their northernmost range in the Chisos; others still, like the bigtooth maple, ponderosa pine, Arizona cypress, and Douglas-fir, reach their southernmost extremity here.

The most surprising and personally satisfying tree for me was the Texas madrone (*Arbutus texana*). Its shiny brown peeling bark, glossy leaves, and red berries were so familiar because it is closely related to the Pacific madrone (*Arbutus menziesii*) which on the West Coast we call simply the arbutus tree.

More intriguing was the Chisos agave, a century plant endemic to these mountains. Like the lechuguilla, which is found only in the Chihuahuan Desert, the century plant stores food within its basal rosette of fleshy daggerlike leaves for fifteen to thirty-five years (not a century) before it shoots up a flowering stalk that sends out branches as it reaches perhaps thirty feet into the sky. *Shoots* is an apt word, as the tall spike grows as much as a foot a day. Peterson described the century plant best when he said, ''It is like a stalk of asparagus stuck in an artichoke.''

We wound upward through the woodland for three hours, stopping to peer into bushes, to whisper "pish" into the shady branches, to play a tape recording of its call, but we had almost reached the Pinnacles and still we had not found the Colima warbler. I kept peeking through the trees at the burnt orange walls of the Pinnacles, hoping to find a panther lounging on a rock ledge. Marie, I think, was wondering if she really wanted to climb to the end of the trail, Colima warbler or not. Ironically, Marie and I were the ones who found the bird. Not one Colima warbler but two; not one species in the tree but several, a real bonanza. It was worth not seeing that panther. Well, almost.

"Yes, they are certainly Colimas," said Gus triumphantly when they showed themselves clearly. "They're like Virginia's warbler — chestnut cap, gray back, yellow rump, but a lot bigger."

"We're lucky," said Marie. "Even Peterson and Fisher didn't get a Colima warbler on their trip."

We had got more than Colima warblers. While we were looking at the warblers, two noisy gray-breasted, or Mexican, jays rushed into view, one dangling a lizard from its beak. While we were watching those, a mystery bird brushed past my sleeve, flew around the oak, and hunched down on a branch with its head buried in its body as if it had no neck. It was one of three kinds of goatsuckers, but they all look alike when camouflaged behind a screen of large oak leaves. Tess was sure it was a whip-poor-will, but Gus insisted it was a chuck-will's-widow, a unique sighting here on the western side of the 100th meridian, and not on the official Big Bend checklist.

A light rain persuaded me to stash my cumbersome cameras and awkward notebooks in my daypack, and for the next three hours I wandered as free as the birds we were watching. It was different, and relaxing. I had more time to notice things: brown and rufous-sided towhees scratching for insects in the leaves at my feet; an antelope squirrel holding its tail over its back like an umbrella and flashing its white underside, enough like an antelope to give it its name; holes in oak trees plugged tight with acorns put there by acorn woodpeckers; tiny black-crested titmice heads sticking out at eye level from a hole in the limb of a pinyon tree; band-tailed pigeons and black-headed grosbeaks.

For most visitors to Big Bend, sunset signals the end of the day. Ours had just begun. We were going to visit elf owls. Gus knew their address. "Elf owls come out when the sun goes down," he said after supper. "We should find some by the stables or the cottages."

As we were skulking around outside the Chisos Mountains Lodge, a band of very aggressive javelinas — collared peccaries — rushed out from behind one of the cottages and started butting and bunting each other with their sharp canines. With one look at their raised bristles, I declined to get close with my camera.

Javelinas are pig-like animals native to North America. They were once hunted almost to extinction for their hides and meat, but are now protected by regulations. Their populations have recovered, although in a more restricted range.

The javelinas came to us that night but the owls did not. We saw their eyes, but could not get close.

"No matter," said Gus cheerfully as we returned to the parking lot. "We'll look for lesser nighthawks and poor-wills along the road."

"I'd give my eyeteeth to see those," said Tess enthusiastically.

The common nighthawk and pauraque, which we had already seen, the chuck-will's-widow which confused us that day, the poor-will and lesser nighthawk, which we hoped to see tonight, are all members of the goatsucker family, nocturnal insect eaters with large, flat heads, enormous mouths, and distinctive white patches in their wings or tails. Their eyes are only slits during the day but are large and round at night.

By the time we had reached the desert, Tess did not have enough eyeteeth to fulfill her promise. We saw (some of us in varying degrees) not one poor-will and lesser nighthawk, but dozens. They skimmed the road so close to the van that I thought we would surely hit them. We saw the poor-wills first, at higher elevations. Like the pauraques we had stalked on foot along the Rio Grande, the grayish, nondescript poor-wills sat on the ground, fluttered a few feet into the air like silent moths, then landed on the road again to be caught in our headlights. In contrast, the lesser nighthawks flew higher, looping and skeining back and forth across the headlights, wheeling, changing gears acrobatically, displaying their distinctive striped wings.

It was midnight by the time we got to Lajitas. The day must have set some record — twenty hours of straight birding. Gus went to his room to complete his checklist, Tess to her room to write in her journal, and Marie and I to our rooms to sleep.

Next morning we were up early and enthusiastically looking forward to hiking the Santa Elena Canyon in search of the canyon wren. Our goal was a massive block of flat-topped rock almost two thousand feet high, split in two by the Rio Grande. We jounced south along a dirt road, over dry arroyas, through a jumble of painted rocks, paralleling the thin trickle of Terlingua Creek that was also bumping its way through the desert to meet the Rio Grande at Santa Elena Canyon.

Like "the boys," we nosed the van as far as possible into a grove of cottonwoods and willows at the edge of Terlingua Creek, for the day was scorching. But unlike "the boys," we could not cross the creek dry-shod. A sticky sludge of slow-flowing caramel marshmallow mud four inches deep and fifty yards wide overlay the stones on the creek bed. Carrying our shoes and trying to step in the footsteps of the one ahead, we waded across to the canyon on the other side. For those with endurance and a head for heights, the rest was easy as we wound along a fantastic trail cut by park workers from the canyon walls: sometimes our stone pathway was a ramp, sometimes steps. Back-hugging the walls behind, we sidled a vertical slab on the U.S. side, but so thin was the slit of the river, so overhung the gorge, that I felt we could touch Mexico on the other side.

Whether it was from an American wren or a Mexican one I didn't know, but the most wonderful cascade of sounds suddenly burst into the canyon. To hear a canyon wren for the first time is unforgettable. Some ornithologists call its song a bugle, but for me that is too harsh a word to describe such a ripple of notes tumbling down the scale faster and faster till arrested at the bottom with a final upturned flourish.

"You hear a hundred more than you see," said Ray Stiles, the park naturalist I met on the trail. "I've heard them here every day, but I haven't seen one for weeks."

The song continued as we carried on along the three-quarter-mile-long trail. Leaving the others to look for birds, I walked with Ray down the canyon wall and along the narrow, sandy floodplain, in and out of tamarisk, or saltcedar, bushes, through willows and honey mesquite, past catclaw acacia. The bottom of the canyon was an oven, though it was not yet summer; we sheltered in the shadows of tall boulders. Attracted as always to water, I tried to reach the olive-colored river, but there was too much mud and too many reeds. Bermuda grass, river cane, and tree tobacco decorate the banks but hinder movement. Getting to the Rio Grande was like struggling through a bamboo forest.

We talked of cougars and attitudes toward them. Ray told me he was the son of a rancher from Langtry. "I'm caught in the middle," he confessed. "I go home to Langtry and my ranching friends think I'm a traitor. Back here at the national park, my colleagues think I'm a killer. The two extremes still exist in Texas, but in recent years farmers and ranchers are being trained in scientific land management and encouraged to take an ecological view." Ray agreed that overgrazing, especially after World War Two, had devastated the Texas grasslands, but that Texans were now making concerted efforts to upgrade them.

"There's been a similar turnaround in attitudes to predators, though perhaps not to the same extent," he continued. "Ranchers don't *hate* a mountain lion. They see it as a competitor to be eradicated in the best interests of their business, to protect their livestock. I do admit, though, that many consider it a macho thing to kill a cougar."

The two goats on the Mexican side at the end of the trail reminded me that Big Bend was Wild America Reclaimed. If wildlife was still threatened on private lands in Texas, at least in this huge national park panthers were back and so were their prey; pronghorn have been reintroduced, mule and white-tailed deer have survived, peccaries are increasing, and there are even beaver in the Rio Grande.

We were leaving the Chisos Mountains, but we were bound for other island mountains looming from the desert lowlands — the Davis Mountains, the Guadalupe Mountains, the Chiricahua Mountains. Unlike "the boys," who had to abandon part of their itinerary while their desert chariot was being overhauled, our van — and the sole driver — needed only a short siesta in mid-afternoon. We stopped just south of Alpine for Gus to point out a ferruginous hawk on one side of the van, and on the other a house finch, a black-throated sparrow, a western kingbird, *and* a "newie," the uncommon phainopepla, a silky flycatcher with a wild red eye, an all-black body (except for white wing patches), and a long tail. The phainopepla reminded me of a cardinal in a black cloak.

On the outskirts of Big Bend, the ghost town of Terlingua, once a thriving quicksilver mining community and now a sun-baked collection of crumbling roofless rock and adobe buildings, is being revived. The general store has been restored as the Chisos Mining Company Motel and Restaurant. Realty companies advertise the sale of half-acre lots of desert. Outback Expeditions advertise float trips on the Rio Grande. And once a year, usually in November, some 5,000 people converge on this desolate area for the World's Championship Chili Cookout.

"We want to make this area the Palm Springs of Texas, the Fun Center of the Rio Grande," said Mr. Moore, manager of Lajitas, the tiny Wild West border town next door to Terlingua. "We started with a hunting camp, but people needed more. So we restored the original buildings, added a swimming pool, a golf course, a fully serviced campground, condominiums, an airstrip, and we are selling lots in subdivisions. Soon we'll add a health spa, a museum, and arboretum."

The travel brochures say that more people have spent the night at the bottom of the Grand Canyon than in Lajitas. By the way the desert is being developed, that should be a temporary situation.

Wild America was being reclaimed in another way.

"Be prepared to see lots of wildlife today," Gus said next morning when we met him at the van. "An extra sugar lump in your coffee for the first person to see mule and white-tailed deer or pronghorn antelope. And an extra pickle in your sandwiches if you see all three bluebirds — the eastern bluebird, the western bluebird, and the mountain bluebird."

The day's drive from Fort Davis, Texas, to Carlsbad Caverns National Park, New Mexico, through the Guadalupe Mountains was a beautiful one over rolling hills and between mountains at an elevation that averaged 5,000 feet. It was billed as the highest mountain road east of the Rockies. We breakfasted picnic-style by a sign that read "Mount Livermore, second-highest in Texas."

I think if James Fisher had seen Carlsbad Caverns National Park as it is today, he would have been impressed as much with its interpretation facilities as with its bats and swallows. To get to the bottom of this immense hole in the ground — or at least the lowest level allowed — visitors either walk into the hole through the natural domed entrance and then switchback down by a ramp for a three-mile hike, or else take an elevator. Although you can have your own guide in the flesh, most people pick up the electronic kind — a portable radio receiver — at the top of the hole. At intervals, as you pass points of interest that transmit radio signals, your handset guide is triggered to talk to you. But perhaps the ultimate luxury for a natural wonder is the restaurant, gift shop, and post office at the bottom.

Descending the equivalent of an eighty-three story building was the same as climbing the Empire State Building in reverse. In semi-darkness we strolled along the cold corridors and through the various chambers, past stalagmites that looked like totem poles, and into rooms with names like King's Palace, Queen's Chamber, Papoose Room, Temple of the Sun, and Painted Grotto. The most impressive chamber was the Big Room whose floor area equaled fourteen football fields and whose height equaled that of Washington's Capitol building. It reminded me of walking to the bottom of the sea.

We did not see any wildlife. Cave bats and swallows live in the cave, but in a part that is off-limit to visitors. Sloths once lived there, and fish and salamanders are supposed to live there still. The wildlife extravaganza at Carlsbad Caverns would not begin till sunset. Over a thousand people gathered that evening in an open-air amphitheater above the gaping hole at the entrance to the cavern to see the bat flight. Nobody knew when the bats would come out of the cave, but the park naturalist answered questions as anticipation mounted.

Bats have been longer on earth than humans, perhaps as long as fifty million years. They are not birds but mammals, with fur and teeth and milk. Look at a bat's black crepe-paper wings and you see that they are hands with arms, and fingers lengthened, with the thumbs clawlike hooks. By hanging upside-down, a bat can drop into the air at the first hint of danger and begin flying immediately. It is the only mammal that can fly.

Three million bats have lived in Carlsbad Caverns, but as many as thirty million have lived in other caves in the southwestern United States. The most common species of bat at Carlsbad is the Mexican freetail. As its name suggests, its tail dangles freely. It spends part of its year in Mexico, as well as the southwestern United States. Although a few bats sometimes hibernate in Carlsbad Caverns, most freetails spend their winters in Mexico or perhaps Central America. They come back here in March. The male bats tend to go to other caves or bridges; the bats at Carlsbad are mostly pregnant females. About 40,000 bats were currently in residence, but a quarter of a million were expected to arrive by early June, to remain until October or early November.

"They're coming," whispered Marie on the bench beside me. "The bats are coming," echoed a thousand people in thought and voice as a wave of excitement rippled through the crowd.

Out of the chasm below us poured a stream of black fragments, each "Like a glove, a black glove thrown up at the light,/And falling back." The words of D. H. Lawrence's poem filtered back from childhood. There was ". . . An uneasy creeping in one's scalp/As the bats swoop overhead! Flying madly. . . . Wings like bits of umbrella. . . . A twitch, a twitter, an elastic shudder in flight." Unlike Lawrence, this audience was silent, awed. The only sounds were the thrumming of wings, the squeaking of bat voices, the clicking of cameras.

The bats whirled from the cave as if from a centrifuge, spiraling into the sky like a moving river, and were supposed to stream off to the south and east. But it seemed they did not come and they did not go. From the first moment they emerged, they were always there, filling the stage in front of us like a huge vat of boiling, buzzing bees. Forty thousand, we were told. Gus thought millions.

We watched till dark, till all others but the park naturalist had gone to their beds. We watched for an hour and still the bats filled the sky overhead. Alone in the amphitheater with the bats, we cupped our hands at our ears to hear the whirring of their wings intensified.

Some people think that the return flight at sunrise is even more spectacular. The bats seem to appear from all directions, then merge high over the entrance, bank in formation, pull in their wings — and at twenty-five miles an hour, they plummet into the hole.

Despite their seeming abundance, Mexican freetails at Carlsbad have declined since an estimated eight million in 1924 and two or three million in 1953. Their numbers were reduced by DDT and when guano miners blasted shafts into their roosting cave. Researchers believe that this has changed the bats' microclimate. Their numbers now seem stabilized at a quarter of a million.

Cave swallows, on the other hand, have increased, from three pairs in 1966 to 3,000 in 1986. Although cave swallows do not compete with the bats for space, they are encroaching farther into the caverns and are trying to nest on some of the limestone formations.

Roller-coasting down from Cloudcroft across the Guadalupe and Sacramento mountains through the Lincoln National Forest and down to the Rio Grande was like driving the Appalachians again. One moment we were high in the sky in the coolness of an emerging spring; the next we were baking on the plains in summer. The seemingly endless dunes of snow-white gypsum that lined the highway through White Sands National Monument only made the desert seem hotter. But always on the horizon isolated mile-high mountains rose like islands, reminding us that we could climb to cooler temperatures. Crossing the Continental Divide at 4,584 feet on a flat desert between Deming and Lordsburg, Arizona's islands in the sky — and our search for the elegant, or coppery-tailed, trogon — awaited.

We had time to visit two of the islands, the Chiricahua and the Santa Rita mountains. As we had found climbing the Appalachian and the Chisos mountains, weather, vegetation, and wildlife changed with increasing altitude. Temperatures drop generally about one degree Fahrenheit for every 300 feet gained, roughly equivalent to a north-south difference of 300 miles for each 1,000-foot gain in elevation. Weldon Heald, who lived and wrote about the Chiricahuas, called this phenomenon the climate ladder.

With their proximity to Mexico and their altitudinal variety, the Chiricahuas are considered by many birders to be the best birding spot in the United States. Mac Cutler, a naturalist friend of Gus's who we phoned in Portal, told us that he came to live in the Chiricahuas after reading *Wild America.* ''I camped here for three weeks on my honeymoon in 1957, then came back and bought a house.'' Weldon Heald has said that ''when good birders die they undoubtedly go to a sky island heaven resembling the Chiricahuas.''

Another supporter of the Chiricahuas is the American Museum of Natural History, which bought Weldon Heald's Painted Canyon Ranch near Portal for its Southwestern Research Station. ''There is probably more natural history within eighteen miles of here than anywhere else in the world,'' said the chairman of the museum's Department of Insects and Spiders at the time of the purchase. The cottages and laboratories snuggle together along a stream beneath towering rose-colored cliffs and surrounded by parkland, an appropriately sylvan setting for natural history research.

This is where we spent the night. People were as friendly as the scenery was dramatic and the wildlife abundant. Dr. Stuart Pimm from the University of Tennessee was studying the feeding behavior of hummingbirds. A group from the University of Texas was studying lizards. Denise Frank from Cornell University was studying social behavior and communication in grasshopper mice (so called because they eat insects). Margaret Thornburg and Marie Sweadner, naturalists from San Diego, had come to see birds.

Although our main interest was trailing trogons, we accepted Mac Cutler's after-dinner invitation to look for owls outside his house in Portal. His wife, Ginny, was the first to hear an elf owl—''a dear little creature'' we all agreed as Mac froze it in his flashlight. Gus picked out two horned owls, which Mac told us had just fledged three weeks before. We did not see any western or whiskered screech-owls, but we could hear one. Denise, who tracks her radio-collared grasshopper mice at night, told me she had seen two mountain lions on her way home from work. However, I had to be content with seeing four striped and one hog-nosed skunk and a rare Mexican native species, the Apache fox squirrel.

Next morning Mac met us at nine o'clock to walk the South Fork of the Cave Creek Canyon for trogons. ''In 1977,'' he said, ''four eared trogons arrived here in the fall from the Mexican mountains, probably because we had such a bumper crop of madrone berries. People came from all over the world to see them. Eared trogons are still very rare, but one or two have been seen almost every year since then.''

Trogons, long-tailed birds in dazzling contrasting pinks, oranges, browns, and greens, attract attention. The most famous trogon, the quetzal of Central America, the sacred symbol of Quetzalcoatl, nature god of the Toltecs and Aztecs, is considered by many to be the most beautiful bird in the world.

Although about thirty-five species may be found in the tropical regions of America, Africa, and Asia, only one nests in the United States — the elegant, or coppery-tailed, trogon — and then only in the forested canyons of four Arizona mountain islands, the Chiricahuas, Huachucas, Santa Ritas, and Atascosas. Although the first trogon was seen in 1885, it was not till 1939 that a nest was found. Peterson and Fisher did not mention trogons when they birded in the Chiricahuas in 1953, and Weldon Heald said in 1967 that the odds for seeing a trogon were about the same as hitting the jackpot in Las Vegas. Cachor Taylor, who wrote *The Coppery-tailed Trogon: Arizona's Bird of Paradise*, estimated in 1980 that fewer than fifty pairs nested in the United States. However, James Lane in 1983 commented that although numbers fluctuated and the species was still uncommon, elegant trogons (they're all elegant!) were appearing in new canyons, and their numbers were increasing. Cachor Taylor estimated that at least 25,000 people come to Arizona each year to seek a glimpse of an elegant trogon.

Cave Creek Canyon is the trogon capital of the United States. Gus said this narrow "painted" canyon between Portal and the research station is reputedly the most beautiful in North America. It was very picturesque and reminiscent of outback Australia in its boldly contrasting colors: the towering red rhyolite rock columns encrusted with bright green lichen, the smooth white trunks of the Arizona sycamore trees beneath, and the brilliant blue sky above.

It was pleasant strolling the canyon, looking up at caves and soaring peaks, listening to the gurgling stream winding among the live oaks and sycamores, picking up western wood-pewees, brown-crested flycatchers, white-breasted nuthatches, bridled titmice, and the vociferous gray-breasted jays. But no trogons.

"Let's drive up to Rustler Park at 8,500 feet," Mac suggested. "Trogons are people watchers, and we might see some in the campground there."

"Every day here is outstanding," Mac told me. "There haven't been many changes in this wilderness in the last fifteen years, just a lot more visitors. Especially this weekend. I'm surprised there are still so many birds."

And bird watchers. I was amazed by both their numbers and variety. Schoolchildren. Young couples. Retirees. The park was crowded, but not with trogons.

Cape St. Mary's gannet colony, Newfoundland. The gannets look like pearls from this far away.

Relaxed viewing at Cape St. Mary's, Newfoundland

Atlantic puffins in Witless Bay, Newfoundland

Hope it works the other way around! Alligators in the south are making a come-back. They may pop up anywhere — beside the road, by a golf course, or on a space shuttle runway.

Steve Beissinger shows Gus Yaki a snail kite's nest in the saw grass on the Tamiami Trail.

Brown pelicans have learned to hang out on wharves for a free feed when fishermen bring in their catches.

Please do not feed the pelicans

ENTERING PANTHER HABITAT

Tess Kloot takes a photograph of the author looking for a Florida panther on the Tamiami Trail. Underpasses are to be built in the hopes that fewer panthers will be killed by traffic.

It's birds first when Gus Yaki, Emily Hamilton and Tess Kloot land by float plane in the Dry Tortugas in Florida.

EACH WHOOPING CRANE FAMILY OCCUPIES A LARGE AREA OR TERRITORY DURING THEIR STAY ON THE REFUGE. THE FAMILY DEFENDS THIS HOME GROUND FROM THE INTRUSION OF OTHER WHOOPING CRANES. THE EXPANSE OF GRASSY FLATS SEEN FROM THIS TOWER IS USUALLY PART OF THE TERRITORY OF JUST ONE FAMILY OF CRANES.

HERE IN PEACEFUL ISOLATION, THEY HUNT FOR THEIR FAVORITE FOODS... BLUE CRABS, MARINE WORMS, CLAMS AND OTHER SMALL MARINE CREATURES. IN ADDITION, THEY MAKE FREQUENT FLIGHTS INLAND TO SEEK SNAILS, INSECTS, ACORNS AND PLANT TUBERS.

Many whooping cranes spend their winters at or near the Aransas National Wildlife Refuge in Texas.

Doris Winship and Chuck Kaigler have worked hard to protect least terns on local beaches at Rockport, Texas.

Charlie, a great blue heron, seeks a free feed from a fisherman in Rockport, Texas.

Big Bend National Park, looking toward Mexico

One would think by the number of times Gus Yaki has "birded" at the Grand Canyon that a viewpoint had been named after him, but the reference is purely coincidental.

Johnny Guerro tells the author stories at Canyon de Chelly in New Mexico.

A round-tailed ground squirrel has learned to co-exist with people at the Salton Sea in California.

A sea otter on the west coast of California. These animals are often seen
close to shore in kelp beds floating on their backs with flippers raised.

California sea lions at the Monterey Coastguard Station

Gus Yaki once called himself "just a little boy who likes birds."
Here in Olympic National Park the birds (a gray jay) come to him.

Robert Bateman entertains children in New Chevak by sketching their portraits.

The author and Robert Bateman taking notes
by fish drying racks in the Yukon-Kuskokwim river delta, Alaska.

Robert Bateman shows one of his prints to Theresa and Mac Cutler, Old Chevak.
The print was delivered from Florida to his tent on the tundra at Chevak.

Old Chevak, Alaska

Bateman and the author look at sea birds on cliffs of Pribilof Islands.

A tufted puffin on cliffs of Pribilof Islands brings grass to its burrow.

A bull fur seal looks suspiciously at the photographer.

A bull fur seal with his group of cows. He spends the summers maintaining his territory of cows.

The dean of birders, Roger Tory Peterson, chats with other naturalists on St. Paul Island in the Pribilofs.

The Chiricahua National Monument was fantastic. I remembered Peterson's words to Fisher: "We mustn't miss this. Lots of geology." Fisher had described the forest of rocks as "a mad maze of pillar architecture, a ruined town of a thousand roofless temples that have known no denizens but wild creatures; it teems with turrets and teeth; spires, steeples, and spindles stand in serried steps along, above the canyon sides, soaring sharply into the sky, or towering to titanic toadstool heads, terrifyingly balanced, tempting the traveler to topple them with a thrust."

We headed now through Bonita Canyon. From the lookout at Massai Point at 6,850 feet, the views over valleys, canyons, and forests were grandly wide-angled. This land was an almost impregnable natural fortress for the Apache Indians. For two centuries, until Geronimo, the last battling chief, surrendered in 1886, the Apaches had fought off the invading white settlers and soldiers, then retired to hide in these rock labyrinths.

Marie and I dashed down to a platform giving a bird's-eye view of the whole area. We seized the opportunity to frame a few of the fantastic rock columns that loomed above us. Fifteen million years ago perhaps, the ground shook, split open, and spewed out flows of molten lava that cooled into solid rock which was later slowly lifted and tilted to form mountains. Weather and water made cracks, cracks widened to fissures, fissures grew to breaches, and soft rock columns were undercut by further erosion into the spectacular shapes of the Chiricahua National Monument today.

A few minutes later, Marie and I got in another shot of some teetering rocks when Gus braked for a photograph of the beautiful red bark of the manzanita. And then it was back to the desert again, to head for another mountain island in the sky, this time the Santa Rita Mountains rising out of the hot Sonoran Desert, and the Saguaro National Monument south of Tucson. "The boys" had quenched their thirst and assuaged their curiosity for the Wild America of Movies and Legends by stopping en route at the commercialized ghost town of Tombstone, but I had the feeling that this would be too frivolous for Gus. Anyway, the owls and trogons of Madera Canyon were waiting.

Arizona's Madera Canyon is one of the best-known and most frequently visited birding spot in the state. Even for those who are not interested in birds, its rocky streams and cool oak woodlands provide relief at 5,000 feet from the hot cactus desert below. Santa Rita Lodge, with its "Welcome Nature Travel" sign and its quiet unlocked housekeeping cabins complete with individual bird feeders, obviously catered to bird watchers. Strolling the grounds were several friendly birders who were wearing — in addition to their ubiquitous binoculars — T-shirts advertising well-known birding spots.

Owling is a nightly ritual at Santa Rita Lodge as birders march through the surrounding woods with their flashlights and tape recorders, hoping to attract great horned, elf, spotted, long-eared, and flammulated owls, and western and whiskered screech-owls. Elf owls, the smallest of all the owls, normally nest in holes hammered by woodpeckers out of giant saguaro cacti and at a lower elevation. But for many years an elf owl has nested in a telephone pole right in front of the lodge. An elf owl and a woodpecker were having some sort of altercation outside our cabins when we arrived, but we were too busy unpacking at the time to catch the details.

"The boys" had heard a "Mexican spotted owl," "a Mexican spotted screech-owl," a flammulated owl, and a great horned owl, and had seen a couple of elf owls — five species in one night. Nevertheless, we went to bed happy to have seen four elf owls, a whiskered screech-owl, a western screech-owl, and to have heard, among the many owl calls, the single toot of the rare flammulated owl. Only in southeast Arizona do western screech, whiskered screech, and flammulated owls occur together.

Now all we wanted was that trogon. We stalked it from dawn next day all through the canyon. No trogon.

"Let's go down to Tucson," said Gus finally. Trogons would have to wait.

And then, just as we were getting into the van, Gus heard one call — faintly from somewhere up the canyon. We scrambled out to the parking lot and ran down to the trees along the stream.

Troink! troink! troink! croaked the trogon continuously from somewhere close by in a grove of trees. It was as if the bird had come down from the upper canyon to meet us.

"There he goes! Over our heads," called Gus excitedly.

Tess shook her fist with joy. "Fantastic!"

"He's landing in that sycamore tree," said Marie quickly, groping for her camera. "What a shot!"

"He's sure got excellent taste!" I agreed admiringly, firing off a couple of slides despite some obstruction from long-fingered sycamore leaves. And then he flew to a better position. A photographer's dream. He sat resplendent in the sun on a white sycamore branch against a brilliant blue sky. I was glad our one trogon was a male, for female plumages are more subdued. His colors — nine of them — were so exactly delineated that his plumage looked artificial. Scarlet breast and emerald green throat divided cleanly by a white bar, orange eye-ring and yellow bill set against a black face, smoky-gray wings, and his unique black-edged coppery tail.

Arizona's bird of paradise was a fitting climax to our fiftieth day around Wild America.

Roseate Spoonbill
Ajaia ajaja

Chapter 5
The West
May 31–June 21

"Subduction leads to orogeny," said Tess next morning as we left Tucson. Well, at least, that's what her T-shirt said. "My children gave it to me before I left Australia but I realize it is a bit suggestive," she confessed apologetically.

"No matter, Tess," I laughed. "Actually, it's quite appropriate. We're going to be doing a lot of that sort of thing over the next few weeks." My companions raised their eyebrows. "Yes," I teased. Lots of geology. You know, the Grand Canyon, the Painted Desert, the Sierra Nevadas, the Olympics. Now that we're in the real west we'll be climbing mountains all the time."

One of our two new traveling companions from Toronto looked pained. "Oh no, don't remind me," moaned Elizabeth Robertson. "I want to see the birds. Wish that they didn't live in the mountains. I get dizzy just thinking of heights."

Elizabeth, a Toronto matron with a pale complexion, frail figure, and long gray hair swept up in a bun, looked as if she should be presiding over tea and cucumber sandwiches rather than joining us to discover Wild America. But Elizabeth is a doughty woman who, despite her fear of mountains, nonchalantly rides her bike in rush-hour traffic instead of taking the subway. A real character, some would say. Many times over the next few weeks I was to enjoy her dry sense of humor.

Our second new traveling companion, Kay Forbes, a retired geography and geology teacher, was looking forward to mountains, deserts, and canyons. Kay's snow-white hair, shy smile, and gentle manner belied her zest for exploration. She was always ready to follow a trail, cross a river, climb a mountain.

Few in Tucson, Arizona, were awake at five in the morning, when we tried to beat the heat of the hottest month in the Sonoran Desert by leaving at dawn and climbing above town to the Santa Catalina Mountains and the Coronado National Forest. Few, that is, other than the wild animals.

Despite the fact that desert animals camouflage themselves by freezing when they sense danger, rest in their dens during the day to conserve water, and stay out of sight of predators, many were out and about foraging around the visitor center in the comparatively cool part of the morning. A Gambel's quail, teardrop topknot nodding as he ran, scurried away from the van when we got out to walk the trail. Whole families of round-tailed ground squirrels stood to attention, stared at us for a moment out of big black eyes, then scampered on broad hind feet into nearby burrows when we passed. Desert spiny lizards snapped up insects. Cactus wrens (the official state bird of Arizona) sang scolding territorial songs from the tops of cholla cactus. A Gila woodpecker looked out the window from its nest in a saguaro hole. A gilded flicker hammered on a telephone pole. A curve-billed thrasher perched photogenically beside a saguaro flower, but never when I was ready to photograph him.

The green-stemmed paloverde, the staghorn cholla, and barbed-wire teddy bear cholla were aflame with yellow flowers, but it was the blooming saguaro cactus, the state flower of Arizona, that gripped our attention. One mammoth, accordion-pleated saguaro, with up-raised arms reaching to the sky, looked like a person, a strange, headless robot, a green primeval monster.

White-winged and Inca doves fed upon the nectar of the saguaro's yellow-centered, creamy-white blossoms. They had to be quick. By noon the flowers that opened for the first time only the night before would probably be closed, never to bloom again. The creatures of the desert — birds as well as bats, moths, ants, wasps, and butterflies — had less than twenty-four hours to feast on the saguaro flower. Later on in June, the red pulpy fruits, each loaded with a couple of thousand seeds, would be preyed upon by even more creatures — birds, insects, mice, pack rats and kangaroo rats, squirrels, foxes, skunks, javelinas, and coyotes. People would use them to make jellies and wine.

The saguaro is more than the most arresting symbol of Sonora and the Southwest, it is a miracle. The largest member of the cactus family, it has expandable ribs that can suck up a ton of water when it rains, and it can live on its storage tank for several years. Roger Tory Peterson remarked that ''not even a camel could do that.'' And whether it is dead or alive, the saguaro provides food and shelter for a variety of desert creatures. Birds like Gila woodpeckers and gilded flickers carve out nest holes in its arms or trunk, and these cavities are often taken over by screech- and elf owls, purple martins, and brown-crested flycatchers. Harris's hawks often build nests in the forks of its branches and use its tall arms for perches. Pack rats use its thick stem for shade. Rattlesnakes forage for food among its roots.

The saguaro is able to protect itself from some of this attention. Its shallow roots splay out a hundred feet or more to absorb water quickly when it does rain. Its multitudinous spines deter most marauders. They also shade it from blistering heat and shield it from drying winds. If a saguaro is old enough to produce arms and flowers and fruit, it has managed to survive not only a host of predators but extremes of climate, drought and flood.

A saguaro grows very, very slowly: at fifteen years it is less than a foot high; at fifty, when it is old enough to produce flowers, it is seven or eight feet high; at a hundred, when it grows arms, it may only be twelve feet high.

Conservationists are concerned that too many saguaros die before they are given a chance to propagate themselves. In addition to natural threats, cattle nearly destroyed the saguaros of the Sonoran Desert. With the recent popularity of the southern deserts for northern "snow-birds" (*homo sapiens* relocating to warmer climates), bulldozers clear saguaros for building projects if developers think they can get away with it. And people sometimes use them for target practice and for wood to make tools and building materials. The noble saguaro needs an educated public more than it needs laws.

When "the boys" went through, the Sonoran Desert was not as well organized for interpretation. There were no trams and shuttle rides to get people to the top of Sabino Canyon, no smart visitors' centers with sophisticated audiovisual displays such as those at the Saguaro National Monument. The Arizona–Sonora Desert Museum — more a zoo, aquarium, botanic garden, geology center, and research institution than a museum — had scarcely been built in 1953.

As we twisted up the side of the Santa Catalina Mountains, from Tucson at 2,389 feet to Mount Lemmon at 9,185 feet, we left the saguaro and creosote bush community of the Lower Sonoran Life Zone and climbed into the Upper Sonoran, marked by evergreen oak, pinyon pine, mountain mahogany, and alligator juniper. Elizabeth was so entranced by the birds that she almost forgot she was driving up a mountain. A Cassin's kingbird valiantly chased a raven. A lesser goldfinch swung upside-down on a swaying thistle. A young phaino-pepla, its crest awry, begged its parent for food.

By the time we reached the ponderosa pines of the Transition Zone at 7,000 feet and then the Douglas-firs and white pines of the Canadian Zone and the Englemann spruce of the Hudsonian Zone at 8,000 feet (a mixed conifer community at this elevation), Elizabeth was beginning to see mountain slopes, not mountain birds. Gus did his best to distract her by calling observations. A pair of bridled titmice went nonchalantly about their business, gathering fluffy seedpods for nesting material. A gray vireo, nervously twitching its tail like a gnat catcher, responded to our taped call, and Tess happily noted minute differences between it and other vireos.

This was a Warbler Day, specifically a Girl Warbler Day.

"Last spring," Gus said, "I was sitting at this picnic table with Bob Bateman and there were so many warblers we couldn't concentrate on making our sandwiches. Not so many this year."

As he spoke, a Grace's warbler flashed past a ponderosa pine. And then we got the rest of the family — Virginia's warbler, Lucy's warbler, and the most uncommon one of all, the Olive warbler, in the forest at 8,000 feet, twisting like an acrobat around the branch of a Douglas-fir.

We stopped often on the road up Mount Lemmon. At 9,000 feet we were still in the forest. The city of Tucson, baking and shimmering in the desert far below, was glimpsed only occasionally through the cool spruce woodlands.

We saw plenty of birds on our way to the top, but none of us wanted to see what was next. "Primitive Road. Not Maintained for Public Use," proclaimed the battered sign on the turnoff to Oracle. "The twenty-eight-mile Oracle Road is dirt, rough and seemingly endless . . . the type of road that you take only once," said James Lane in his *Birder's Guide to Southeastern Arizona.* Peterson tells us that Fisher "seemed to relax in the sheer pleasure of maneuvering a big car on a difficult little road that darted into canyons, nudged around spurs, changed its mind and wriggled uphill, thought better and slid down again."

I can say for sure that none of us, not even Gus and certainly not Elizabeth, relaxed as we descended to the desert on the other side of Mount Lemmon. The Oracle Road had deteriorated badly in the past thirty years. We eased over mud-baked ruts, sidled around boulders, dug out of sandy patches, squeezed between trees, and skirted dropoffs. At one point there was no trail at all, just washboard and boulders cascading downward. Uncharacteristically, we all stayed silent, too petrified to talk. And nobody, not even Tess, was watching for birds.

To everyone's great relief, we survived Oracle Road unscathed. We scissored erratically through the Salt River Canyon, a canyon that, according to "the boys," would be as well known as the Grand Canyon if it were located anywhere else but in Arizona, where all landscapes are so dramatic. It was not the canyon but a canyon wren that had me spellbound. Gus heard it when we stopped at the Salt River Bridge.

Surely the most appealing of all bird songs, it rippled down the scale like a cascade, bringing back memories of Santa Elena Canyon. And then we saw it singing from a Mormon tea bush. Its white throat looked like a white pompom bobbing about in the green leaves, a sharp contrast to its rusty red belly and tail.

Another picturesque but silent bird in the Salt River Canyon was the Lewis's woodpecker. We watched entranced as it hopped up a dead pine tree, its plum-colored breast feathers flapping and fluffing in the breeze like a cloak in marked contrast to the sheen of its dark green back and black rump. With its neck hunched forward to gain momentum, it humped up the tree, then disappeared.

Unlike Peterson and Fisher, who toiled over the Mogollon Rim, we sped on shiny smooth highways through the Fort Apache Indian Reservation (one quarter of Arizona is Indian land) and over the rim to look down on an African-like veldt scene of yellow grass dotted here and there with blue sage bush and gray-green juniper. I expected to see elephants; instead I saw cattle. The rangeland passed, and then we were into the desert again, or more aptly, desert grassland, where grass and sage and yucca are not continuous, but separate themselves competitively over the bare ground.

We drove through the Petrified Forest and Painted Desert National Park for twenty-seven miles, stopping at overlooks, strolling short trails, examining exhibits at visitors' centers. But there is much more petrified forest and painted desert, much more wilderness, than can be seen from the thin strip of asphalt that shoots most visitors across this bejeweled ground. Nearly a million people a year drive the highway, but fewer than a thousand venture into the wilderness.

We were overwhelmed not by the color of birds and plants, but by the incredibly brilliant color of stone. Even the trees were stone. The lunarlike landscape rolled and heaved and stretched toward the distant horizon in a jumble of buttes and mesas, cones and pyramids. It looked bare, barren. Its beauty lay not in abundant wildlife or lush vegetation, but in shape and color. Wrinkled hills of mud, silt, and clay were layered like candy cane but in more muted tones, mineralized rainbows of mauve and mahogany, russet and gray. Vertical pleats and horizontal bands of sandstone were softened by erosion into shapes to stimulate even the most sluggish imagination — umbrellas, mushroom caps, ice cream cones.

Badlands, they call these landscapes, yet beautiful badlands made colorful by bejeweled trees that looked like sun-glinted peanut brittle. Strewn across this pockmarked painted desert as if dropped by a giant lumberjack, were thousands of logs, stumps, chips — sawn, carved, shattered — and made dazzling by crystals of quartz and jasper, agate and amethyst.

It was hard to visualize that 200 million years ago, the Painted Desert and Petrified Forest once looked like parts of the Everglades today, that this was jungle, marsh, and volcano. In the late Triassic Period, streams flowed into this basin from the Mogollon Highlands, carrying logs and burying them in silt and mud and volcanic ash. Slowly the logs were impregnated with solutions of silica, filling each cell with crystals till the logs turned to stone. Minerals in the silica produced the famous rainbow colors seen in the Petrified Forest today: iron gave the yellows and reds; copper, the blues and greens; manganese and carbon, the black; quartz, the white and gray. Many logs are still buried by sediment, but others have been lifted, exposed, and eroded to delight both scientists and laypersons today.

A warden stopped the car ahead. The officers were searching for a couple accused of stealing a few pieces of petrified wood from the park. Visitors have hidden such souvenirs in unusual places — bikinis, diapers, hairdos, and garter belts. Offenders face stiff fines. But this was not always the case. Petrified logs were once blasted open for quartz, amethyst, and agate, once crushed to make grinding powder. Petroglyphs, crude figures pecked into the patina of sandstone cliffs and boulders, were once winched, dynamited, and carted away. When ordinary people complained, President Theodore Roosevelt in 1906 protected part of the Petrified Forest as a national monument. The Painted Desert was added, and the monument became a national park in 1962, with more land added in 1970.

In the past, people worked to preserve these natural features for aesthetics, not science. Now there seems to be more practical reasons for their preservation. A few months before our visit, paleontologists had discovered previously unknown dinosaurs — amphibians, reptiles, and mammal-like reptiles — fossils that added to their knowledge of evolution. Astronomers had found places where sun shafts and shadow lines had fallen on geometric petroglyphs with such precision that they believed these solar calendars allowed prehistoric peoples to measure winter and summer solstices, spring and fall equinoxes. Perhaps it does not matter why we preserve our wilderness areas. Certainly, the more reasons we have, the easier it is to do so.

Not that these southwestern deserts are wilderness in the most pristine sense. Native Indians have lived in them for fifteen centuries, building homes of petrified wood and farming the streamside soils.

We visited the Puerco River Ruin, the remains of an Anasazi Indian pueblo with 150 rooms, probably two stories high and enclosing a large plaza containing several underground ceremonial chambers, or kivas. A couple of hundred people lived there in peak periods.

We headed north to Chinle and the Canyon de Chelly National Monument, traveling through the vast Navajo Indian Reservation. There were very few signs of civilization — perhaps an Indian sitting on a ridge, gazing at a flock of sheep or standing by a truck at the roadside; an occasional hogan, or house built of wood or stone; a red dirt track cleaving through the treeless plain.

Pronghorn antelopes and prairie dogs grazed grass hummocks. A family of kit foxes sat in front of their red-earth burrows, squinting in the evening sunlight. Kay picked out a burrowing owl on a log. Gus called sage thrashers singing from a fence and mountain bluebirds flying over the van.

We slept that night at Justin's Thunderbird Lodge in Chinle amid a grove of cottonwood trees, green lawns, and flower gardens — an irrigated, civilized oasis at the entrance to Canyon de Chelly. Part of the lodge was once a trading post built in 1896 to serve the Navajo Indians who lived in the canyon. It was still a trading post and working ranch in 1953 when "the boys" stumbled in late at night.

"Peterson and Fisher wouldn't recognize the place now," said Joe Duncan, who has owned Thunderbird Lodge since 1964. "In those days you wandered all over the reservation on dirt roads with no signs and got nowhere. Only hardy adventurers made it to Canyon de Chelly."

This national monument is unique in that people live and work inside it. Native Indians — the Basketmakers, the Pueblo, the Hopi, and the Navajo — have been doing so since the first century A.D. The Navajo now use it as their summer home, coming onto the canyon floor in early spring to plant corn, melons, and squash, tend their peach trees, and graze their sheep and goats.

Some say too many people come into the canyon. Nevertheless, Canyon de Chelly, a national monument since 1931, is strictly controlled, more so than a national park. Signs said: "It is unlawful to enter the canyons in Canyon de Chelly National Monument unless accompanied by a National Park Service ranger or authorized guide."

I was enchanted with Canyon de Chelly — or was it with Johnny Guerro, a Navajo Burt Reynolds who has been guiding visitors through the canyons for almost a quarter-century? Johnny himself was well worth the tour price, even without the twenty-six-mile-long Canyon de Chelly and the thirty-five-mile-long Canyon del Muerto, whose salmon sandstone walls rose a thousand feet above the farms on the canyon floor, and even without the cave dwellings, pictographs, and petroglyphs of the Anasazi, or "Ancient Ones." A flamboyant, black-moustached ham, he kept us entertained for a full day with nonstop patter that was both informative and jovial, a happy mix of the reverent and the irreverent.

His jeep's eight huge rubber tires sloshed through several inches of water in the stream bed that acted as a road through the canyon. The stream, normally dry above-ground, was now swollen from an unusually high spring runoff and heavy late-spring rains. The high water table and shady canyon walls were two reasons why the Navajo returned each summer to farm the canyon floor. Now grassed, fenced, and treed, sprinkled with occasional people, hogans, and livestock, this national monument is scarcely wilderness.

Yet it was still wild. Its sheer vertical walls rising cleanly above the stream bed looked as if some giant had sliced them from a massive apricot sandstone cake with a sharp knife. It seemed impossible that people had found enough tiny finger-and toe-holds to get themselves to the top. "Desert varnish," looking like wet streaks after a rainstorm, draped many of the smooth rock faces in dark veils of stain — red from iron, blue-black from manganese. Windblown sand had polished them to a patina that glowed when the sun caught them. I thought of all the natural forces that had sculpted Canyon de Chelly for 200 million years, and I felt humble.

Swifts were our avian highlight for the day. Gus counted a hundred of them putting on a spectacular flying display near the rim of the canyon — coming together, breaking away, chasing, twirling, climbing, tumbling. Swifts fly continuously all day long, doing everything on the wing — feeding, drinking, collecting nest material, probably courting, perhaps copulating.

We were lucky to get the opportunity to see one of those aerial acrobats up close. One of our group, Asgar, ran from the river with a little swift in his hand. "I found it drowning in the water," he said breathlessly as we all huddled together looking at a soggy little bird with pointed wings like a swallow and a wide mouth like a nighthawk. "I'll put it back beside the canyon wall when it's dry."

"It'll be more comfortable if you get it cling to your shirt in an upright position," suggested Gus. "It's more natural. Swifts are used to clinging to cliffs and chimneys."

Even Johnny was intrigued by the notion of someone playing foster father to a tiny chick clinging to his shirt like a black-and-white tie pin. So was Gus, but for a different reasons. "It's rare for a swift to make a mistake but that adult must have hit the cliff face, been stunned and dropped into the water.''

We continued through the canyons, stopping often while Johnny pointed out where prehistoric people had once lived on high cliff ledges in long, interconnected, flat-roofed, stone apartments called pueblos. Many were multistoried and allowed the Anasazi to climb the canyon walls from one roof to another.

When we left Johnny, we headed for the Grand Canyon, the most popular geological wonder of all. And we wanted to get there before sunset. West we flew across the Navajo Reservation, across the Hopi Reservation, past First Mesa, Second Mesa, Third Mesa, past ancient Hopi villages perched on precipices that rimmed the sky. A long-haired Indian youth in loincloth and sweatband jogged the ridge of a flat-topped rubble pile. Satin-bloused, hoop-skirted women gathered from the ground their rugs, their jewelry, their baskets, and folded their sheets. A coyote dragged his long tail through scented sage bush. The sun wrinkled the sidehills red in the Painted Desert. The evening shadows came all too soon.

We tried to read how Peterson and Fisher came to the Grand Canyon. But anticipation, a feeling of impending awe, kept us unusually silent. Even Tess, who had not seen a new bird all day, put her field guides away and seemed absorbed by other things.

It was almost dark, almost chilly, when we stopped at Desert View. Silently we pulled on sweaters and long pants and left the van. Each, as if alone, walked toward the chasm. I remembered Fisher's words. ''The world ended; began again eight miles away. Between the ends of the world was a chasm . . . the greatest abyss on the face of the earth.'' Yes, the world as we knew it, a thin skin of soil and plants and trees, had indeed ended, and the world beneath had bared its soul. But the chasm was not a steep, straight-walled, flat-bottomed cleft in the ground like Canyon de Chelly, with emptiness in between. It was a wave-tossed ocean of plateaus and pinnacles that rolled and rippled across the naked bowels of the earth, black and blue and purple in shadow, rust and pink and red in the alpenglow of the setting sun.

The Grand Canyon at last. Tess and I hugged each other in one impromptu silent moment. When one feels magic in the wilderness, one must share.

Next morning was not the same. Twenty-five miles west, at Grand Canyon Village, we entered another world, a world of bustle and noise, motels and hotels, shops and restaurants, banks and post offices, service stations and laundromats, billboards, pavement, and shuttle buses. Grand Canyon Village was more like Grand Central Station. Much more popular, much more expanded since Fisher expressed his admiration for the dignified administration of this national park, the Grand Canyon is now fodder for the masses. We stood in a crowd of camera-clicking internationals at Yavapai Point, waiting for the sunrise over the canyon, and I felt no awe.

"There's a mountain chickadee behind you," said Gus half-facetiously. "That's as good as a ditch." He wandered away from the view and Tess followed.

"I'm glad the emotionalism of yesterday is over," she whispered. "Now I can get back to birds."

Kay and I waited till the sun came over the North Rim, and watched while it kindled each band and butte, giving life to each shape and shadow. I looked around to see Elizabeth hovering among the junipers, well away from the edge. "Elizabeth, you can't come to the Grand Canyon and not see it," I admonished. "There's a railing right here." But Elizabeth knew her mind. "I'm just fine," she smiled sweetly.

You can see the Grand Canyon by riding a mule down a switch-back trail to its bottom, rafting the river that coils through its gorge, or flying between its walls in a plane or helicopter. National Parks Rangers are experts at interpretation, and the system is perhaps the best in the world, certainly more advanced than Australia, according to Tess.

There are many ways to describe the Grand Canyon. Fisher called it "a marvelous piece of luck." I like the story of the cowboy who went looking for cows and found himself looking down into the Grand Canyon. "Something has happened here," he said laconically. The ranger at the visitor center talked about the factors — climate, uplift, rivers, rocks, time — that combined to make the great gash, 277 miles long, ten miles wide, and one mile deep. He said that eventually the Colorado River will carve the canyon so wide that the rims will be so far apart that to the human eye they will not be connected at all. (Reportedly, pollution makes it look that way now, a hundred days a year.)

We lunched among the Gambel oaks and pinyon pines near Yaki Point. While my companions scooted off into the bushes to watch pinyon jays, red crossbills, and pygmy nuthatches, I tried to photograph a tassel-eared squirrel. It was clinging to the trunk of a ponderosa pine about three feet from the ground and seemed almost buried under its enormous bushy tail. But tassel-eared squirrels, called by Fisher "the Beau Brummel of all American squirrels," are famed more for their tall, tufted ears.

The formidable barrier of the Colorado River and the Grand Canyon divides the species into two: the Kaibab tassel-ear of the North Rim, with its all-white tail and black belly, and the one I was watching, the Abert's tassel-ear of the South Rim, with its gray tail and white belly.

Gus and the rest of the crew came back bubbling over their bird list. Birds are numerous (280 species) and extremely diverse at the Grand Canyon, a consequence of its many changes in elevation over a short distance. Humans have had a hand in increasing both the number of birds and their habitats. Since 1976, thirty-four species of new birds have been added to Grand Canyon's checklist, all because of human creations such as dams and sewage lagoons.

I could not visit the Grand Canyon without thinking of mountain lions. My friend, biologist Harley Shaw, had been studying them on the Kaibab Plateau on the North Rim for several years. But now all lion research in Arizona had shut down for lack of funds. Harley was pleased, however, that for the first time in Arizona's history, a restricted hunting season had been recommended. "Numbers of lions are probably stable, as long as Arizona retains large areas of rough public domain," he said. "But I think they need this extra protection."

As we switchbacked down to the desert through the Prescott National Forest, close to where Harley had studied cougar-cattle relations, I thought of his last words. "I'm working on desert bighorns right now. Frankly, I find them dull compared to cougars, but much easier to study."

There is something about this cat of many names that gets you hooked. I had not found one in the Appalachians, Florida, or Arizona. Perhaps I would in California.

We entered California at Blythe on Highway 10. Peterson had called the nearby San Bernardino Mountains "a searing hell hole." And so it was for us. Our destination for the morning was the Mojave Desert and the Joshua-trees of the Joshua Tree National Monument, but like "the boys," we were deterred by the heat and the long detour to the monument's northern end. We had to be satisfied with seeing Joshuas on its outskirts.

We photographed a few Joshuas, tree-high, twisty-limbed yuccas of the lily family, in a farmer's field. They looked like scruffy Sesame Street characters. One had a hawk's nest on top. To the Mormons seeking refuge in the West, the Joshua-tree's "wildly gesticulating limbs," to quote *Wild America*, each crowned with a mop of stiff bayonetlike leaves, were the arms of Joshua beckoning them to the Promised Land.

The Joshua-tree is found in California, Arizona, Utah, and Nevada, but it thrives best in the Mojave Desert. It characterizes this desert as the saguaro characterizes the Sonoran Desert. And like the saguaro, the Joshua-tree provides food and shelter for a myriad desert creatures: birds nest in its wide-spreading branches and perch on top to scan the desert for meals or probe for seeds or insects; yucca night lizards scurry under its bark and dead debris looking for termites; stinkbugs nibble on decaying fibers in its trunk, and antelope ground squirrels feed on its flowers.

But the most amazing creature to use the Joshua-tree is the *Pronuba*, or yucca moth. Deliberately, intentionally, the moth collects the heavy yucca pollen from one blossom, carries it in a ball on her head to another blossom, and forces it onto the stigma to pollinate the flower. Then she lays her eggs in the flower's ovary. When the fruit forms, her larval offspring will have ample and easily available food. The Joshua-tree (or any of the yucca species) and the *Pronuba* moth, helping each other, are a perfect example of mutual symbiosis.

Early Spanish explorers called the Salton Sink the "Valley of Torture." Hollywood used it to film *Dante's Inferno*. It is reputed to have the hottest, driest climate in the United States, with less than two inches of rain a year. With the sink at 235 feet below sea level, we did not expect to find much relief from the heat, which reached the century mark by midmorning.

The Salton Sink extends from Palm Springs south into the Gulf of California. It used to be dry. Then in 1901 a forty-mile canal was built to bring in water from the Colorado River to irrigate this desert. Soon mesquite and paloverde, salt bush and thorn bush gave way to date and citrus groves, asparagus and avocado fields. We drove through Mecca in the Imperial Valley, one of the richest agricultural regions on earth, and the town seemed aptly named.

How it got that way is a dramatic story well told by Peterson in *Wild America*, a story of man against a river to produce a sea. In 1905 the Colorado River burst its artificial channels, and for two years, despite dams, dynamite, and dredges, it poured full-force into the valley, causing a great sheet of water to rise several inches a day. The Salton Sea, thirty-five miles long and fifteen miles wide — California's largest inland body of water—was born. As James Lane comments in *A Birder's Guide to Southern California*, "what had been a land of burning sand with a few rock wrens became a lush valley filled with birds."

Gull-billed terns, now uncommon visitors to the Salton Sea in spring and summer, once nested here. Peterson and Fisher expressed their amazement that gull-bills, along with laughing gulls and white pelicans, crossed hundreds of miles of vast deserts and high mountain ranges to nest on the Salton Sea. The birds were attracted by salt water and fertile fields.(Unlike other terns, which plunge into the sea after fish, gull-bills dart after insects.) In 1953 "the boys" counted 207 gull-billed tern nests on a "secret island . . . one of the most curious bird islands in North America." But Peterson feared that the birds were vulnerable, that predation could destroy the colony.

Since then the colony has been destroyed. Bill Henry, biologist for the Salton Sea National Wildlife Refuge, told me that the continually rising waters had inundated the little island. Gull-billed terns, laughing gulls, and white pelicans did not nest there any more.

Although gull-billed terns and laughing gulls are rare, many thousands of white pelicans flock to the Salton Sea in winter. "We counted 18,000 white pelicans at the south end of the sea in February 1985," Bill said.

To see large concentrations of waterfowl in the most bearable temperatures, winter is the best time to go birding at the Salton Sea. Between January and March there may be half a million ducks, fifty thousand geese, many thousands of shore- and landbirds. The Audubon Christmas Bird Count often reports the highest numbers for the continent, especially for species such as ruddy ducks, pintails, eared grebes, long-billed curlews, long-billed dowitchers, mountain plovers, red-starts, rough-winged swallows, and orange-crowned and yellow-rumped warblers. Millions more pass through in spring and fall, migrating through the Pacific Flyway. Summer brings in interesting visitors from Mexico, which is just twenty miles away: roseate spoon-bills, wood storks, brown and blue-footed boobies. The Salton Sea has the highest population of doves west of the Rockies, including mourning doves, white-winged doves, and Mexican ground-doves.

And after the birds come hundreds, thousands, of birders, many of whom were there today. The Salton Sea refuge at the southern end of the sea has 258 species on its checklist, and we were to see about seventy of them that day, including a glaucous gull, a new listing for the refuge.

We lunched at Niland Marina with the van door open to attract some breeze off the water. I had another use for the door — as a blind to photograph families of round-tailed ground squirrels who came up to nibble on our banana peel linings. They were engaging creatures, popping in and out of sandy burrows beside our van, sending sand flying as their back legs whisked away the earth to widen their tunnels. I was intrigued by their neat and almost naked little tails. These little squirrels were well used to people.

Unlike Florida, the Salton Sea suffers not from too little water but from too much — and of the wrong kind. The waters had begun rising when "the boys" were there, reducing the refuge land by a third. Fisher thought it was due to the spongy subsoil reaching saturation after so many years of irrigation. The condition was aggravated, however, when farmers tried to leach out salts from the alkaline desert soil by running fresh water over their already sodden fields.

Since then, according to Bill Henry, the sea has risen "tremendously," particularly since the 1970s, cutting out still more land used to grow forage crops for birds. "We have lost a lot of nesting habitat for gulls, terns, and white pelicans, including that little island you said Peterson and Fisher visited. And with increased channelization, we've lost a lot of natural edging. We've got concrete along our waterways now instead of bullrushes."

Another problem is the sea's increasing salinity. Fisher said that the salinity level in 1953 was "3⅓ per cent — near that of sea water." Bill Henry said that it had now risen to 10 percent, much more salty than the sea. "So we have lost a lot of our original wetlands, our freshwater marshes. And that reduces habitat for birds like the Yuma clapper rail, which is already an endangered sub-species."

When birds are compressed into shrinking wetlands surrounded by contaminated drainage water containing salts, selenium, and other pollutants leached from farmers' fields, they develop diseases commonly referred to as western duck sickness. In the summer of 1983 at the Kesterson National Wildlife Refuge in California's San Joaquin Valley, the young of several waterfowl and shorebird species developed deformities like misshapen beaks, bulging skulls, clubfeet, and stubby wings. Biologists believe that these abnormalities were due to selenium poisoning. "The fish in the Salton Sea have too high levels of selenium already. We shouldn't be eating them ourselves," Bill Henry said.

Since "the boys" were at this refuge, habitat for wildlife has deteriorated in both quantity and quality. Refuge managers struggle constantly to buy or lease land so that diversionary crops like barley, vetch, and millet can be grown to feed wintering waterfowl rather than risk the ire of neighboring farmers. Nevertheless, there have been some gains. Numbers of birds have increased, especially Canada geese, great blue herons, white pelicans, and cattle egrets. Barnacles have been good for ducks, and tilapia, a fish introduced to control the weed hydrilla, has been good for herons. Bill Henry looks into his glass ball and is ''a little pessimistic'' about future gains, but he concedes that at the field level, dedication is strong, and as a result of the losses, many more people are now working to solve the problems and insist on solutions.

From below sea level and above century heat, we climbed to over 4,000 feet through mountain passes on our way west to the Pacific Coast. A red-shouldered hawk carrying a snake above a vast and busy shopping mall seemed to illustrate the contrasts we would find in California.

California not only has the largest human population of any state in the Union but it also has the largest reported mountain lion population. With 3,000 or so of these cats in the state, the only western state that forbids lion hunting, and one where mountain lions have been seen in cities like San Diego and Los Angeles, perhaps I would find a wild cougar there. The status of many animals in California has improved in the last three decades — the mountain lion, elephant seal, gray whale, and sea otter, to name a few — and much of the credit is due to the insistent lobbying of the general public.

Dick Weaver, a biologist with the Department of Fish and Game, believes that the cougar's California status is healthy, but he does not expect the maximum population to exceed the 3,000 estimate by more than 800 to 1,000 animals, even under the best of conditions, because of habitat constraints and the animal's solitary nature. One of the main reasons why the mountain lion's status is reasonably secure in California (besides its loyal and lobbying friends) is that much of the wildland it prefers is either in public ownership or not particularly vulnerable to development. If I could not see a cougar in California, then I was glad to know that it was there, and I looked forward joyfully to exploring its main Californian habitat, the wild country of the Coast Range and the Sierra Nevada.

But first, the wild country of San Diego. Thirty years ago San Diego Zoo, in Fisher's words, was simply ''one of the most attractively landscaped zoos in the world.'' Now it is perhaps the best in the world — in every way. Thirty years ago there was no Sea World or Wild Animal Park. Since then such spectacles have proliferated all over America, all over the world. But the best are still in San Diego.

Since then too attitudes to animals and animal interpretation have changed phenomenally. Millions of people visit these parks annually to be entertained. It is hard for North Americans not to get enthusiastic about wildlife when they have such intimate and entertaining ways to view it in zoos and oceanariums: monorail and aerial tram rides, photo caravans, summer camps, behind-the-scenes tours, walk-in aviaries, moving sidewalks that take people right into the midst of animal habitats.

But the new emphasis is on education and research. Entertainment is limited to the natural behavior of animals. No more belittling them by cutesy, saccharine narration, no more dressing them like dolls. Animals perform and are displayed, but people learn about their biology and their geography at the same time.

We arrived in San Diego at the right time to see two important events in the zoological world: the opening of a state-of-the-art penguin display at Sea World and the birth in captivity of California condor chicks at the Wild Animal Park. Both are excellent examples of the three aims zoos and oceanariums use today to justify their keeping of animals in captivity — education, research and conservation through captive breeding.

At the penguin display, people see not only penguins but also the other animals that share the same ecosystem. They see scientists doing research they could not possibly do in the harsh conditions of Antarctica. They see endangered penguin species raising their young. So Wild America can be found in zoos too. And I think King Penguin himself, Roger Tory Peterson — nicknamed after his favorite bird — would be pleased.

It is easy to love a penguin, but very few people find a condor appealing. Literally translated, its Latin name means "the bald vulture of California," which aptly describes its naked, yellow-orange head and sickly pink bulbous neck. It looks as if a barber had gone mad with a razor and shaven his victim raw. Even more incongruous, the condor has a black fringe of feathers which it raises around its neck like a shawl, reminding me of a jaundiced bald man in a high-necked black evening cloak.

Yet to the Indians, the California condor, soaring, gliding, hanging high in the air on nine-foot wings, was a demigod who symbolized immortality. Ironically, it is now the world's rarest bird and symbolizes white society's destruction of a species that has been around since the Pleistocene epoch.

In 1986 less than half a dozen birds remained in the wild. Condors declined primarily because their food supply declined. Historically, condors fed on beached whales and deer carcasses. Nowadays, whale populations are down, and with increased fire protection, brush areas have expanded and deer carcasses are difficult to see. From 1800 to 1850 the hide and tallow trades left many cow carcasses, so condors thrived. Between 1850 and 1939 cattlemen, careless in animal husbandry, put their cattle out in the spring and gathered their survivors in the fall, so condors continued to thrive. However, after 1939 cattlemen became more careful with their stock and left fewer carcasses, which was good for business but bad for condors. Ranchers also poisoned cattle carcasses to get rid of predators they did not want.

There are other reasons for the decline of the condor. Gold prospectors killed them to make gold dust containers from their quills. Ornithologists collected their eggs and skins. Hunters shot them for trophies. Fishermen killed them to make flies from their feathers. Developers reduced their wild habitat by constructing roads, towns, networks of electric wires, and oil wells. People killed them just because they were there, just because they were ugly.

Dr. James Dolan, Curator of Mammals at the San Diego Zoo, confirmed that with their low numbers and reproductive rate (not breeding till five to seven years old, and then only producing one egg every other year), condors *will* become extinct in the wild unless "we take drastic measures to breed them in captivity."

Those measures were being taken in 1983. It was the Year of the Condor in California, and Jim was jubilant. "There has been a 180-degree turnaround in attitude," he told me. "The National Audubon Society used to be against condors in captivity, but now they are working together with us, with the state, and the feds to develop a captive group of condors that has genetic representation from all five breeding pairs in the wild."

I joined the crowds excitedly pressing against the glass windows of the nursery at the Wild Animal Park to watch Sisquoc and Tecuya, the first condors ever hatched in captivity, pecking at their hand-puppet mothers for a feed of skinned mouse. They looked like little Yul Brynners. Two more condors had just been hatched at the zoo from eggs collected in the wild, but they were not on display. Nine more chicks would be hatched by 1986. They would soon be released into large flight pens called — what else? — condorminiums, and then eventually into the wild in habitat that allows them to survive.

Like the peregrine falcon, whooping crane, and Andean condor experiments that preceded it, the California condor project continues to be a success, with twenty-four condors in captivity in 1986. However, there has been a constant reduction of condors in the wild: from about sixty in the 1950s when Peterson and Fisher did their trip, about fifty in 1970, nineteen in 1983 when we did ours, thirteen in 1984, and only six in 1986. Spurred at the last minute by the deaths of six wild condors since 1984, including the shooting and lead poisoning of the last wild breeding female, government wildlife workers decided to round up the last six condors and add them to the captive breeding project. By the time of the roundup, there were only five.

Being, like Fisher, a lover of seabirds and islands, I was disappointed that we were not able to visit the Mexican Coronados Islands, which are only twenty-five miles from San Diego. However, my host, David Acuff, a fellow cougar researcher, updated me on a couple of the conservation success stories on those islands and others off the Baja California coast. Since "the boys" boated to the Coronados with Dr. Carl Hubbs of La Jolla's famed Scripps Institute of Oceanography, numbers of California sea lions and elephant seals had increased considerably. Elephant seals on Guadalupe Island had grown from 4,548 in 1952 to 80,000 in 1985, causing overcrowding. Brown pelicans, which suffered drastic declines between the 1950s and 1970s as a consequence of pesticide poisoning (virtually no young in 1970), had rebounded well and, said David, "hundreds of young are now being produced annually."

Meanwhile, Tess made an exciting discovery in San Diego — a Brandt's cormorant in rarely described and seldom-seen nuptial plumage. Birders know well the Brandt's breeding plumage of fine, hairlike white streaks scattered about its head, neck, and back. But this Brandt's had two large, silky-looking ear tufts that were longer and denser on the right-hand side. (Tess and the rest of the women were so intent on recording the strange white plumes that they failed to hear an approaching train; Gus pulled them clear with only seconds to spare.) After months of research, Tess solved the mystery with the help of Dr. Gerry van Tets in Australia. Gerry confirmed that both sexes have these particular plumes only until there are eggs in the nest. Then, as the season progresses, they abrade, leaving only the plumage that is commonly seen.

Our first destination beyond San Diego was to look for a wild condor in the Sespe Condor Reserve near Fillmore. But first we had to get past Los Angeles. I smiled when we read that Fisher had insisted that Peterson drive him through downtown Los Angeles and Sunset Boulevard. Peterson had ventured to the heart of Los Angeles only to show Fisher a Chinese spotted dove with an address on Figueroa Street. Gus cannot have felt the same as ''the boys'' about Chinese spotted doves; he swung into the traffic stream on the Golden State Freeway and rolled with it to the north.

For an hour we hairpinned back and forth along steep-walled treed canyons up into a misty sky. We were only thirty-five miles from downtown Los Angeles, yet we could have been in a different world. It was rugged, forested, and wild — except for trucks and oil tanks that shared the road with us. Surely there were no oil wells in a condor reserve! In 1953 Peterson thought oil drilling would not happen at Sespe because of the rugged terrain. Conservationists effected a compromise whereby no drilling could be undertaken within one-half mile of an active condor's nest, but they could not stop it altogether. Side roads off the public access road we were enduring led to oil rigs, and we could clearly hear the drilling of the ''gas trees,'' as Fisher called them. For several fascinating moments we could hear three different kinds of drilling sounds at once: the gas trees, the delicate electric drilling sound of the wrentit, and the firm whacking sounds of the acorn woodpecker.

We parked above jungly cloud and mist at Dough Flats amid mountains that looked like folded green shag rugs. On the way up we had found the ground carpeted with purple mint, white sage, purple phacelia, scarlet larkspur, yellow monkey-flower, and evening primrose. No wonder there were so many hummingbirds.

Elizabeth stayed at the flats, but the rest of us, beckoned by blooming yellow yucca candles, walked easy switchbacks through the chaparral to a bench overlooking bluffs where condors sometimes soar. Gus had seen them twice before in November. ''Extra tomato slice at lunch for the one who sees the first condor,'' he promised, scanning the blue sky. Wings flew by, but they did not belong to condors. Nor were they golden eagles, turkey vultures, or red-tailed hawks, alternative silhouettes illustrated on a plaque by the viewing bench.

We did not find a condor. Considering that there were so few left in the wild, I was not surprised. It is ironic really that condors often choose to nest in poor places when better sites are available, that they sometimes lose their eggs through clumsiness or by letting ravens harass them. In 1986 one egg of the last condor female in the wild was found thirty feet below the nesting cliff; the second one was hatched successfully in the San Diego Zoo. Wild America has its hazards. As I gazed across the spacious skies, I prayed that soon there would be captive-bred condors to fill them.

After lunching with lizards on the back of the van door, we felt fortified for the descent. Down we went 4,000 feet, lurching along the puddled, rutted track again through swirling mists and between knife-edged ridges.

Elizabeth was relieved and I ecstatic to hit the ocean at Ventura, which coincidentally is the home of the Condor Research Center. We now headed north again, this time along the Coast. At Carpinteria I was even more enthralled to see a black swan, the symbol of my home in West Australia.

It was crowded at the Andree Clark Bird Refuge in Santa Barbara, not only with birds — mallards and mallard mixes, western, ring-billed, California, and Heermann's gulls, double-crested cormorants, great blue and black-crowned night herons — but with people feeding them.

As we left Santa Barbara I looked wistfully out to sea, remembering a summer fifteen years before when I had visited the nearby Channel Islands. These eight small mountain-tops sticking steeply out of the Pacific between eleven and forty-five miles offshore are a natural-history paradise. Santa Barbara Island has the largest nesting population of the Xantus' murrelet in the nation, if not in the world, and is the only nesting place in America for the black storm-petrel. Anacapa Island is the only place in the western United States where the endangered California brown pelican breeds regularly and is slowly increasing. San Miguel Island was for a long time thought to have the only breeding colony of fur seals south of the Bering Sea. In 1972 a second colony of fur seals, now 6,000 animals, was discovered on Castle Rock, a mile northwest of San Miguel. Its population was growing rapidly, with more than 700 pups born annually. A friend of mine found one of these pups on her beach in the Queen Charlotte Islands, British Columbia. Fur seals more commonly migrate southward from the Bering Sea, not the other way around!

San Miguel not only has fur seals but California sea lions, Steller's sea lions, harbor seals, elephant seals, and Guadalupe fur seals as well, which make it the most diversified seal and sea lion rookery in the world.

Fifteen years ago the Channel Islands were bombarded by an oil spill in the breeding season. San Miguel, owned by the Navy, was also a target for bombs. Then in 1980 — perhaps because of the catastrophe and ensuing controversy — five of the Channel Islands, including the sea for six miles around, became a national park.

I was anxious to stop farther up the Coast at Morro Rock, a 576-foot high monolith called the Gibraltar of the Pacific, where I had watched peregrine falcons nesting in 1970. I wondered if, despite the decline in peregrine populations everywhere since then, they might be nesting there again. Suddenly above the sound of the surf came the clear, unmistakable *kack kack kack kack* of a peregrine falcon. My adrenaline rose. The falcon was so close, it must have flown over our van.

Gus followed the falcon to Morro Rock. Just then the sun broke out of the morning fog. People were tending their boats, fishing, and feeding gulls. Only one person was looking up, intently observing four falcons threading across the blue sky, two adults and two fledglings chasing, screaming after their parents, begging for food.

"I'm on twenty-four hour watch making sure people stay away from the peregrines," Stephen Thorston said shyly when I posed the question with my tape recorder. "I work for the Predatory Bird Research Group and the Peregrine Fund at the University of California in Santa Cruz."

Peregrines declined dramatically on the West Coast between the 1950s and 1970s, presumably from the effects of DDT. By 1970 less than five active eyries were known, indicating a 95 percent decline, with similar crashes in Washington and Oregon. Then, with DDT banned, the peregrine recovered from less than ten known pairs (all in California) in 1975 to eighty-two known pairs in 1985 (California seventy-seven, Washington four, and Oregon one).

Researchers on the West Coast are concerned because some still do not hatch, or else they break under the incubating parents, and pesticide levels are still high in the migrant birds that peregrines eat. However, they believe that even with increasing urbanization, decreasing wetlands, and the perennial pesticide problem, the three Pacific states could support more than 300 nesting pairs, not just the eight-two they have now.

"Yes, the peregrine's doing pretty well along this Coast," Stephen confirmed. "We have fifteen eyries between Monterey and Pismo Beach, a distance of 150 miles or so. That's improved to historic levels. But it wouldn't be okay without man doing things for them. This Morro Rock pair resides here, so they don't bring back DDT themselves. They're getting it from the prey birds wintering in Central America and the chemical residues we still have in the environment. The female here laid bad eggs, so we gave her dummy eggs to incubate. We couldn't take a chance and give her good eggs in case something happened to them. Then when the proper incubation period ended, we gave her two chicks eight to ten days old that we'd hatched ourselves. She went ahead and fed them. They're the two chicks you're watching now."

While I was talking to Steve, the others were scoping the bay. Their bird list was well worth stopping for: brown pelicans, Brandt's, pelagic, and double-crested cormorants, common and red-throated loons, black-crowned and great blue herons, surf scoters, western, ring-billed, and Heermann's gulls, oystercatchers, violet-green swallows, and white-throated swifts. The whole Morro Bay estuary is a sanctuary.

And then I saw a sea otter. He was lying on his back by a weed bed, bent into a C-shape more dexterously sustained than a gymnast touching his knees at exercise class. He held up two stubby front paws stiffly like a hand in a mitten; occasionally, languidly, he circled his hind feet like a flaring fan. The sea otter is clothed in the densest fur coat of any mammal, but it has learnt to float still and high in the water, holding its unfurred snout and palms to the air, ridding its body of excess heat — thermoregulating, the scientists say.

The Big Sur Coast stretches from Morro Bay to Monterey. Very little has changed along this spectacular coastline in the past thirty years, very little since the Spanish considered it the Graveyard of the Pacific two centuries before that. Very little is expected to change in the next hundred years, thanks to environmental activists and environmentally conscious governments, who after a decade of debate have finally agreed on a zoning plan to protect this national treasure from development. Local residents opposed a proposal that it become the Big Sur National Parkway, similar to the Blue Ridge Parkway through the Appalachians, because they feared that national park status would bring too much publicity and too many tourists. In the present plan some houses (about 800) may be built, but only in canyons, lowlands, or other sites where they do not intrude on the view. Man, as well as rugged landscape and winter weather that often washes out communication, will ensure the isolation and the natural features of the Big Sur Coast.

The road was like a roller-coaster — soaring, plunging, leaping streams, hugging gorges, slicing mountains pitched steeply to the sea. It was as if the hills themselves had tumbled pell-mell into the ocean, cracking into cliffs, shattering into offshore stacks and needles, churning the sea to foam. There are no safe harbors here, few inviting beaches: Big Sur is an inaccessible, unprofitable land from the human point of view. Perhaps that is why sea otters like it.

Originally, sea otters ringed the Pacific from northern Japan through the Aleutian Islands to California. By the beginning of the twentieth century hunters methodically searched for months trying to find a single otter, and many believed the species to be extinct. And so they were in most of Alaska, all of British Columbia, Washington, Oregon, and, it was thought, California. But hidden for a hundred years by formidable mountains, hazardous shores, and vast sprawling kelp forests, a few California sea otters managed to survive. They were rediscovered accidentally in March 1935 by a couple testing a telescope. Frieda and Howard Sharpe watched in amazement as ninety-four sea otters floated together in a raft off Bixby Creek on the Big Sur coast near Monterey.

From that small pod of ninety-four, the California sea otter population grew steadily till it reached an estimated 1,800 in 1977, at which time it was officially classified as a "threatened species." Since then it has not significantly expanded in numbers or distribution. The annual spring count is now between 1,300 and 1,400 animals. However, in the spring of 1985 there was a bumper crop of pups (236), the highest number of pups recorded in six years. Other colonies have grown too since the days of decimation: over a hundred thousand in Alaska, a count of 345 in British Columbia, fifty or so in Washington, but probably none in Oregon.

Despite the success of thousands of otter lobbyists like Margaret Owings of Friends of the Sea Otter, sea otters are still threatened in California: by increased offshore oil drilling and tanker traffic, by increased toxic pollution in the sea, by direct, malicious killing—and now a new threat, accidental death by drowning in fish nets. It is estimated that a thousand have died this way in the past decade. Conservationists have long planned to transplant otters to San Nicolas, the outermost of the Channel Islands. This proposed colony would be far enough away from the sea otter's current habitat, along 200 miles of central California coast, that a major oil spill would not wipe them out.

Some people, such as fishermen and abalone divers, do not want the sea otter to increase, and they vigorously oppose a second colony in the Channel Islands. The values of fishermen, divers, oil drillers, businessmen, naturalists, and tourists are being weighed constantly along the California coast, and only the future will tell which way the scales will tip.

We lurched to a stop just south of Villa Creek, where Gus saw a huddle of sea-battered redwoods in a gulch. They snuggled down beside live oaks in rocky canyons. Yet these were the famous redwoods, the largest, tallest trees in the world. Some sixty million years ago, contemporary with dinosaurs, there were about forty redwood species. Now only two survive: *Sequoia gigantea*, the giant sequoia of the Sierra Nevada, and *Sequoia sempervirens*, the coast redwood which grows just inside the summer fog belt from San Francisco north to the Oregon border. The coast redwood species we were looking at along the Big Sur coast could grow as high as 350 feet and live to be 2,000 years old. Redwoods grow old because their thick red bark is able to resist fire, insects, disease, and birds, but it cannot resist man. Loggers say that more than twenty average-sized houses can be built from one large redwood tree. Fortunately for those who believe that there are other values, Sequoia and King's Canyon national parks and Redwood National Park (new since Peterson and Fisher's trip) protect these largest of all living things. And as sea otters have guardians from the general public in Friends of the Sea Otter, the trees have Save the Redwoods League.

"The road's washed out from here to Monterey," said the man in the homemade bus with the intriguing license plate BAD INFLUENCE. "El Nino strikes again. You'll have to go back and take the Naciemento road inland."

By the time we had taken the long way around to Carmel, we had to cancel our intended drive around the Monterey Peninsula. Fisher called this coastline the most picturesque in the United States, "the finest surviving example of the near-pristine, unspoiled community of plants and animals once characteristic of the California coast [where] flowers grow in the profusion that the first Spanish settlers saw." Francis McComas called it "the greatest meeting of land and water in the world."

It is still pretty and pristine, thanks to private and state protection. Point Lobos State Reserve, one mile south of Carmel, is known particularly for its offshore colonies of California sea lions whose barking sounds like dogs (or wolves), its rafts of sea otters, its naturally whitewashed offshore rocks for cormorants and brown pelicans, its viewpoints for watching gray whales on winter migration. Seventeen-Mile Drive, a private, strictly controlled road along the rocky coastline, is like a miniature Big Sur but more accessible. It is famous for its seals and sea lions, birds and sea otters, but distinctive for its original groves of picturesque wind-buffeted Monterey cypresses. Flat-topped, gnarled-limbed, tight-twigged, these weather-twisted trees lodged in granite by the curdling shore look like hands sending platters sky-ward . . . or anything you want them to be.

Marie and Kay were certainly thrilled next morning to get an intimate look at the California sea lion rookery at Monterey. From the parking lot of the Coastguard Station, the rocks had looked as if they were covered with a crawling carpet of massive banana slugs. Standing beside them at the gate to the breakwater, we could see clearly the differences between the bulls, cows, and newborn pups. The larger bull-necked males, their crests raised and saliva foaming from open jaws, lumbered across the slender, diminutive females as if they were rocks. Other females, propelling themselves from the water with their long front flippers, squirmed out of the way of the bulls and slumped to rest on the heaving pile. Scarcely a foot away, skinny week-old pups with concertina-like skin lay on pilings and cross-struts along the wooden wharf and looked up at us with limpid but alert eyes.

Other sea lions were playing offshore, swimming on their sides doing some sort of an Australian crawl, rolling like corkscrews. Some looked like paddle-wheelers, back flippers churning the water as they dived, frothing in circles when they surfaced. These animals, breeding virtually in downtown Monterey, were well used to people—and judging by the number of sea lions we saw tagged and transmittered, were well used to scientists too.

The California sea lions, with their ability to rotate their flippers and even gallop along the ground, were much more agile than the harbor seals bobbing out in the kelp beds. Harbor seals have their hind flippers permanently turned backward, so they must wriggle over the ground or through the water using muscular contractions. California sea lions belong to the eared seal family, as did Sam, my northern fur seal, and the northern, or Steller's, sea lions we would soon be seeing in Alaska; harbor seals belong to the earless seal family. To make it even more complicated, the differences are not really a matter of whether they have ears or not: it is just that you can see the tiny external ears of the eared seals, whereas the earless, or true, seals look as if they just have holes.

California sea lions have been increasing steadily in California in the last thirty years, so much so that many males have moved to British Columbia, at least for the winter. Their barking at the end of my garden overlooking Mill Bay is distracting, but I enjoy knowing they are there. Scientists are not sure if they have expanded northward because of population pressure in the south or if they followed the warmer waters brought by El Nino. There were 4,500 California sea lions in British Columbia in the winter of 1984, a dramatic increase since 1980.

Gus swung away from the coast and headed across the hot Central Valley of the Sacramento–San Joaquin rivers to the Sierra Nevada — and Yosemite.

Many roads lead to Yosemite. The Sierra Nevada is one of the most accessible of American mountain ranges, and being only a few hours' drive from San Francisco and Los Angeles, it is accessible to many people.

Water is what Yosemite is all about. And after El Nino's heavy rains and the deepest snowpack in history, Yosemite's rivers were bursting, its waterfalls tumultuous, its meadows more like lakes. The Merced River rushed down the valley to meet us. Like a giant spilled milkshake, it boiled around boulders, frothed and curdled over bushes, thrilled the rafters racing by our van. And then at 4,000 feet, on the floor of the Yosemite Valley, it leveled to a lake, meandered through flowering grassy meadows beneath a shady arch of trees, and almost disappeared.

We could only see tree trunks from the windows of the van: green lichen snakes over the red-barked ponderosa pine, showers of white bracts on the Pacific dogwood, cinnamon limbs and graceful feathery droops from the incense cedar. To appreciate the grandeur of Yosemite Valley, we needed to lie flat and look up to the sky. Half a mile above, waterfalls plunge over the rim of the canyon, plummet down polished rock faces, and cascade in clouds of spray. Yosemite has the grandest collection of waterfalls in the world, concentrated and spectacular. Yosemite Falls, Sentinel Falls, Ribbon Falls, El Capitan Falls, Bridal-veil Falls, the Cascades, the Giant's Stairway—their faces are as famous as their names. I remembered scissoring up the side of Yosemite Falls alone, 2,700 feet in three and a half miles; plodding up the Giant's Stairway by Vernal and Nevada Falls in a group, one hiker behind the other, 2,000 feet in one and a half miles.

We had approached the Grand Canyon from above and had looked down on mountains that rivers had carved. Now we approached Yosemite from below and looked up at mountains that glaciers had gouged. Yet some of Yosemite's famous faces have been sculpted by more than glaciers, more than erosion. Massive granite rocks once buried as much as ten miles below the surface of the earth have been uplifted, relieved of their enormous pressure, and expanded. Now exposed to air and water, heat and cold, the rock has cracked in layers, peeling and flaking off in shells like the scales of an onion, or the leaves of a cabbage, leaving rounded domes. Sometimes, as in Half Dome, which looks as if a giant knife had sliced it clean, cracks or joints have been eroded in addition to exfoliation by load-relief.

John Muir, Yosemite's greatest publicist at the turn of the century, said: "No other mountain chain on the globe, as far as I know, is so

rich as the Sierra in bold, striking, well-preserved glacial monuments
. . . or gets more light . . . everything shines. It should be called the
Range of Light, not the Snowy Range.''

Hot coals were once pushed over its cliffs in a flaming fire-fall to
persuade people to come to Yosemite. A million visited in 1953, two
and a half million thirty years later. It is so popular, so congested, that
customers reserve space in the park by Ticketron at shopping malls
throughout America. Rangers set quotas to limit hikers on the trails.
The "village" in its valley is more like a town.

There are 750 miles of trails, many paved, and 266 miles of primary
roads in this national park, yet the valley occupies only seven of its
1,189 square miles. "Nearly all the park is a profound solitude," said
John Muir almost a hundred years ago. That is true if you leave the
frenzy on the valley floor and climb through the park's several life
zones to the High Sierra above timberline at 11,000 feet.

We could not drive to Glacier Point as "the boys" had done to see
Yosemite's finest view, because many of the roads and trails were still
impassable. I was tempted to take the shuttle bus to Mirror Lake where a
mountain lion had been seen two weeks before but I decided to stay
with my companions. We hiked up through the snow to see another of
Yosemite's wonders, the Big Trees, *Sequoia gigantea.*

For three and a half hours we dawdled along the trail to the Upper
Grove, reveling not in the sequoia symphony that awaited us at the
top, but in the overture that preceded it. James Fisher was an enthusiastic
admirer of sugar pines, "those clean, stalwart, straight trees, growing
among the sequoias, showing that all life can be big." Called sugar
pines because their sap is sugary, these soft pines are the tallest of the
American pines and have the longest cones.

I was fascinated by the incredible snow plant stretching foot-high
blood-red candles through the drab debris of the previous fall. Sapro-
phytic scavengers, but one of Yosemite's showiest plants, their red
fleshy asparaguslike stalks and bell-shaped flowers looked painted or
plastic.

There was no dearth of birds. Solitary vireos, Oregon juncos, pygmy
nuthatches, hermit thrushes, and a bevy of warblers — Townsend's,
MacGillivray's, Audubon's, Virginia's, and Nashville, yellow, yellow-
rumped, and orange-crowned, and a new one for the trip, the hermit
warbler with his distinctive plain yellow head and black bib. Gus thought
he saw a calliope hummingbird. The scoop of the day for Tess was a
Cassin's finch atop a sugar pine.

Douglas squirrels and Sierra chickarees busy feasting on the fleshy scales of sequoia cones scolded us with bird-type calls as we passed beneath their trees. Mule deer returned our gaze with alert but solemn eyes. A coyote limped away through the trees.

Two hundred giant Sierra redwoods awaited us. They were instantly recognized by the cinnamon-red color of their foot-thick fibrous bark, twisted like a man's knuckle. In 1852 promoters stripped the bark off these sequoias and shipped it East. The General Sherman tree in Sequoia National Park is the largest sequoia, but the Grizzly Giant tree in Yosemite was massive enough for us to appreciate the grandeur of the species. Probably standing for 2,700 years, it is 209 feet tall at its snag top (it used to be taller), 96 feet round at its base.

People will not be blasting tunnels through the tall trees any more as they did to attract visitors to the Wawona Tree in 1881. Attitudes have changed. Today, that would be called desecration. Our understanding of fires has changed as well. Forest managers now realize that sequoias (as well as several other species) need fire to survive. Fires destroy competitors, burn litter on the forest floor to let sequoia seeds sprout, and clear the limb canopy, letting sunlight down so that seedlings grow. Today, fires are prescribed and controlled.

White-headed woodpeckers kept circling the trunks of some of the big trees, particularly the ponderosa pines and incense cedars. Gus was hoping to see a great gray owl, a bird of the Northwest with a southern outpost in the Sierra Nevada. Or a dipper, the incredible little water ouzel that walks under water. But it was mainly a warbler and woodpecker day. Still, aided by Gus's ever-observant eye, we did add thirty-eight of Yosemite's 200 species to our bird list.

Although Yosemite is called the Valley of the Grizzly Bear, we knew we would not see those any more. People have not left enough space for grizzly bears. Still, Yosemite is surviving, despite the enormous pressures of millions of visitors a year. The fact that most people remain on the valley floor and that those who do go into the backcountry are regulated helps the park to retain its wildness. All who go to Yosemite leave imbued with some degree of conservation philosophy. The Sierra Club was founded on such a premise.

I almost wept when we learned that El Nino had struck again and we could not leave by way of the Tioga Pass. The road was closed after the worst snowfalls in recorded history. We would not be able to surmount the 14,000-foot high, 400-mile long, eighty-mile wide Sierra Nevada; we would have to sneak around its edge.

We lunched by a mulberry tree in full fruit that attracted an incredible number of birds: Steller's jays, band-tailed pigeons, robins, rufous-sided towhees, a black-headed grosbeak, a lesser goldfinch, an unidentified hummingbird, and a new woodpecker, this time Nuttall's.

An hour and a half later, in the snow at 8,000 feet, we were still counting birds. Green-tailed towhees, fox and white-crowned sparrows, Oregon juncos, and hermit thrushes hopped through the underbrush for insects or seeds. A Townsend's solitaire perched on an artistically gnarled two-toned juniper as if in a Robert Bateman painting. Pine grosbeaks and Wilson's and Audubon's warblers flitted from branch to branch in a bigger juniper above. Then onto the top twig of what we felt sure was a stunted bristlecone pine (the oldest tree species in the world) flashed a Clark's nutcracker, a somber-colored bird in black, gray, and white, but with a bright personality like a crow or wood-pecker. Even more personable was the pika, or rock rabbit, that darted out of a boulder burrow at my feet. He tolerated my stare for several minutes, probably wanting me to leave so he could get on with the summer's business of cutting and drying hay.

The strong scent of artemisia wafted toward us when we came down from the Toiyabe National Forest onto sagebrush country. Common snipe, birds of the meadows and marshlands, were instantly recognized by their zigzag flight and the tremulous winnowing sound made by air rushing through their spread tail feathers and rapidly beating wings. One of these game birds obligingly pitched down on a pole to give us a good view of his striped head, which, if he had been on the ground, would have looked just like the grass.

Another bird to greet us in the open country was the black-billed magpie. Like the yellow-billed magpie, this is a handsome bird that appears black at a distance, but whose long tail and wings are really iridescent green. Only the scissor-tailed flycatcher we had loved in the South had a longer tail relative to its body.

"Welcome to Nevada" said the sign, and most people headed for Lake Tahoe and Reno think of resorts, entertainment, and gambling. I suppose that Wild America is indeed in the eyes of the beholder, but I could find it in Lake Tahoe too. Snow-peaked mountains rearing 10,000 feet out of an incredibly clear blue lake and flanked by forests of pine and fir. Two common mergansers preening on a sun-warmed boulder by Sand Harbor State Park, breeding males in startling field-guide plumage—their heads really did look green, their beaks and feet impossibly red. Our first golden eagle for the trip, being harassed by two screaming red-tailed hawks. Black blobs turning into mountain blue-birds when the sunlight struck them. Belding's ground squirrels emerging from the snow melt by fence posts to forage among still sodden grasses. The straggly tips of fir trees against a polarized blue sky at the Mount Rose Weather Observatory. Ants struggling over a rock with the remains of a moth's wings.

And then near Reno, the mystery bird of Red Rock. "Look at that pintail, at least I think it's a pintail," said Gus quickly, bending over his scope. We all trained our binoculars on the duck to see the usual pintail features — slender neck, needle tail — but it did not have the neck-stripe of the common pintail, *Anas acuta*. "It could be *Anas bahamensis*, the white-cheeked pintail, a West Indian vagrant some-times seen in the East," pondered Gus, leafing through his field guides. "If so, then it's highly unusual to find it here in the West. Probably a record." A local birder Gus phoned that evening agreed that things were topsy-turvy in the bird world this Year of El Nino.

"I'm not convinced that bird is the white-cheeked pintail," said Tess, brooding over her notes and sketches. "It didn't have that much white and its beak was too light." Several months later in Australia, indefatigable Tess devoured the bird books of several countries and concluded that our mystery bird was *Anas georgica*, the yellow-billed, or brown, pintail. It did not come from the Bahamas but from Chile, and as far as we knew, had never been recorded this far north.

We were now crossing Lassen Volcanic National Park. The Land of Fire was still the Land of Ice, and many roads in the Cascades were closed as they had been in the Sierras. We drove as far as the snow allowed. The names along the way — Devil's Doorway, Chaos Crags, Chaos Jumbles, Hot Rock, Devastated Area — reminded me that Nature was not quiescent as it seemed to be in the Grand Canyon and Yosemite. The forces that build our landscapes and wear them down are still at work — visibly — and leave us a legacy of spattercones, lava plugs, gurgling mudpots, steam vents, hot springs, caves, cones, and chasms. Lassen Peak last erupted in 1921.

It was humbling to drive through piles of rubble, walk into dark lava tube tunnels, throw snowballs where so recently flaming lava had flowed. It was hopeful to see that life returned. Pairs of evening grosbeaks, Townsend's solitaires, house wrens, and pygmy nuthatches courted among the Jeffrey pines. Hairy orange caterpillars, with black circles making striking patterns down their backs, spun gray webs around themselves. Mule deer browsed among carpets of showy mule's ears in yellow flower and shiny greenleaf manzanita in pink blossom. Rock wrens chiseled insects out of spattercones with their sharp-pointed bills. Golden-mantled ground squirrels, looking like chipmunks but without stripes on their faces, bounced around the jumbled rockfalls. A forest of dwarf conifers, some more than 250 years old, grew from rubble piles.

Mount Lassen is only one of the snow-capped volcanoes that pimple the Cascade Mountains in a long line from California through Oregon and Washington to British Columbia. We had yet to see Mount Shasta, Mount Hood, Mount St. Helen's, Mount Rainier, and the one I see from my bedroom window, Mount Baker. We wound upward through the Shasta-Trinity Forest on well-graded roads till at 10,000 feet our way was barred by ice.

It was an impeccable day, and we had the mountain to ourselves, a world of blue and green and white. The snowpack on either side of the road was cratered thickly like a frozen bubble bath. Each dark green fir and spruce tree sat in its own basin of meltwater. Such a silent, bright, still world, a world of carved, shiny marble. I wanted to close my eyes and revel in the sun.

The track at my feet galvanized me to movement. Four rounded pads stared at me from the snow. The town of Cougar was not far away. Panther Meadows was close by.

"Peterson and Fisher saw 900 bitterns at the Lower Klamath and Tule Lake national wildlife refuges," Gus reminded us as we drove to one of the oldest waterfowl refuges in North America. "A free dinner at midnight for the first one to see three adult bitterns together."

We did the auto-tour of Lower Klamath and Tule Lakes, just two of the six units making up the Klamath Basin National Wildlife Refuge, also a National Natural Landmark. It was like driving in a boat: lake on one side, water impoundments on the other. Canals and dikes interlaced with green fields of barley and alfalfa patterned like a checkerboard. Manipulated water, manipulated land, necessary manipulation to bring water back to the desert after historic lakes had been drained for farmland, necessary manipulation to grow crops for wintering waterfowl.

In summer, water is managed to provide irrigation for agricultural crops, to prevent flooding of nesting habitat, and to maintain marshes in a healthy condition. In winter, when farmers do not need the water and birds do not need nesting sites, much of the refuge is flooded to provide lakes for the huge rafts of birds that rest and feed here en route between summer breeding grounds in Canada, Alaska, even Siberia, and winter refuges in California. The Klamath Basin, surrounded on all sides by mountains and forests and deserts, is a natural bottleneck on the Pacific Flyway. "More birds funnel through Klamath over a longer period of time than any other place on the Pacific Flyway," said Marti Collins, the assistant manager of the refuge.

For those who like spectacles, such a refuge provides bird watching at its best. The Klamath Basin refuges are one of the few places in North America where you can still see skies blackened by ducks or lakes whitened by geese in stunning concentrations. Bird numbers peak in late October and mid-March, during the fall and spring migrations, but 180 of the 275 species seen at Klamath stay around to nest. Perhaps 60,000 ducklings and goslings may be produced in a good year. It was mid-June, not peak season, but we saw birds everywhere: in the air, on the water, crossing the levee in front of the van; individuals, family groups, and flocks. There were flotillas of ducks and geese.

I agree with Fisher — the most exciting birds were the western grebes. They sailed across the pond, necks stretched tall but pliant, long yellow rapier bills pointed forward, eyes glowing like red rubies. The time had passed when pairs did their spectacular wedding dance, treading water together, rushing forward side by side, then facing each other, breast to breast, rising from the water, bills pointing to the sky, and offering weeds to each other. Most were now tending eggs on floating nests of reeds. Many had hatched their young, and downy gray chicks now rode on their parent's backs (almost like a marsupial), snuggled down into a pocket formed by their wing and back feathers. When the parent dived, the chicks went underwater too.

I did not see any bald eagles, although they are present all year round. An estimated four dozen pairs of eagles nest in the northern part of the Klamath Basin. The refuge has the largest wintering concentration of eagles in the contiguous forty-eight states, perhaps six hundred birds in January and February, attracted by the wintering waterfowl.

Sundown found us in hillier terrain by Lava Beds National Monument. Marsh hawks quartered across the fields doing a midair ballet. We saw one male passing food to the female, and off she went toward the bluffs, perhaps to carry it to their young. We were looking for owls, short-eared owls that "the boys" had tried to see without success.

Ironically, and unusually, when we did find a few individuals sitting in the grassy fields or along the sandy canals, blinking their big yellow eyes, they stayed there so long returning our stares from the van that we moved on before they did. We saw a dozen altogether, beginning their nightly patrol. Also foraging at dusk in the sagebrush country were California quail, chukar partridges, yellow-bellied marmots, many mule deer, and four antelope, one nursing her young.

We had not seen a bittern, so nobody got a free dinner that night. But we had seen more birds in numbers than any other day around Wild America. Gus reckoned that we had seen several thousand. However, when Peterson and Fisher visited the Klamath refuges, their hosts reported birds nesting in the several thousands, migrating in their hundreds of thousands, particularly pintails, who were measured in their millions.

Since then, despite management, waterfowl numbers have drastically declined. According to Marti Collins, a total of 687,600 ducks, geese, swans and coots used the Lower Klamath and Tule Lake refuges on a peak fall day (October 29, 1985). In comparison, refuge staff in 1953 reported a peak of seven million birds of just eleven species. "Pintails, white-fronted geese, and cackling Canada geese seem to be way down," Marti said by phone, quoting 163,000 pintails, 73,000 white-fronted geese, and 1,920 cacklers, compared to 5.2 million pintails, 340,000 white-fronted geese, and 71,500 cacklers reported to "the boys." Except for mallards and Canada geese, which are now resident on the refuge, all species seemed to show declines.

Why? Nobody wants to say for sure, but Marti pointed to some of the possibilities. "The species that nest in the Arctic and migrate through here show the greatest declines, species like white-fronted and cackling geese and pintails. We haven't lost any acreage in this public refuge, but wetlands held privately are diminishing. Too many birds crowd onto small areas in the winter, greatly increasing disease problems, and crowding may contribute to a general decline in the population." Heavy hunting pressure, both in the lower forty-eight states and in Alaska, is considered to be another factor by refuge staff.

Realizing that there have been tremendous losses in breeding, migrating, and wintering habitats, particularly on the prairies, through urbanization, industrial expansion, and the draining of wetlands for agriculture, the Secretary of the Interior for the United States and the Minister of the Environment for Canada launched a North American Waterfowl Management Plan in November 1985. Waterfowl species and waterfowl habitat will be monitored scientifically and reported at five-year intervals to at least the year 2000. Present land will be improved. More land will be purchased. Farmers will be given financial incentives to preserve wetlands and nesting cover. Hunting will be curtailed where necessary. This plan is the most important conservation initiative since the Migratory Birds Convention Act of 1917.

We continued north along the Cascades. The ghost of El Nino followed us to Crater Lake in Oregon. Instead of driving for thirty-five miles around the rim of the deepest, purest lake in Wild America, the bluest blue lake in the world, we were restricted to glimpsing this shimmering caldron through a window cut out of a snowbank. Still, Crater Lake for me is the single most memorable view in Wild America: it was breathtaking when I first saw it twenty-five years ago, and it is breathtaking still.

We left the volcanic ice cream cones of the Cascades at the Columbia River, which Roger Tory Peterson thinks is "unquestionably the most beautiful river in America," and headed West to the Coast. Rain and rainforests. Sea and salmon. Fiords and fish ladders. Salal and white rhododendrons. We had reached the Pacific Northwest — home for me.

"Some miles beyond Portland we noticed all the trees silhouetted against the skyline were dead," Roger wrote in *Wild America*. "We found ourselves in a ghost forest, where great tree skeletons, charred black, gestured in agony with their stubs of branches." He was talking of the Tillamook Burn, a fire that in 1933 devoured a virgin wilderness of nearly 500 square miles. Despite twenty years of regenerative growth, Peterson commented that "in places the Tillamook seems so sterile that one wonders whether trees will ever take root again."

They certainly did. The Tillamook Burn is now the Tillamook Forest, and trees are ready to be harvested. "It's a thick carpet of green," confirmed Clair Kunkel, biologist with the Oregon Department of Fish and Wildlife in Tillamook in 1986. "We have deer, elk, bear, even cougar and mountain beaver, which are usually rare. We have good runs of salmon and steelhead. Except for a dead snag here and there, you could never tell there was a burn."

We were headed for an even greater "burn" — Mount St. Helen's which had erupted on May 18, 1980. The earthquake, registering 5.0 on the Richter scale, triggered the collapse of the mountain's near-perfect dome. Gases equal to ten megatons of TNT exploded and blew away a cubic mile of the mountain's summit. A sled of earth, a hail of ice and boulders, a fiery blanket of suffocating ash, swept 230 square miles of land into oblivion, obliterating trees for miles, tossing others like matchsticks into the world's biggest clear-cut, triggering mudflows, blackening skies for hundreds of miles around with dark, abrasive clouds, flooding valleys, destroying lakes and streams, creating others, flattening fields, burying houses, vehicles, and people. The eruption killed an estimated two million birds, fish, and mammals.

We followed the story of the devastation along the North Fork of the Toutle River for twenty-seven miles by a new road to the official observation site, where the river is dammed by earth, preventing our farther progress. The actual blown-off cone of Mount St. Helen's is another ten miles away.

Despite the gray of land and sky, the debris, and the foreboding signs shouting "Evacuation Area" and "Potential Hazard," there was an almost festive air at the Lewis and Clark Visitor Center, a new tourist attraction. Bus tours took you closer, helicopters closer still, and films and displays closest of all, albeit vicariously. I persuaded Tess to take home a souvenir of Mount St. Helen's ash in soapblock form.

Surprisingly, there were birds. "An incredible list for standing still by the van," said Marie in amazement.

"I'm only identifying 50 percent of what I see flying in and out of the bushes," said Gus.

Red-breasted sapsuckers and downy and hairy woodpeckers were foraging around the red elderberries. Cedar waxwings, robins, western tanagers, hummingbirds, Steller's jays, and red-breasted nuthatches were feeding on the foxgloves. Song sparrows and western wood-pewees were singing by the sword ferns. An osprey flew overhead.

It will take perhaps forty years to rebuild the food chain, but life is being resurrected at Mount St. Helen's. Millions of new trees have been planted. Avalanche lilies, blackberries, lupines, fireweed, ferns, and alders are growing again. Deer, elk, gophers, and ground squirrels have reclaimed the wasteland. Blue-green algae proliferating in volcanic-rich water provide a chemical broth for new life.

Because of its unique and diverse terrain — mountains, glaciers, volcanoes, rainforests, lakes, rivers, and seacoast — Olympic National Park, which takes up most of the Olympic Peninsula, has been designated a World Heritage Park and Biosphere Reserve. Mount Olympus, named after the mythical home of the god of rain, is the wettest spot in the continental United States, with about 200 inches of precipitation per year, mostly in the form of snow. Yet Sequim, only forty miles to the east, is the driest area north of southern California, with less than seventeen inches. Because the climate is mild, the mountains are so close to the sea on three sides of a peninsula, and there is so much rain and coastal fog, the Olympic National Park grows record-sized trees — Sitka spruce, Douglas-fir, Alaska cedar, western red cedar, red alder, and western hemlock. Roger Tory Peterson commented that the Olympic rainforest is by far the largest and densest of any rainforest outside the tropics, so lush that it may contain the greatest weight of living matter, per acre, in the world.

Statistics do not convey the grandeur and mystery of a West Coast rainforest, an almost impenetrable, three-dimensional world of green: tall columns of trees soaring to find the sky, light filtering down as if through stained glass windows, a ground hidden in a profusion of ferns and flowers, a tangle of salal and hanging gardens, a cathedral-like stillness.

The park is possibly the wildest, most pristine part of North America, excluding Alaska. Although it has the densest population of Roosevelt elk and black-tailed deer in the United States and the densest population of cougar, its very wildness make it impossible to see this elusive animal.

We left the rainforest and drove north to lunch along the seashore. On the horizon five miles out to sea loomed our destination — Destruction Island — but we had no way of reaching it. "It is no small project to get out there," Peterson had said in *Wild America*, thinking of treacherous seas and special permits. Gus agreed. Fortunately, I had been to Destruction Island before on scientific visits and was to go again. First I had gone by rubber boat on an unusually calm day, so calm I could have got there by log; twenty years later, I was to go by helicopter. Destruction Island is jointly administered by the Coast Guard as a light station and by the U.S. Fish and Wildlife Service as a refuge. Between my visits, the Coast Guard boys had been replaced by an automated light, the buildings had been torn down, the ladder to the top had been abandoned, and Destruction Island was given back to the birds.

Especially rhinos. Say "rhinos" to most people and they will have an instant image of massive, horned mammals lumbering over the African plains. Rhinoceros auklets also have horns — but these are alcids, seabirds that, like puffins and murres, can swim with their wings. With their chunky black bodies, pale orange beaks, white whiskers and plumes, and their habit of nesting in burrows (or caves), rhinos should be called "puffins," not "auklets."

They are the most numerous seabirds in Washington (over 69,000 breeders), but people rarely notice them because they come to land only in the nesting season and then only under the cover of darkness to bring fish to their young. Even the Coast Guard boys on my first visit to Destruction Island lived right in the midst of rhinos without knowing they were there.

So how do you see them? You wait on the island till night as they wait at sea, and you grab them from the air — either with a mist net strung in front of their burrows to catch them as they come in or with your bare hands before they dive down. James Fisher was struck by their silence — just a whirr, then a crash to the bushes. I was struck by their growls, especially when, in my case, I had to steal their fish (for pesticide analysis). The night flight of the rhinos is unforgettable, and you wear the scars on your hands forever.

Rhinos are tough little critters and are doing very well all along the Pacific Coast, increasing both in numbers and range.

Another island in the Washington Islands National Wildlife Refuge system is Protection Island which, like Destruction Island, is an example of Wild America Reclaimed. Lying only a mile and a half offshore from the Olympic Peninsula between Sequim and Port Townsend, it is one of the most important seabird rookeries off the Washington coast. It has the largest colony of glaucous-winged gulls (5,000 pairs), the fourth-largest rhinoceros auklet colony in the world (16,000 breeding pairs and 16,000 nonbreeding birds), and the only colony of tufted puffins in inshore waters (thirty-four pairs). It has nesting pigeon guillemots, black oystercatchers, pelagic and double-crested cormorants. Seventy percent of all Washington's inshore seabird nesters find a home on Protection Island. It is also a major pupping area for harbor seals. We saw some of its abundant wildlife from Diamond Point through Gus's telescope, but we did not land. I was to visit it later.

Protection Island used to belong to people and sheep. Now, like Destruction Island, it belongs to the birds. In 1986 it was designated a national wildlife refuge, thanks to decades of effort by a few dedicated bird watchers.

Zella Schultz, Eleanor Stopps, and Lorna Campion pestered, pressured, wheedled, and lobbied till enough money was found to buy the island for the birds. People contributed $10 for a gull, $25 for a rhino, $50 for a puffin, $200 for a black oystercatcher. At last word, Eleanor was working on getting stiffer protection. "Being so close to towns and marinas, the birds are still vulnerable," she told me. "We need a wide buffer zone around the island."

We spent our last day together before Gus and I dropped off the rest of the crew and picked up new recruits driving up Hurricane Ridge above

Port Angeles, into the ramparts of the Olympics. This jagged line of snow-capped peaks looking like white cardboard cut-outs makes a spectacular background on the skyline for Victoria and Vancouver Island. It was only an hour and a quarter by ferry across the Straits of Juan de Fuca to my home. I lived within a few easy miles of some of the wildest scenery and most abundant wildlife in North America.

Hurricane Ridge in Olympic National Park is one of the few places anywhere where you can drive from sea level to a mile above sea level in just forty-five minutes. The scenic eighteen-mile road winding to a day lodge set beside subalpine meadows at the top was just being constructed when "the boys" strolled through the rainforest at its base. Despite its proximity to the cities of Victoria, Vancouver, and Seattle, Hurricane Ridge puts you intimately amid unspoiled glaciers, mountain peaks, and deep forested valleys, it lets you walk among untouched luxuriant wildflower gardens and observe some of the most approachable wildlife anywhere. There are no campgrounds or overnight facilities along Hurricane Ridge. It is a place where people and wild but fragile habitat coexist well.

Mountain goats, wearing bright red ear tags but looking decidedly dishevelled with their winter blankets hanging scruffily around their shoulders, grazed rocky outcroppings. They had been introduced to the area in the late 1920s for meat and sports hunting and did too well in this new niche, spreading throughout the park and destroying the native subalpine plants that had evolved there. Since 1981, 200 of the 1,000 goats in the park have been removed from the densest areas. Pending public hearings, more or all may be removed in the future.

The park had not yet officially opened, so we were alone with Wild America. The wind swirling the snow at our feet and the rain drizzling through leaks in our ponchos seemed to make Wild America even wilder. A black bear lumbered along a ridge beneath us. Olympic marmots, looking like two-toned honey-brown shag rugs, sat in front of the packed-earth porches of their burrows, contemplating busy spring activities of courting, playing, sunbathing, and putting away fat for their long winter of hibernation. I kept looking for cougar tracks in the snow.

Olympic National Park was a wildlife wonderland, an optimistic and fitting climax to our search for Wild America below Alaska. "It's an island," Bruce Moorhead, the park's enthusiastic wildlife management biologist, told me later. "We're lucky it's pristine. We've been protected because there's been no easy access, no good harbors on our western flanks, no easy way to log our forests."

Bruce agreed that the park was probably the wildest, most rugged part of America we had yet seen, but he warned of threats at its edges. Logging has been "running amok" around its boundaries since ways have been found in the last twenty years to "rape" steep forested slopes. Elk are no longer isolated but are often attracted to the clear-cuts outside the park, and are killed by hunters. Rare spotted owls, creatures of mature forests, are killed by horned owls or compete for food and nesting sites with the barred owl, which has been aggressively expanding its range westward.

Capt. John Meares named the peninsula's highest mountain Mount Olympus because it seemed to be a fitting place for the Greek gods. As we left our island in the sky and drove toward Seattle, I hoped that the legendary wisdom of the Greek gods would also prevail in our battle to maintain Wild America.

Tufted Puffin
Fratercula cirrhata
(upper birds)

Horned Puffin
Fratercula corniculata
(lower bird)

Chapter Six
North To Alaska
June 22–July 8

A sea of islands, a sea of mountain peaks, lured us northward and westward to a wilder frontier, a wilder America in Alaska. Fiords, rivers, and glaciers, runways of water and ice, cut into the coastline looking like black snakes and white snakes from our vantage point in the clouds.

Flying over Canada was a journey back in time for me, reminding me of old stories I had written. Flying and boating around Vancouver Island and the Queen Charlotte Islands with eagles and seabirds. Flying and climbing into the Chugach and St. Elias Mountains with Dall sheep and goats. Boating among the islands of Prince William Sound with raccoons and sea otters. Beside me on the plane, Vi Debbie was reading one of those stories, *There's a Raccoon in my Parka*, Midge Rowley was reading another, *There's a Seal in my Sleeping Bag*. For more than a decade I had traveled this precipitous, deeply indented, island-splashed coastline between Washington and Alaska in a tiny rubber raft. Now I was flying high above it with nineteen companions in a plane.

We were headed for Anchorage, but this city was to be merely a launching pad for a journey further back in time. West to the Yukon Delta and the Bering Sea where humans — and animals — used the Bering land bridge to enter the New World; west still to the Pribilof Islands, where twenty years before, when I first entered the New World, a fur seal I called Sam had inspired me to a love of natural history. This final segment of our journey looking for Wild America would be the climax of our expedition, but also a personal homecoming for me.

Gus Yaki had picked up a large group of naturalists for the last segment of our Wild America odyssey. Many, like Susan Harvey of England, Ruth Delaney and Anne Macdonald of Toronto, and Jack Bryans of Ottawa, were friends from previous trips; some, like Kay Forbes of Niagara Falls, Ontario, Vi Debbie, Midge Rowley, and Gerry Breitenback of New Jersey, and Mac Cutler of Arizona, we had already met on our expedition; a few, like Donald and Joanne McRobbie of Saskatchewan, Dennis and Darlene Dalke of Oshawa, and Edge and Betty Pegg of Ontario, were new friends, and John and Joyce Pratt were ornithologists from Australia. Co-leading with Gus was wildlife artist Robert Bateman, who with his wife, Birgit, would soon be leaving Ontario to live on Saltspring Island in British Columbia. Roger Tory Peterson would be meeting us in the Pribilofs.

From Anchorage our packed Twin Otter sped across the pristine Alaska of every southerner's imagination. We could sneak a look north to Mount McKinley, North America's highest peak, then west across glaciers and a frozen meringue of mountains, the Alaska Range, the Taylor Mountains, and the Kilbuck Mountains. Then we flew down the delta and across the Kuskokwim River to land at Bethel, headquarters of the twenty-million-acre Yukon Delta National Wildlife Refuge, which did not exist when Roger Tory Peterson and James Fisher came this way in 1953.

Gus started calling out birds immediately, but most of us were noticing the town. Bethel, begun as a Moravian Mission in 1885 and largely forgotten till after World War Two, is now the administrative hub for the Yukon-Kuskokwim River Delta, a busy trans-shipment point by bush plane, barge, and flat-bottomed skiff for fifty-two outlying villages. It was the usual, sprawling northern hodgepodge of plywood houses built above the permafrost on blocks or pilings, kickers (outboard motors), ditched cars, and building materials strewn along the river bank. Sled dogs and fish drying racks sat beside taxis and snowmachines. The modern hospital and shiny satellite dishes stood apart as if their architecture did not belong. "A bit depressing," murmured Ruth. But the people, 3,500 of them, native and non-native alike, were among the friendliest I had yet encountered in my many trips north.

There was a tundra meadow downtown. "Don't fall off the birch trees you're standing on," joked Gus on a prebreakfast bird walk. He pointed out Lapland longspurs feeding their young in the arctic cotton-grass by the Moravian Church, a red-necked grebe swimming in a tundra pool close by, fox sparrows at the log museum, a least sand-piper on the roof of Bethel Cablevision, and a gray-cheeked thrush flitting around the shacks. Hoary redpolls, bank and tree swallows, parasitic and long-tailed jaegers looped and swooped overhead. A northern waterthrush greeted us at the door of the hotel. Twenty-five species in the streets of Bethel — more than you would expect in the usual town.

"The boys" said they were unable to find New Chevak, the village we were winging to next, on their maps. It is located on the ocean edge of the 250-mile-long by 250-mile-wide Yukon-Kuskokwim River Delta, one of the largest floodplains in the world, which is still totally road-less terrain. Part of the vast Yukon Delta Refuge, New Chevak would be the starting point for our boat trip to Old Chevak, where Peterson and Fisher had camped.

Clouds scudded by to give us intermittent glimpses of brown chocolate streams snaking around green reed-fringed ponds, shimmering blue lakes, lush green meadows, and rusty-yellow mudflats. Cotton-grass and white flowers pepper-and-salted the higher ridges. "The most exciting-looking terrain he had ever seen," was how Peterson described his friend Finnur Gudhmundsson's reactions to this delta.

Others would say it was barren and desolate, but I always feel excitement on the tundra. I like the feeling of being isolated some-where on top of the world where few others have been, of feeling challenged and being renewed spiritually by that challenge.

And although you would never know it looking down from a plane, the tundra is filled with wildlife. The coastal marsh area of the Yukon-Kuskokwim Delta is the summer home for about half a million ducks, geese, and swans, and many species of shorebirds, which probably outnumber any other species group. It is a major nesting area for sandhill cranes and more than 30,000 tundra swans, 50 percent of all the world's brant, 80 to 90 percent of all cackling and emperor geese, and prob-ably all the white-fronted geese that migrate along the Pacific Flyway. There can be more than a hundred broods of Steller's eider ducks per square mile, more than five arctic loon nests per square mile. Although only ninety-six species of birds have been recorded since official field studies began in 1963, their abundance in each habitat was "almost unbelievable," according to a 1976 U.S. Fish and Wildlife report. Peterson commented that it was "the greatest goose nursery in North America."

The Yukon-Kuskokwim River Delta seemed more defined than the Mackenzie River Delta in neighboring Canada. It was the same intricate mosaic of rivers shattering into a million fragments and sending snakes of water coiling through a maze of ponds, meadows, and tiny spruce forests like a child's finger painting. But the main channels of the Yukon and Kuskokwim Rivers cut more precisely, more obviously through the mosaic. More villages lined the river banks — over a hundred dot the delta altogether. Jack Bryans, following an almost impossible map, called out the ones we passed en route to New Chevak — Atmautluak, Nunapitchuk, Old Kasigluk, Kasigluk. All were part of the wildlife refuge.

This is the land of the Yup'iks, translated as "genuine persons," and there is a greater concentration of Eskimos here on the Yukon-Kuskokwim Delta than anywhere else in the world. The Yup'iks have been isolated longer than most other Eskimos. At the time of Peterson and Fisher's visit, the Yup'iks lived a traditional life of subsistence hunting and fishing, although some went out to work in salmon canneries. Most lived in barabaras (semi-subterranean sod houses), a few in one-room log cabins chinked with mud. They traveled by dogteam in winter and kayaks or small dinghies in summer. They cooked in fifty-gallon drums over open fires. They were independent but officially poor, "among the poorest spots in the United States," said politicians who visited the delta in the mid-1960s. "We didn't know about being poor till outsiders came and told us we were," said one of the Yup'iks. Then came the Alaska Native Claims Settlement Act of 1971, and the Yup'iks, now masters of 35.8 million acres and $165.2 million in cash, were thrust into a modern and vastly different economy.

How would we find Yup'ik country now? And how would all this wealth, all these people in a fragile habitat, affect the wildness of this last part of Wild America?

Gus had made arrangements with the villagers for tents, food, and boats. Paul Ayuluk introduced himself and his two brothers, Bill and Johnny, as our cooks, and we followed them across the tundra to our campsite. We set our tents along an escarpment overlooking the delta. From a height of perhaps seventy-five feet, we had a grandstand view of the marshland, the coiling river edged with boats, oil drums and fish drying racks, and the village itself. Our nearest neighbor was a line of staked-out sled dogs. About eight miles away were the hills at Cape Romanzov and the Bering Sea.

Gus began calling birds, and people set up scopes before choosing their tent spots, although sometimes the two activities were simultaneous. Ann and Susan found a hoary redpoll nest of four blue eggs swinging in a willow bush hammock beside their tent. Betty eagerly drew our attention to a pair of Lapland longspurs feeding five young a few feet from the cooktent. Their nest of soft sphagnum moss lay in an opening between two tussocks of dry grass with a handy pink flower nearby to warn us where not to step. The parent birds did not seem to mind nosy new neighbors training cameras and binoculars on their home and offspring. They went about their feeding rounds unfazed. The male would always fly straight to the nest, but the female took a circuitous route from tussock to tussock for several minutes before she would land. Meanwhile, Bill the cook stretched forward on the ground and offered the chicks a fistful of mosquitoes. Immediately, camouflaged downy blobs became gaping red abysses. The young longspurs did not mind from whom their next meal was coming, just as long as it came.

Several pairs of yellow wagtails, recent arrivals from Siberia and lifers for probably all of us, chittered and hovered constantly along the ridge like big yellow butterflies. They and savannah sparrows obviously had nests nearby. (One yellow wagtail had its nest in plain view of our portable privy tent.) A pair of greater scaups and a family of green-winged teal sailed the pond directly below the ridge. Two dozen tundra swans sailed the lake by the airstrip. Mew gulls, arctic terns, long-tailed and parasitic jaegers flew by overhead. Dunlins and black-bellied plovers probed the mudflats at low tide. So did cinnamon-breasted, bar-tailed godwits, the only godwits regularly seen in Alaska and probably also lifers for most of us. Eskimo kids throwing stones at the birds along the beach caused Gus to comment dryly, "They don't like leaving a tern unstoned."

Unfortunately, mosquitoes were as abundant as the birds. We lathered ourselves lavishly in repellent, and Joyce beat us all in fashioning stylish headnets.

The rich delta soil formed from centuries of sediments deposited by the Yukon and Kuskokwim rivers supported an abundant plant life too. Camped as we were on the upland tundra, we walked on a bouncy carpet of moss and lichen, ground willow, dwarf birch, and crowberry. We not only had to avoid trampling birds' nests, but a veritable garden of tundra flowers too, pink northern primrose, creamy Labrador tea, yellow saxifrage, arctic milk vetch, and the beautiful blue Jacob's ladder.

It took a couple of days to organize our trip to the abandoned village of Old Chevak and half a day — on Eskimo time — to get under way. Without the high tide to help us, it was a mucky business putting down boards in the thick chocolate mud to load the boats. Finally, at 1:30 P.M., we had stowed our gear, put on ponchos to protect us from imminent rain, and boarded the two boats, one an open flat-bottomed scow driven by Jacob Nash and the other a small Starcraft cruiser skippered by Paul.

We set off down the narrow river channel lined on each side with skiffs and smokehouses — bound at last for Old Chevak. When we entered Hooper Bay, the only division between land and sea was a thin line of green. Sky and water were one. Birds became more abundant, lines of black brant, skeins of geese, flocks of ducks, eruptions of shore-birds were difficult to identify in the shimmering glare. By 3 P.M. we turned our backs on the Bering Sea and entered a channel leading to the Kikleevik River.

"There it is," called Bob three and a half hours later, pointing to the horizon. Focusing our binoculars, we made out on one side of a channel one red-and-white-roofed building, another flat green building, an outhouse, and on the other side a tent frame and some oil drums. This was Old Chevak, where we would be birding for the next several days.

Paul nosed us into the bank on the west side of Old Chevak Slough beside the tent frame and oil drums. Peterson and Fisher had camped on the other side in a one-room wooden shack that was once the Kashunuk people's church. Biologists were now using it as a bird study station. Paul took Gus across in the boat to introduce our contingent.

"Let's set up here on the bank where the slough and the river meet," I suggested to Ruth, who was scrounging driftwood for tent pegs. "It's got a good view of everything and is a scenic spot for pictures."

It was also, as we found out afterward, near the nests of a western sandpiper and a savannah sparrow. Behind our tent was a pond with a family of red-necked phalaropes darting in and out of the reeds at the edge, and an arctic loon with her chick in tow sailing languidly ("Like pharaohs," said Darlene) across the middle. Black turnstones wheeled overhead, flashing their dramatic black-and-white-striped flight patterns and making sounds like video games, I thought. It was difficult to concentrate on putting up tents when so many birds were competing for our attention — and we were competing for their territory. I leaned down to tie my bootlace by a guy rope and *whoosh!* flushed out a female willow ptarmigan.

Camouflaged by dwarf willows but within two feet of the Pratts' tent in a little hollow scratched out of the moss and lined with dry grass and leaves, was a nest of ten reddish eggs. We worried that the mother ptarmigan would not return, but the Pratts reported that she was seen on the nest again several hours later. And so she remained for the time we camped at Old Chevak.

From our chosen position on the edge of camp, Ruth and I had to run an obstacle course past the western sandpiper nest, past the savannah sparrow nest, past the willow ptarmigan nest, and also try not to tread too heavily on the newly emerging flowers. It was still only June and the plants were not yet at their best, but already the path to our tent was strewn with fragrant valerian, yellow mustard and lousewort, blue

Jacob's ladder, pink cranberry, arctic raspberry, ladysmock, starflower, and Labrador tea.

After supper that night our neighbors, the two biologists from across the slough, Dr. Dennis Raveling and Jim Johnson from the University of California at Davis, drove over in their dinghy to tell us about their study of local geese.

"The Yukon-Kuskokwim Delta is the heart of goose country," Dennis began. "Four main species nest here — cackling Canada geese, Pacific white-fronted geese, emperor geese, and brant. In 1951 it was described as America's greatest goose-brant nesting area, and one of the early U.S. Fish and Wildlife Service biologists who began making systematic surveys in 1956 said the numbers were overwhelming. Well, since the early 1970s there has been an alarming decline in cackling and white-fronted geese, one-tenth to one-third the numbers in the 1980s compared to the late 1950s."

Dennis gave me the statistics: 450,000 white-fronted geese, now down to 81,000; 350,000 cacklers down to 26,000; 150,000 brant down to 121,000; 150,000 emperors down to 100,000. Later still in 1986, Ron Perry, the manager of the refuge, gave me more statistics. Emperor geese were down further to 41,600; cacklers had stabilized at 32,000, although still only 10 percent of their former population; white-fronted geese had stabilized at 93,000, although still a long way down from their former abundance; black brant had stabilized at 126,000, slightly down from the last count.

However, other species and subspecies of geese nesting in other parts of Alaska were steadily increasing. The problem geese appear to be the ones that nest on the Yukon-Kuskokwim Delta. Almost all geese except emperor geese winter down south in Washington, Oregon, Texas, Mexico, and particularly California's Klamath Basin, where we had just been.

"Basically, the story is this," continued Dennis. "The geese put on 50 percent of their body weight in fat in California, they fly thousands of miles to Cook Inlet in Alaska to replenish, then they fly to the Bering Sea to lay their eggs, usually within twelve days of arrival between, say, May 16 and May 30, just after the snow melts. If they have to wait too long, they lose a lot of body weight and suffer losses to predators. Last year the cackling geese had a nesting success of only 7 percent — this was catastrophic. We felt that it was due to predators — mink, fox, gulls, jaegers — and hunting."

Hunting has been curtailed or, in the case of cackling geese, eliminated entirely on southern wintering grounds, but neither biologist wanted to talk about excessive hunting on the northern nesting grounds. Yet in 1984 Dennis reported in *Transactions of the Forty-ninth North American Wildlife and Natural Resources Conference*, "The clear implication is that harvests of geese on the Y-K Delta are excessive for all geese and alarmingly so when combined with harvest in California. This is correlated with a 42 percent increase in the human population of coastal Y-K Delta villages between 1960 and 1980 and rapid advances in availability of modern technology. In the 1950s, many people on the Y-K Delta still lived in sod houses and used kayaks and even a one h.p. motor was a luxury. Dog teams were a major means of travel for the spring goose hunt in the 1960s. By 1972 about 2,000 boxes of shotgun shells were sold in one village of about 550–600 people. Boats now commonly have motors of 25–75 + h.p. (often twin engines). Most families now have a snowmachine whereas they were a relatively scarce luxury in the mid-1970s. This technology enables even short-term hunts to commonly exceed twenty miles in distance from villages. Biologists studying geese on the Y-K Delta have witnessed large-scale shooting when geese arrive in spring, flushing geese on nests with snowmachines in order to drive them to hunters, shooting geese on nests, taking of eggs, and shooting or capture of geese with broods."

On the Yukon Delta National Wildlife Refuge, established in 1980, native hunting is allowed as long as it is not detrimental to wildlife. In Bethel I had talked to Jay Ballinger, then the refuge manager, and Chuck Hunt, a kindly Eskimo liaison officer, who are trying to educate natives to conserve geese.

They agreed that the Migratory Bird Treaty of 1916, which forbade the hunting of waterfowl on their nesting grounds, was not being enforced. As Chuck put it, "What do you do if the whole village says, 'Arrest me? I've got a duck, arrest me'?"

Eventually, in 1985, the treaty was modified to allow the legal, regulated harvest of birds and eggs in spring. "What's needed," Jay had told me, "is everybody pulling together instead of everyone standing around pointing a finger at somebody else, hunters in the South blaming the hunters in the North, and vice versa."

Ron Perry, who became the next refuge manager, reiterated Jay's philosophy. "Hunting is only detrimental if the population is low. We're trying to collect facts. Let's see how many birds are killed by foxes, by jaegers, by people, and then work together to solve the problem and preserve the birds."

Amazingly, education at the school and village level worked. In 1985 attitudes had changed to such an extent that the Mekoryuk people on Nunivak Island, another national wildlife refuge in the Bering Sea, twenty-three miles offshore from the delta, voted to charge three of their villagers for illegally taking cackling Canada geese. This was a unique and historic occasion and could not have been anticipated in 1983.

For the first time, in 1985, native households were asked to tell how many birds they had killed. Ron reported a total of about 58,000 for the 1985 season, an amount which did not unduly worry him, although he conceded that others could interpret the data differently. What does seem clear is that attitudes have changed. Natives understand the problems facing the geese, and many people no longer gather their eggs. Everybody realizes, both in the North and the South, that co-operation is needed, or else the geese could disappear forever.

Dennis believes that there may be more factors involved in the decline than predation and hunting. Jay and Chuck had suggested changeable weather conditions and habitat loss in the South. Dennis and several other biologists on the refuge were monitoring the eating and nesting habits of geese to see if these could be factors. They were marking individual geese, so they could identify them later, both in California and in Alaska.

"It's fascinating how four different species of geese share the same environment, but use it slightly differently," Dennis said. "Brant feed on the mudflats on delicate grasses; emperors feed on the mud too, but eat invertebrates; white-fronted geese with big bills eat coarse sedges and grasses on the edge of sloughs; cackling geese with delicate bills eat delicate grasses. We raised some geese ourselves and took them into the meadows to watch what they ate. We saw how they selected particular species, right down to individual shoots. It's uncanny how the young hatch right at the time of the best quality vegetation."

He told us that just as the different geese species used different feeding places, so they used different nesting habitats. "Even three to five centimeters in elevation on this tundra gives rise to different plant communities and thus different niches for different birds. The cacklers nest on islands in ponds, the white-fronts on the high banks of the sloughs, the emperors on peninsulas in lakes, and the spectacled eiders in meadows or lowland ponds."

Magic words. "Where will we see spectacled eiders?" was the question on everybody's lips. Spectacled eiders, well named for the large, white, black-rimmed spectacles around their eyes, are rare birds in North America. Because they summer on the Bering coast and winter on the Aleutians, few birders get to see them. Most of us would have just this one chance to add a spectacled eider to our lists. We probably would not see the males, who had gone off to a communal area to loaf and molt, but we hoped we would see the females now sitting on eggs.

At midnight a scow and a family of eight Eskimos and a dog pulled into the bank, quietly unloaded their gear, and proceeded without introduction to set up their camp and their fish nets by the cooktent. I had hoped it might be Jack Paniyak, the Eskimo who had guided Peterson and Fisher, since this was his land and he had promised to meet me here. But it was an older woman with seven children, Jack's relatives, who were camping here for the summer.

Next morning, one of the children, Theresa, introduced me to her mother, Julia, and told me how shocked they all had been to find so many strange people camping on their land. " 'Unbelievable!' said my little brother when he saw all your tents — 'one, two, three' — he started counting them from far away. My Mum was worried that you were the Fish and Wildlife Service and were going to take her land away. She was relieved to learn that you were only bird watchers."

Theresa came with us for the day's boat trip on the Keoklevik River toward the coast. "A baked Alaska for the first person to see a spectacled eider," teased Gus as Jacob cast off. "Three baked Alaskas if you see an Aleutian tern, not in the Aleutians where you should, but here where Peterson and Fisher did."

We did not see the rare and very localized Aleutian tern, but we did see forty-nine different species over the next couple of days, including Alaska specialties like the emperor goose, which summers on the delta and winters along the Aleutians. From our low perspective in the boat we usually saw emperor geese walking the skyline in family groups of two parents and half a dozen gray, downy young, or scrabbling up the slick gray mudbank to the marsh above. Sometimes we just saw their giant tracks in the mud. The emperor goose of the field guide is a handsome goose with a white head and pearly gray scaled back. But all the adult geese we observed had their white heads stained a rusty yellow from the iron content of the water in which they dipped to root around for bottom vegetation.

On one occasion, emperor geese came to us. We rounded one of the innumerable bends in the river and cut across a family. Parents and most of the goslings scattered, but two of the brood made straight for our boat. We resisted the temptation to get closer; Jacob veered away, and Gus assured us that the two chicks would reunite with their family once we were gone.

We did not see any white-fronted geese (or speckle-bellies, as the hunters call them, a more appropriate term, I think). But we did see dozens of cackling geese and their families. Unlike the more commonly known and larger Canada geese, which weigh up to thirteen pounds, the cacklers are little bigger than a mallard duck and weigh only two or three pounds. The cackling subspecies get their name because their call sounds more like a cackle than a honk.

Closer to the coast, the darker, shorter-necked brant were numerous, skittering with their families through the mud as our boat approached. We stopped at a little side channel and walked the tundra, the wet lowland tundra closer to the river and the higher upland tundra farther inland. Bob and Birgit with their slide cameras and sketch pads, Susan with her movie camera, and I with my cameras, notebooks, and tape recorder made the most of every moment when we stopped. Like Gus looking for birds, our eyes had to be everywhere, not just to see them but to record them too.

"There's a red phalarope," called Birgit excitedly, pointing to a lone twirling bird on a pond. We had seen several red-necked, or northern, phalaropes, but red phalaropes, with their bright rusty red breasts and yellow bills, are much less common. This one did not seem to mind our approach at all, twirling, bobbing, spinning in circles as phalaropes do to stir up plankton and small marine invertebrates to the surface of the water where they feed. These two species of phalaropes are sandpipers that spend most of their year at sea. In the breeding season, the female is much more colorfully clad and more aggressive than the male. After she has laid the eggs, she leaves her more drably dressed partner to incubate them.

Another bird we enjoyed was the pectoral sandpiper. This is one species that has become more abundant on the delta than when "the boys" visited. A pectoral sandpiper's most intriguing feature is its voice. We heard it often in the constant orchestra of the tundra. In the breeding season, the male pectoral sandpiper inflates his throat and breast to twice its normal size and sends out a hollow, booming sound that some listeners have described as froglike.

The highlight of the day was the bird we had all been hoping for since we arrived — the spectacled eider, a life bird for us all, even Gus. Bob sketched it immediately, one eye on his pad, the other on the bird through the scope. Birgit was constantly at Bob's side to tell him what the eider was doing. We saw five more that day, as well as two common eiders, all females as we expected. The males were gone to the loafing grounds.

That night after supper I joined Dennis and Jim to check goose nests. Three of us would better be able to get closer to the geese without disturbing them than a large group could. We left Old Chevak in a small dinghy at high tide from the Kashunuk River through a narrow reed-fringed slough called Kootuk, which Dennis said was named to honor a local Eskimo for his help in finding goose nests. Almost immediately we heard the loud ringing trumpeting of sandhill cranes. Obviously they had a chick, and they were determined that we would not find it. They did not know that we were looking for geese, not cranes. However, the adults put on an intriguing show, trying to distract us away from their chick with a display like a killdeer's broken-wing act. With wings outspread, they wobbled around awkwardly as if crippled, fell over themselves as if they were all legs, necks, and wings.

"I call this the City of Destruction," Jim said as we walked toward Emperor Goose Nest Number 25. "About twenty nests have been destroyed by some predator; we don't know what. They were all on good islands that foxes can't usually get to. There are no messy eggshell remains that would indicate jaeger predation. We think it might be mink."

Jim and Dennis visit the nests of cackling, white-fronted, and emperor geese every two days to find out the exact date the eggs are laid, incubated, hatched, and the young fledged. If the eggs do not hatch or disappear, they try to find out why.

I watched while Jim waded to Emperor Goose Nest 25. The female had sneaked away long before he arrived to check the grassy tussock on the tiny island. He counted the eggs and listened for cheeping, but there was none. They would not hatch for at least two more days. Before he left, he covered the eggs with leaves and other debris to protect them from the ever-circling gulls and jaegers.

At the next nest Dennis found a broken eggshell. He could determine if the eggs had hatched naturally or if they had been destroyed by a predator by looking at the membrane. "If it peels off easily and you find a little dropping inside, then you know it was successfully hatched," he explained patiently.

He can also determine the order in which eggs are laid. "We number the eggs on the end," he said when I caught up with him at an abandoned white-fronted goose nest on another island. "When the female lays the first eggs there are no feathers in the nest, so they sit wet and damp in the bowl. She adds down after the third egg, so eggs progressively get more down and are thus more insulated. They're also whiter later, not so dirty. As we have numbered them, we know which hatch, which don't, and we try to relate the order of hatching to hatching success. Looks like they all hatched here but this one, which could have been lost to predators.''

As we trudged to another pond, to another island, Dennis said that productivity this breeding season promised to be much better than the disastrous year before. So far, it looked as if the white-fronted geese were 65 percent successful, the emperors about 45 to 50 percent successful, and the cackling geese only about 30 to 40 percent successful.

"This is the last nest we'll do tonight," Dennis said sympathetically, noticing the difficulty I was having stumbling through the mud in my borrowed oversize hip waders.

"Okay, I'm going to photograph this one," I declared purposefully, hitching up the slipping rubbers, hoisting my cameras on my shoulders, and slogging into the knee-high bog. The "primordial" mud grabbed my feet like a magnet, I tried to stride forward, the brain was willing but the body too weak. I teetered, then collapsed in the water, instinctively holding my cameras aloft like some wet, bedraggled Statue of Liberty. Jim and Dennis were at my side instantly to rescue the cameras and pull me to my unsteady feet — in between much laughter.

With their help I reached the nest. But the mother had crept away and taken her chicks with her — all but one. Squeaking, flapping its little wings like flags, the gray, downy emperor goose chick scurried toward me, following me in and out of a thick forest of red mare's-tail growing on the island's edge. Dennis scooped up the little fluffball — an incongruous image of big bearded biologist with tiny chick — and kept it warm in his parka while we pondered what to do. Finally, he said, "Let's try to adopt it out. There's another emperor goose nest close. We'll add it to that clutch."

Unfortunately, the potential foster home was not ready for our boarder. It would be another two days before its eggs hatched. We would have to raise our little gosling orphan ourselves.

"Let's call it Lyn," grinned Dennis, "because she—and the goose— are always in water."

Back at the old church, warm and dry again, Jim fed coffee to me and mosquitoes on the end of a toothpick to the little orphan.

It was one in the morning and still light when Dennis drove me back to our quiet camp. The tents were silent, still, but I wondered how many of my friends were actually sleeping. The birds did not sleep. All day long, all night long, ducks, swans, geese, cranes, marsh birds, and shorebirds, maintained a continual chorus, "a real orchestra," Gus had called it. It intensified at about four in the morning, just before dawn. Most memorable for me was the delicate undulating winnowing of the snipe, the bugling, froglike gurgling of the sandhill cranes, the hollow booming of the pectoral sandpipers, the mournful wail of the loons, and above all, the beautiful whickering of the bar-tailed godwit. Cuckookwok, the Eskimos called it, and that is just what it sounded like. Early ornithologists had said the calls of the godwit were "dinful," and certainly they were noisy, but it was a noise that I could have listened to all night — and did.

It was time to leave. As usual, Ruth and I were the last to get our gear packed and down by the boat. And I hadn't yet taken a picture of the willow ptarmigan nest by the Pratt's tent. "You can go closer," said Joyce helpfully when I set up my camera at the nest site. I ventured forward a yard, leaned down in the grass and tried to find the female's eye amid the cottongrass and camouflage. "Kwow, kwow, kwow". Suddenly, the mother stoop up, alert, watching. From the grass beside her rose one fluffy yellowish-brown chick and then several more. She had hatched her brood during the night, perhaps earlier that morning.

"Chicks!" someone called out and within seconds, the birds were surrounded by cameras and binoculars. "Poor bird," commented Anne drily as she passed. The ptarmigan, didn't appear to mind and a few minutes, later, Paul called us to the boats.

I ran back to my tent site to take a picture of a western sandpiper. Andrew, one of the Eskimo boys, raised his three-pronged spear and pointed it at the female still sitting on eggs. "No!" I yelled spontaneously. The words were drawn from me, unthinkingly.

He looked at me for one quizzical moment, aimed deliberately, and threw. The prongs closed around a flutter of feathers. The hunter had made his mark.

What to say? "Why did you do it?" I said, still unthinkingly.

"To practise my new spear," he said proudly. "Look! I broke its wing." I forced myself to look at the huddle of quiviering feathers, the bloody useless wing, the eggs that would soon die.

Reason came slowly. What did it matter to lose a family of sandpipers, there were plenty more. This wasn't my land, not even by invitation. Julia and her family had been gracious.

"Please only kill if you are going to eat it," I lectured Andrew, despite my reason. "Try target practice on something dead." He looked at me amusedly as I picked up the still fluttering carcass and wondered what to do with it. "Last call for the boats," called Paul. I lay it in a little gully and rejoined my companions.

Teresa met me at the riverbank. "I'm sorry I criticized your brother," I said lamely. My eyes pleaded for her understanding. "Andrew," she said seriously. "You eat that bird or you give it to the dog. Go get it." Hesitantly, I looked at Julia. She came over and kissed me good-bye.

As we pulled away, one of the children let loose the dog which had been chained during the time we shared the family's campsite. Our last view of Old Chevak was a dog running after the family of willow ptarmigan. Some of us were horrified.

"It happens in our society too," replied Gus, keeping us on track. "When I was a kid I went out with boys with 22s, not even BB guns, and they shot just for the sake of it."

We were into the third month of our journey around Wild America with only a week to go. We had probably driven 30,000 miles and flown 4,000 more. But for me, the trip was just beginning. We were flying to the Pribilof Islands in the Bering Sea, 800 miles west of Anchorage. The Islands of Seals, the Islands of Seabirds. Mecca.

Beside me on the Reeve Aleutian Airway Lockheed Electra, just across the aisle, sat Roger Tory Peterson, the bird guru himself, the coauthor of the original *Wild America*, the man who had inspired our journey. Tall, striking, with somewhat unruly silver hair, dressed in a bright red shirt and an orange cap, wearing glasses and binoculars, he was recognized instantly. Avid bird watchers of all ages, including two eager little boys from Massachusetts, approached respectfully to get their field guides autographed.

We stopped briefly in the Aleutians to refuel, then sped north across the Bering Sea. Somewhere below that cloud blanket were five tiny, fog-shrouded, storm-swept volcanic rocks, the Pribilofs. We in our silver bird had modern technology to find them, but the Russians in their little ships searched the Bering Sea for more than a decade looking for the place where the fur seals went to breed. It had been forty-five years since Vitus Bering had mapped the Alaskan coast and claimed it for Russia. Forty-five years for the Russians to enslave the Aleuts to hunt for them. Forty-five years for the sea cow to become extinct, the spectacled cormorant soon to become extinct, the sea otter launched on the same path. Now it was the fur seal's turn—if the Russians could find it.

Then in 1786, through the dense fog, above the cold wind, Fleet Master Gerassim Pribilof heard the roaring, bleating, and trumpeting of thousands upon thousands of fur seals. He named the island where he landed St. George, after his ship. The following year, forty miles to the northwest, the Russians found a second island — bigger, and with five times more seals. They called it St. Paul. These islands, with three smaller ones — Walrus, Otter, and Sea Lion Rock — became the Pribilofs. The Russians brought Aleuts from their Aleutian Island homes, and the decimation of three million fur seals began.

The slaughter was accelerated after 1867, when Russia sold Alaska to the United States. It became disastrous when several countries, faced with declining numbers of sea otters and whales, shot the fur seals at sea. By 1909 the population was thought to be as low as 200,000 — the lowest recorded.

And then in 1911 came the turnaround. Russia, the United States, Japan, and Great Britain (for Canada), countries who either owned the rookeries or the waters the fur seals swam through, signed the International Fur Seal Treaty. They agreed to stop pelagic sealing, share the sales of the pelts, and study the animals' biology. Only bachelors — males three years old and between forty-one and forty-nine inches long (rules vary annually) — would be killed. By 1953 Peterson and Fisher were told that the fur seal population had increased to 1.75 million.

"Welcome to the Pribilofs," said the pilot as we dropped through a hole in the clouds and shuddered onto the runway at St. Paul.

I had come to the islands for the seals and seabirds. I was not prepared for the flowers. I was dazzled by their color before I had stepped from the plane. The rust-red cinder-built runway was bordered with bouquets of yellow arctic poppies, blue lupins ("A blue to break your heart," said one visitor), and tall purple lousewort.

As our guide, John Tillotsen, drove us by bus into the village of St. Paul, the contrasts of color continued to be overwhelming: the red of the road, manmade from scoria and cinder; the black sand of the beaches naturally formed from ancient basalt; the vast emerald green of grasses and sedges rolling to the horizon over gray, compacted ash (greener still where arctic foxes have lived and fur seals have died); the multi-colored mats of mosses, lichens, and subarctic alpine flowers seeking root on the black lava nodules and boulders pimpling the shoreline; the shimmering rugs of seaweeds, anemones, and sea urchins hooked to rocks at the tide zone — and almost everywhere, patches of creamy angelica, purple monkshood, pink thrift, blue gentian, and showy yellow ragwort.

I saw my first fur seal not among thousands in the chaotic sprawling confusion of a colony, but one lone subadult bull peering out of the long grass by a road sign that said "Seal Crossing." "It'll be dead next week when the hunt gets to this rookery," said John succinctly, reminding me rather grimly of the reason people live here.

The Pribilofs have been called the Galapagos of the North, not just for their spectacular wildlife concentrations, but for the ease with which people can see them. Between June 1 and October 15 each year, guides authorized by the National Marine Fisheries Service lead visitors to observation blinds built on platforms overlooking two of the seal rookeries. At Reef Rookery a solitary fur seal heaved himself out of the grass and challenged me with a sudden lunge of his concertinalike neck, even before I could step up to the platform. Other nonbreeding fur seals sprawled over lichen-covered boulders at the edge of the colony, almost at whisker level when I looked through pigeonholes in the plywood blind.

A family of arctic foxes with a den in the sand dunes on one side of the viewing platform popped their ears and then their heads over the waving angelica. Arctic foxes come in two color phases, blue and white, and it is the blue phase which predominates in the Pribilof foxes. The adults were in the last stages of molting from their bluish gray winter coat to their sooty gray summer one. They looked mangy, disheveled. Their long brownish tails, some of them almost white, waved like plumes or hung like brooms, looking as if they did not belong to them. The kits, seven of them, were a fluffier brown. Five of them lolled on the ground outside the den entrances: two of them slept. I wanted to belly forward in the grass for pictures, but anything to either side of the blind was strictly off limits. John gave me a warning look.

Patience pays, or perhaps it was luck. When almost everybody else had gone off to the bird rookeries, another fox came to me. I saw him through the plywood hole, an adult in a portrait pose against the backdrop of the village. He stared straight at me with alert piglike eyes. Sensitive to the clicking camera but not seeing me, he paused for a moment on a rock, then trotted in and out of the sprawling fur seals in front of the blind.

A second fox appeared from the sidehill where the nonbreeding fur seals hauled out. It sidled around a boulder beside the blind, then to my amazement and delight, stopped to curl up on another boulder right in front of my peephole. It knew I was there, but it did not seem to care. Its front foot was crippled.

We were to find arctic foxes commonly patrolling the seabird and fur seal colonies, sprinting up cliffs where it was possible to take eggs and chicks or even adult birds, scavenging afterbirth or dead seal pups.

They were not tame, as foxes have become in northern outposts such as oil and construction camps, because on the Pribilofs, Aleuts trap them in winter for their pelts.

Although the animals under my nose were compelling, the chief center of interest was the main breeding colony. The din there was incessant: the roaring and whickering of bulls, the gargling and grunting of cows, the bleating of pups. Thousands of fur seals like huge brown and black slugs ("Sausages," said John), lay sprawled over the smooth, bouldered beach, waving their flippers like fans to get rid of the heat of congestion and intermittent sun. Some rested against rocks with their heads pointed into the air as if sunbathing, although they were probably just saving energy and sleeping. Others had no rocks, but according to John, they "did a rock imitation" by posing imperiously, noses in the air, eyes closed — "like carved statues," said somebody else. A few sat or wallowed in the water.

At first glance, the seal colony was an indiscriminate sea of undulating bodies. But patterns emerged as I watched, patterns in color and behavior, which were determined by age and sex.

A sleek yellowish brown cow splashed out of the surf, passing other seals at the tideline and pushed through the jammed-packed bodies along the waterfront. Not for her, unfortunately, was this prime real estate for fur seals. Her territory was farther inland, entailing a hazardous journey getting there. One bull rushed toward her and she scrambled back to sea. Later, she tried again. She managed to thwart several attempts to move in on her — not only the physical contact of bulls but also the coughs and open-mouthed threats of females.

Rising from the sea of cows and five times larger than any of them, a massive dark gray bull, perhaps six hundred pounds in weight, eyes white and wild, mouth gaping, canines flashing, lumbered over the other bodies like a giant caterpillar. Surely he would crush the smaller females and even smaller pups. Yet in closer focus, he seemed to be feeling his way across the throng, to be elevating himself over those he passed as if aware of his great weight.

Suddenly I saw the object of his movement. At the obvious edge of his territory, he came face to face with another bull. He lunged. Out shot his thickly blubbered neck in a snakelike dart, out rushed a puffing sound something like a locomotive. The encroaching bull reared at the same time, lunged as well, but neither seemed willing to pursue the altercation. For the established bull who had won his territory through fighting in earnest, this boundary display was mere ceremony. It was part bluff, but it worked.

The intruder left, and the established bull settled down to a territory patrol, humping his way back through the mass of females and pups with head low, neck arched, long white whiskers pointed forward, and whickering. Perhaps this wild bull was checking females for their readiness to breed. Or perhaps he was just making sure that everybody knew that this was his territory.

It's a tough life being a bull in a fur seal colony: fighting to get a territory in the first place, maintaining it for four or five months with little chance to sleep and no chance to eat, copulating up to seventy times a summer. Many bulls can not manage and die. No bulls hold territories for more than three or four seasons, and the average is one and a half seasons.

Standing out by color and size from the conglomerate of blacks, browns, brindles, and beiges of the adults were the tiny, shiny black newborn pups. Some lay nursing against their mothers' sides, each consuming as much as a gallon of rich milk at each feeding. (Fur seal milk must be rich in fat because females may have to swim up to two hundred miles from the islands to find enough fish, and so return to feed their pups only about ten times in four months.) Other pups, temporarily abandoned, gathered together in creches, scampered among the rocks in the few places there was space, sparred with each other, scratched themselves with the toenails on the top surface of their back flippers, or slept. Not till the end of July, when they were about a month old, would they move to the tide pools and sea edge to practice their swimming skills.

I was mesmerized. I twisted my telescopic lens till one small pup filled my frame. A bull in miniature: the same arrogant, nose-high pose, the same languid waving of its hind flippers like black kid gloves when the sun came out, the same accordion folds of its fur as it moved. I twisted the lens further till the golf-ball, deep-velvety eyes came into focus. The years rolled away and I was back in British Columbia staring at Sam.

Two days later, with a special access permit from Joe Scordino at the National Marine Fisheries Service, I accompanied biologist Kathy Newell from the Department of Oceanography at the University of Washington to her blind overlooking the Lukanin rookery. Because of their economic importance and international significance, the Pribilof fur seals (65 percent of the world's population) are among the most intensely studied mammals on earth. Richard Peterson and Roger Gentry have been leaders in fur seal research, especially in their recent interpretation of some traditionally held concepts of seal social behavior. "Gentry has years and years of data on St. George Island, but this is the first year for comparative data on St. Paul," Kathy told me. "Basically, we are comparing a hunted population like here with an unhunted one like St. George's, where the harvest was stopped in 1973 and where only subsistence hunting has been going on since 1976."

Kathy's blind was only six feet by four, but surrounded on three sides by glass and overhanging one side of the rookery close to the sea, it was seal study deluxe compared to my peephole in the plywood public blind. She sat at a ledge along the longest window, ticking off on cards things seals were doing — going to sea, returning from the sea, drinking, swimming, interacting with other animals, nursing, copulating, fighting. The list seemed endless, and she had to be eternally vigilant to see order in the apparent chaos. She was also recording the movements of specific animals, counting females that continued to come into the colony daily ("They're not all here yet; I expect another hundred soon"), and drawing the distribution of their territories — and those of the established males — on maps.

Directly in front of us, the rocky, black beach, knobbly rough in some places, worn smooth in others, was divided into a grid eighty meters by twenty meters, with painted yellow lines marking transects for easy mapping. Closer to shore, territories were filled and the ground was totally covered in seals, but here, backdropped by grass, bulls with only two or three females — or none — looked lonely.

Adult bulls winter close to the Pribilofs in the Bering Sea and the Gulf of Alaska, but the rest of the population range as far south as California. They return to the Pribilofs in descending order of age: the older bulls arrive first in late April and early May to establish aggressively a territory, averaging about 250 square feet; idle bulls, adult males both young and old that have no territory, arrive next in mid-June and are forced to take up residence in hauling grounds adjacent to the rookery or on isolated beaches; pregnant females start to arrive in mid-June, about the same time as the bachelor, or subadult, males; younger seals, mostly two-year-old males and females, come ashore in August and September, followed in October and November by a few yearlings of both sexes, although most yearlings and two-year-olds stay out at sea. The seals leave in reverse order, the older territorial bulls after their long fast first starting in August, and lastly, in November, the pups.

To a casual observer — and also to biologists for many years — the territorial bulls, or beachmasters, as they are often called, act like kings or polygamous sheiks, rounding up females and placing them in their harems. The bull goes to where he was born, the female goes to where she was born. He may try to stop her from leaving — in fact, females have been known to be torn apart, literally, in a tug-of-war between competing bulls — but he cannot keep her if she is determined enough. Well, that's the theory. I was to see some of the practice.

Suddenly several dramas burst on the stage at once. This was the thirteen-minute highlight of my journey around Wild America.

The cow nearest me began to give birth. "Oh, my God!" I exclaimed reverentially as I grabbed my camera. I watched in fascination as a black head masked by a white plasticlike birth sac oozed from between her back flippers. The new mother wriggled around in a circle and looked over her shoulder at the emerging pup, but otherwise showed no concern or even interest. Nor did any of the other fur seals.

"Another pup born to the left," called Kathy laconically, ticking off columns on her cards.

I swung my camera to the nine-o'clock position and caught a gull swooping down to pick up the red afterbirth as the next mother bleated, sniffed, and nuzzled her offspring.

"Look above, the eleven-o'clock position," called Kathy again. "Mohammed Ali's copulating."

This was almost impossible to see. With the bulls so many times larger than the demure females, the cow's body had disappeared entirely under her mate's bulk. I thought she was dead. Only her head was visible, and though I was too far away to catch any facial expression, I grinned and said, "She can't be enjoying it. She's probably closing her eyes and in the best Victorian manner, doing it for God and the Empire — or perhaps the Czar."

I was just about to leave the nuptial chamber and return to the nursery when the next drama unfolded at the two-o'clock position. Kathy and I saw it simultaneously. A solitary bull, bereft of cows, sidled over to a neighboring territory where several black pups were gathered, seized one in his jaws, flung it in the air, caught it effortlessly again, hurled it onto a boulder beside the grassy verge, and stood over it, trumpeting. Aghast, I was sure such a heave would have killed the pup. "Happens all the time," murmured Kathy, still ticking her columns.

Back below us on stage number one, ten minutes from the start of the action, a little black sausage of a pup burst from the sac. One of the closer females stretched her long neck curiously toward the newborn.

Seemingly interested for the first time, the mother opened her mouth threateningly, bared her teeth, and coughed and grunted at the onlooker. Returning to her pup, she made a high-pitched gargling or bawling sound, which the pup responded to. Then she began to nip and nibble on its loose coat, continuing the age-old bonding process between mother and young.

"Oh, my God — Kathy!" I yelled, forgetting all about science, or reverence for that matter. It was almost too quick to be believed. A neighboring bull, oblivious to the harem master (now sleeping) of the isolated territory closest to us, suddenly exploded from seemingly nowhere, snatched up the new mother within a few moments of delivering her pup, and threw her effortlessly into his own territory, as if she had been a pup herself.

The motherless pup, still wet from the birth sac and bleating pitifully, took a few waddling steps toward the only figure it knew in its short life of a few minutes — and rolled into a narrow crevice.

"Kathy! What can we do?" I knew the answer before I asked the question.

"Nothing," she said realistically, continuing with her notes. "I wouldn't mind a picture, though, if it turns out."

Several days later, the mother was still a prisoner in the adjacent territory and the pup was still a prisoner of the crevice. And there was nothing any of us could do about it, especially me, who was there under supervision and only to observe. Cow and pup stealing is a common occurrence in a fur seal rookery, and biologists believe that nature must take its course, especially when they are there to document its history. If one of us had walked through the colony to pull the pup from the crevice, warding off aggressive bulls, stepping over nursing females, more damage would be done. And, my reason told me, about 50 percent of all fur seal pups die in their first year, 60 percent by their third year.

The ultimate irony is that despite goodwill and cooperation between four nations in one of the best-kept international treaties ever, and despite intensive research and management, fur seal numbers overall have declined since the early 1970s and are continuing to decline at a rate of 5 percent per year. Roger Tory Peterson recorded between 1.5 million and 1.75 million fur seals on the Pribilofs in 1953 (there were actually two million).

"The population is below half what it was then," said Chuck Fowler, biologist with the National Marine Fisheries Service in 1986. "Last season only about 170,000 pups were born on St. Paul, less than 30,000 on St. George, compared to almost half a million thirty years ago." Researchers now estimate the Pribilof's fur seal population to be less than 800,000, which represents an additional decline in its share of the world population.

Why has the Pribilof population declined so drastically since Roger and James visited?

"It began in the 1950s," commented Michael Bigg, in charge of marine mammals for the Pacific Biological Station, in Nanaimo, British Columbia. Mike has been a good friend and colleague of mine ever since 1963, when we used to mix seal formula together on the same stove. "Biologists, hoping it would lower the mortality of pups, improve the rearing success of the others, and stabilize annual pup production at 400,000, decided to reduce the number of females in the population. Between 1956 and 1963, they had intentionally killed more than a quarter of a million. It was good scientific management at the time, but it was flawed. Part of the problem was that they based their figures on tagged pups, and many of the tags fell off."

Some of the Aleuts were outraged. They did not understand or condone population dynamics as the biologists explained it. For centuries they — and even the Russians in the heyday of hunting — had believed that females should be spared. "In this case, history has proved them right," added Mike, "and some of them still resent researchers today, especially since the harvest was stopped on St. George for additional scientific management."

The fur seal herd never recovered. But the killing of females was only one reason for the decline. Scientists, basing their opinions on ongoing studies, can only guess the others. "I think the main reason now is net entanglement," Chuck said. "Fur seals spend most of their year at sea and they are getting caught in active trolling nets, abandoned fish nets of all kinds, discarded plastic packing straps from cargo boxes, and other debris people throw out at sea. It could cause an annual loss in fur seals of 5 percent or much more."

Biologists are also wondering about a tremendous increase in Bering Sea fishing, changing weather patterns such as warmer waters, marine metal contamination, hunting, predation, and disease. "Perhaps we'll never know the exact reasons," Mike shrugged. "The ecosystem is complicated. It can't be managed that precisely. We can't monitor the whole ocean."

One of those potential factors has been removed. Although I did not know it then, I witnessed the second last time fur seals were commercially harvested on the Pribilofs since the hunt began centuries before. Although the Aleuts always did the actual killing, I saw the last time the United States federal government controlled the operation. In 1984 the islanders took over the entire hunt, harvesting 22,000 three- and four-year-old bachelor seals. In 1985 the hunt was terminated — probably forever.

"The pressure of world public opinion against seal hunting was the main reason politicians stopped it," commented Chuck. "So when the 1911 treaty came up for renewal at the end of 1984, it was not ratified." Ever since the 1960s, organizations such as the Humane Society of the United States, the International Fund for Animal Welfare, and the Fund for Animals have lobbied to stop the hunt.

Other reasons probably had an effect in the decision to halt hunting. Numbers of fur seals continue to decline, and the harvest is not economical, given the low price of seal pelts compared to other furbearers.

But it is the vociferously expressed distaste for killing seals — whether in Newfoundland at the outset of our journey or in Alaska at its end — that finally stopped the centuries-old hunt. "It's part of a pattern of change around the world," said Mike. "People just don't like killing seals and whales. They stopped the fur seal hunt in South Africa, the harp seal hunt in Newfoundland, the gray seal hunt in England, and whaling in America. It's an emotional thing. People want to clean up the environment, to give the animals a chance."

The Aleuts are going to need a chance too. The Russians brought them to the Pribilofs for one reason only, to kill seals. The Americans maintained them there for the same reason. From 20,000, their numbers have declined to 3,000. So the Aleuts are also a threatened species.

If mecca for me was the fur seal rookeries, mecca for most of my companions was the seabird rookeries. Birders flock to the Pribilofs from around the world to see some of the largest and most diverse seabird colonies in the northern hemisphere. The birds are drawn to breed there by the abundance of food in the Bering Sea, an enormous broth of nutrients that some have called an underwater Serengeti. People come to see species such as the red-legged kittiwake and red-faced cormorant, which nest only on the Pribilofs, a few islands in the Aleutians, and off Siberia. And they come to look for rare international accidentals ("Wind-drifted strays," Peterson calls them), like Mongolian plovers, Oriental cuckoos, Polynesian tattlers, and Siberian ruby-throats.

Best of all, the Pribilof Islands earn their nickname, the Galapagos of the North, for the ease with which people can see the birds. You land on the flattish, treeless terrain of St. Paul by plane, live in a hotel, get driven back and forth along twenty-seven miles of easy road, and stroll for as little or as long as you want across grass and wildflower gardens to eye birds a few feet away. For most species, you do not really need your binoculars or telephoto lenses.

I knew the tufted and Atlantic puffins, the common and ring-billed murres, the rhinoceros and Cassin's auklets; now I was to be introduced to other members of the alcid family — the horned puffin, the least, crested, and parakeet auklets — colorful birds that few people ever get to see. Four more seabird species that nest in the steep-walled Pribilof "apartment" cliffs are the red-faced cormorant, northern fulmar, and the black-legged and the red-legged kittiwakes. Glaucous and glaucous-winged gulls nest on open slopes and grassy uplands — if foxes let them be.

Amazingly, they all get along. At first glance, a seabird rookery looks just as chaotic as a sea lion rookery. But ecological patterns exist. Seabirds share the land and the water, so that the Pribilof cliffs and the Bering Sea serve them all.

Red-faced cormorants, one of the very few species to stay on the islands year-round, build their nests of grass, sticks, and seaweed on broad but isolated and individual ledges high on the cliff face. Lines of murres lay their single eggs on longer, more shelflike ledges where crowding seems to motivate breeding: common murres favor broader ledges than thick-billed murres (the common murres sat with their whole foot on the ledge, while the thick-billed murres seemed to hang onto near vertical walls by their toenails). Agile red-legged kittiwakes favor smaller ledges with overhangs, perhaps to avoid the larger black-legged kittiwakes. Tufted puffins scratch out their nesting burrows from the soil under grass clumps; horned puffins are more likely to lay their eggs in large rock crevices. Both crested and parakeet auklets nest in cracks between rocks, but the parakeet sites are apt to be higher. Least auklets cluster around boulders on the beaches (although on St. George they also nest along a mile-long talus ridge inland). Pribilof seabirds also lessen competition by varying the distance they travel to get food and the quality and depth of the water in which they find it.

St. George Island, with seven times the cliff area and higher, steeper slopes, has many more seabirds than St. Paul — an estimated 2.5 million compared to a quarter of a million. But it is easier to get around and see the birds on St. Paul. Its cliffs (none more than 400 feet) are deeply gullied, so you can view and photograph them at an angle across the gully without resorting to lying on your stomach, hanging over the edge, and hoping somebody holds your onto ankles, as Birgit did for Bob.

Bob had a marvelous helpmate in Birgit, who would run ahead along the grassy cliff edge and choose good camera locations. I imagined she told the birds to put their best feathers forward because Bob was coming to sketch them.

Ancient volcanic lava-flows and ash eruptions have left a legacy of landforms in different shapes and sizes. Beautifully fractured basalt columns and wave-worn boulders were sewn with yellow lichen and sprinkled with hairy cinquefoil, scurvy grass, and bird's-eye chickweed. Birds use them now for nesting and perching ledges, or dig into the easily eroded rock for their tunnels and burrows. One particular gully was ideal for the puffins and the auklets, who nested just under the grassy overhang, and for Bob and me, who photographed them against these picturesque backdrops.

Roger Tory Peterson joined us when he returned from accompanying a Lindblad Travel group on the first tourist flight to St. George. He told us that the island and the village still looked the same as they did on his previous visit thirty years before. "The hotel was unoccupied when I was there then. I remember putting our sleeping bags on the floor, and a little blue fox came in the door and took off with a friend's shoes. It's been fixed up since then, but it retains all the original character. The village on St. George hasn't changed a bit, but St. Paul here looks a lot different."

Peterson reckoned that there were four times more birds on St. George than on St. Paul. "But it's hard to photograph them on those thousand-foot-high cliffs." He said that he saw the same variety of species, but that in contrast to the "millions" of murres and the "millions" of least auklets he had reported in *Wild America*, numbers appeared to have diminished.

Three years later I talked to Vernon Byrd and Dave Nysewander, biologists working for the Alaska Maritime National Wildlife Refuge, to get more accurate figures. "It is very difficult to census birds, especially seabirds," said Vernon by phone from St. Paul. "In ten years, we're only just starting to refine our methods. One can't be accurate when we're comparing a single count on a particular day in 1976 with the consistent replications we're doing now. We haven't got enough baseline data yet to know if declines are normal fluctuations or real downward trends."

Nevertheless, the data seem to indicate that murres and kittiwakes, with sharp breeding declines in certain seasons, are declining in total numbers as well. Some biologists go as far as to interpret the data as showing a 35 percent decrease over the decade. The counts of 229,000 common and 1,610,100 thick-billed murres, and 222,000 red-legged and 108,000 black-legged kittiwakes certainly seemed far fewer than Peterson's count, despite the difference in counting methods. "The boys" had estimated that the numbers of auklets in 1953 ran into "millions." A 1978 report gave the numbers of least auklets as 273,000, parakeet auklets 184,000, and crested auklets 34,000; tufted puffins 7,000 and horned puffins 32,000. Counting such burrow nesters as puffins and auklets is far more difficult than cliff nesters such as murres, cormorants, and kittiwakes, so the biologists did not know trends for these. However, it seems reasonable to assume that their numbers have declined as well. One species that is doing well overall is James Fisher's favorite, the northern fulmar.

If biologists are loath to say how many birds are on the Pribilofs, they are even more cautious in giving reasons for decline. It could be that the warm current known as El Nino that swept into the North Pacific for two or more years from the tropics has created a shortage of the fish normally consumed by the birds. Perhaps it is warmer water or warmer air. Or native hunting. Or entanglement in fish nets. "If you were forced to give a reason," Dave Nysewander said, "I guess you might say it was commercial fishing in the Bering Sea." Perhaps it *will* be oil spills. Seismic crews were already exploring for oil and gas offshore from the Pribilofs.

Peterson came back from St. George with the news that he had seen a Franklin's gull, a common gull on the prairie, but the first record for the Pribilofs. He had the same shine in his eye that all birders have when they see a rarity.

One of the highlights of Peterson's 1953 visit to the Pribilofs had been his boat ride to Walrus Island, a flat island of about eighty acres, eight miles due east of St. Paul. He had described "acres of murres . . . a blizzard of buzzing birds, bewildering, countless." Up till 1949 Walrus Island was one of the world's largest murre colonies (Peterson estimated about a million birds). However, after Steller's sea lions took up residence there, murres were either eaten by the sea lions or they moved away, leaving only 200 murres on a sea stack at the island's northern end. Now, it seems that the Steller's sea lions are also declining.

As journalist Bob Krist once said, "Birding with Roger Tory Peterson is like climbing a mountain with Sir Edmund Hillary." One of the nonbirders on our tour quipped, "They ought to change the name of this island from St. Paul to St. Peterson."

Peterson came with us on the bus. Everybody, of course, wanted to ask him questions or get their field guides autographed, but he did have the opportunity too to wander alone along the cliffs, reliving perhaps his time with Fisher, when there were no tourist trips to the fabled Pribilofs.

Like us, Peterson was encumbered by the usual paraphernalia of cameras, a backpack of lenses, binoculars, and a tripod. Like Bob, he takes pictures as references for his drawings. "I enjoy photography. I take many more photographs than I'll ever need, but it is relaxing therapy for me, a delight," he murmured in his gentle voice. "People think that I always draw birds like those in the field guides, giving them the patternistic treatment, emphasizing their essential field marks. But I'm doing more portraiture, even in the guides. I received all sorts of proper training in the arts and I want to get back to the kind of thing Bob Bateman is doing." He is often quoted as saying, "If I could paint like another wildlife artist, it would be Robert Bateman."

Peterson's aim on this bird walk was to take photographs of red-faced cormorants and red-legged kittiwakes in preparation for painting them. I found one red-faced cormorant within touching distance near the locally named "short cliffs" by Southwest Point. It was just as tolerant as the one Peterson had photographed thirty years before, and just as photogenic—a bird, James Fisher said, that was "designed for Kodachrome." A little larger and longer-billed than its closest relative, the pelagic cormorant, it perched on a tiny ledge under the lip of the cliff, preened, and returned our stares with a beady eye. Its black plumage had a distinctively iridescent green sheen, its face was bright red with a blue patch on the base of its bill, it had two crests on its crown, and its thighs were white.

Bob Bateman often says, "Art begins where Nature ends." I walked on, wondering how the two artist-naturalists would portray that red-faced cormorant.

Peterson took one photograph that day that was not of a bird. Gus, who had been assiduously checking all of the gulls in case one in the flock was unusual, was finally rewarded for his patience. "Slaty-backed gull, an Asiatic accidental," he announced, straightening from his telescope. "You won't find any other black-backed gull occurring here regularly." Everybody as usual lined up behind the scope to focus on this rarity. (Coincidentally, "the boys" had found a slaty-backed gull in a flock of a thousand glaucous-winged gulls on their trip.) "In the Pribilofs," Peterson remarked amusedly as he took a photograph of us, "people are more likely to line up for beer, not birds."

During our week on St. Paul we saw, collectively, about thirty-nine of the 210 species recorded for the Pribilofs. For four days we feasted our eyes on Steller's eiders, a species found only on the Arctic coasts of Alaska and Siberia and the Bering Sea. Gus spotted an albino murre for our oddity list. And Joanne McRobbie spotted a McKay's bunting, a species that Peterson had never seen. She tried to find it a second time — for him — without success.

The climax of the week as far as birds were concerned were "the high cliffs" of the west coast. Here the grassy slopes plummeted into the sea like vertical folded green rugs. Where rocky knife edges were too precipitous for vegetation, birds still managed to claw out a perch or a nest. Down below, waves made soap patterns at the pebbled shore. Chunky puffins and more streamlined murres whirred past, their bodies stiff, their webbed feet splayed behind, their short, stubby wings beating busily — so busily, it seemed, that they should be making faster headway in the blustery wind.

Puffins certainly are tough — with that massive, parrotlike bill that can latch onto bare skin with the tenacity of a bulldog, the sharpness of an axe, and the flexibility of a concertina. Despite its incredible beak, the tufted puffin, with its long golden tassels and orange-rimmed eyes, will probably always be my favorite alcid. But the horned puffin is intriguingly new to me. With its black back, white shirt front, lack of tassels, and striped bill, it resembles the Atlantic puffin, except that the horned puffin has a bicolored bill of yellow and red rather than the tricolored one of its eastern counterpart, and that the black "horn" above its eye is more pronounced. The horn that gives this puffin its name is not really a hard horn like the protuberance on the beak of the rhinoceros auklet, but soft living tissue, which the bird can raise or lower at will.

You cannot think about a puffin without calling up words like comical, grotesque, droll, fantastic. They can be both sad and funny, clowns and judges. Puffins have an eye-catching personal style in all that they do, whether they are digging out turf with their pickaxe beaks or sitting outside their burrows with a face full of fish. Perhaps they are playing a part, and the masklike bill which they shed in the fall is just part of the masquerade.

The auklets I met on the Pribilofs were droll in appearance too. The first to arrive on the islands while snow still clads the slopes are the least auklets, the smallest of the alcids. Sparrow-sized, they swarm in like mosquitoes to congregate on the rocks, constantly chittering and chirping. They looked as if they had just come in from the toyshop. Their white eyes were pearl buttons pasted onto the black velvet of their chunky bodies. We were told that the Aleuts put them into pies. Susan remarked dryly, "I wonder if they need four and twenty of them."

The pudgy parakeet auklet sitting alone or in small groups on boulders had pearl-button eyes too. Its chief characteristics are a red upturned bill and white plumes that seem to grow out of its eyes. Despite its name, it did not look as much like a parrot as the puffin.

The crested auklets barked. By far the noisiest of the auklets, they made weird cries like dogs. Other observers have said they honk like geese or yap like foxes. Like all these bizarre auklets, their white eyes looked sewn onto their faces, but the crested auklet's most distinctive feature is a backward-waving black plume that causes some observers to call the bird a sea quail.

The rare red-legged kittiwakes, found only on the Pribilofs and the Commander Islands off Siberia, were sitting on eggs or tamping down their mud-and-seaweed nests. They looked as if their legs were dipped in blood.

"Turn me loose on this island and I wouldn't starve," said Gus as we sloshed through lush edible gardens of angelica, alpine bistort, woolly lousewort, oysterplant, scurvy grass, even chocolate lily. While Gus, Ruth Delaney, and I snacked on plants as we strolled, Susan Harvey was busy with her movie camera recording the flamboyant scene. Tucked in among the edibles were other flowering plants — Siberian buttercup, spring beauty, violets, cinquefoil, monkshood, and the beautifully blue weasel snout.

The lushness of the meadows above the cliffs was repeated below. Each wave-washed boulder was draped in a riot of colorful seaweeds that reminded Birgit and me of hooked rugs. Each tide pool was studded with flowers of another kind, colorful sea urchins and anemones. Such lavishness attested to the richness of the Bering Sea and its abundant wildlife, but it still seemed strange here on these otherwise stark, mist-and-wind-clad volcanic islands. Strewn everywhere on the beach as we walked were washed-up nets that not only catch fish but strangle seabirds and sea lions too. I saw more than one fur seal wearing a lethal green necklace.

I wanted to catch sight of some of St. Paul's 350 reindeer that had been propagated from an introduction in the early 1900s for meat and hides. Finally, for a few brief moments, a dark smudge of animals moved across the skyline of Ridge Hill. Reindeer at last. The Aleuts take about a hundred each year to eke out their meat supply.

The joy of the Pribilofs was not only in masses of flowers, milling seals, and a myriad seabirds. It was also in seeing life on a smaller scale. Sitting on a long black beach at midnight watching seals at play beyond the surf line. Steller's sea lions raising their heads out of the mist on Walrus Island and Sea Lion Rocks. A lone murre waddling awkwardly across the beach on its belly, its wings beating the sand like oars till it reached the security of the sea. A walrus beached forever.

On my last night in St. Paul I had a hamburger dinner in Father Lestenkof's crowded basement, the ''in'' place in town. The priest's family prepared the hamburgers behind a counter inches from where you tried to find a seat, and the priest served them.

''Didn't your travel agent warn you about this place?'' said the lady opposite me with a horrified look around. ''My husband gave me this trip to Alaska as a wedding anniversary present — but didn't tell me where we were going. I thought we were going to Waikiki.''

''Warn me?'' I asked incredulously. ''I've been wanting to come to the Pribilofs for years.''

She looked even more incredulous. ''It's so gray and depressing, so dirty. And there's no nightlife, no restaurants, no boutiques.''

I thought I would skip the seals, the birds, the foxes, the reindeer, the Aleuts, and start with the flowers. Flowers and babies usually have universal appeal.

She listened grimly, then commented determinedly, ''But we have better flowers in Lincoln, Nebraska. I'm glad I'm white and I live where I do.''

After supper I joined the others in the schoolroom to chat with Roger Tory Peterson. Each night we had gathered for our reading of *Wild America*, and I was intrigued to discover that while I had been reading the Pribilof chapters on St. Paul to our group, Peterson had been on St. George reading the same chapters to his Lindblad group. Now we were all together, a fitting climax indeed to our respective discoveries of Wild America.

Peterson talked of course of birds and birding, of how he began, and how it is now. ''My own interest came at the age of eleven when our teacher started a junior Audubon club. She gave me a color plate of a blue jay to copy and an outline to color in. But perhaps it was my first bird walk. I went afield with a friend of mine, Carl Hammerstrom. It was April 8, 1920. We came to a little wood, and there was a flicker on a tree. Obviously it had been migrating, was dead tired, and asleep on the cusp of the tree. I thought it was dead. I touched it, and all of a sudden this brown thing sprang to life, gorgeous red slash here, yellow under the wing there, such a contrast between something that was seemingly dead and such a violent expression of life. I think that that, more than anything, has stayed with me, the feeling that birds are probably the most eloquent expression of the living world. At any rate, I've been birding ever since.''

He talked of how birding had come full circle. "In the early days, we didn't have books that made identification easy. Audubon of course shot birds. He said it wasn't really a good day unless he shot at least a hundred — rather shocking now when you think of the protectionist society in his name. But it was understandable in those days. You had to have the thing in hand to be able to describe it and name it and know what you had.''

By 1895 Frank Chapman and Chester Reed began questioning the Shotgun School. They wondered about putting guns in the hands of increasing numbers of bird lovers. They tried to remedy the situation by producing bird guides that Peterson referred to as ''little checkbook guides'' because of their shape. The format was simple, but the text was too detailed. "Chapman would start describing a bird, starting with its beak and ending with its tail. For example, the robin would start this way — yellow beak, blackish head with three white spots around the eye, three black stripes on a white throat, and only halfway down would he come to the red breast — the words that would be the robin's distinguishing feature.''

The answer of course was in the field guides that Peterson devised himself and began publishing in 1934. "A book that gave me the germ of the idea was *Two Little Savages* by Ernest Thompson Seton, a Canadian, one of the really brilliant naturalists of the Old School. He wrote this novel about two boys who go camping in the woods. They saw the birds, but they had problems identifying them. The hero, Yan, goes to town and finds a dusty showcase with ducks inside mounted and named. He notices that all these ducks were different, they all had blotches or streaks that were their identification tags, like uniforms. So he copies the simple patterns the ducks had in the showcase and looks for the same patterns in the field.''

From then on, bird watchers could look at a bird through their binoculars and reach into their pockets for one of Peterson's many field guides, all of them simple, handy, and to the point. Peterson selected the diagnostic feature of each bird that separated it from all others at a glance or at a distance, then marked it with an arrow. "My whole idea was simplification, but now people want amplification,'' he smiled.

"All these hotshot birders now have Questar high-powered telescopes. They can even see the nasal grooves on a Polynesian tattler. So we're back to bird-in-the-hand birding. Field guides are coming out now in Britain with twenty pages devoted to one species. That means a western guide with 500 species would become a book of 10,000 pages. It's a problem."

When identification was made simpler in 1934, the number of bird watchers increased phenomenally, more than fortyfold, Peterson thinks, since his first guide. There are perhaps twenty to forty million bird watchers in North America, depending on how you define their level of birding. Some birders do more than just look at birds. Hundreds of thousands of people around the world report their observations regularly and provide important information on bird behavior, numbers, distribution, and migration patterns. (This is important, because birds are like ecological litmus paper — they indicate what is wrong or right with the environment.) As a result of their interest in one species, birders also support research and conservation projects for all species. Peterson said, "It is inevitable that the intelligent person who watches birds becomes an environmentalist."

One such birder is Robert Bateman. He told us that it was a copy of Peterson's guide that got him into serious bird watching at the age of twelve. By sixteen he had sketched every hawk and owl in North America. Birds are still Bateman's first love, although he now paints — and promotes — a variety of animals and their habitats. He calls himself a "professional appreciator of the natural world." In turning the general public onto his paintings, he makes them appreciators too. By using his status and donating part of the revenues from his paintings to promote various conservation projects such as funding panda reserves in China, he widens his influence as a conservationist.

As I listened to Peterson and Bateman talking about their motivation and reflected on their influence, I thought of the lady from Nebraska who was so disappointed with the Pribilofs. After all those miles and months looking for Wild America in company with devotees, I needed a jolt back to other people's reality. For some people, it is not the natural jungle but the concrete jungle that is desirable. I could not be too complacent. If we are to be successful in the battle to conserve the natural world, then those people must be recruited too. How?

To become effective appreciators, people need to find their own meanings and values in wilderness. Wilderness means different things to different people. The famous Spanish philosopher Ortega y Gasset called it "a vacation from the human condition." For some, it is what they see in wildlife refuges, ecological reserves, and national parks; or what they do—climbing, canoeing, backpacking and snowshoeing, hunting and fishing. For some, wilderness is far from other people, a place they experience alone and untouched; for others, like Thoreau, who one summer went looking for the wild and found he got no farther than his back yard, it may be as close as their hummingbird feeder.

You have to find the magic for yourself, whether you are John Muir reveling in the Sierra Nevada, Ernest Thompson Seton watching a kingbird attack a crow, or Tess Kloot looking at a scissor-tailed fly-catcher on a roadside fence.

Originally, I had found my own motivation close to home in the company of eagles and seals, murres and puffins, cougars and raccoons. I also found it, one day long ago, before my search for Wild America, far away near the roof of the world.

It seemed the world had stopped that day on the high tundra. The midnight sun hung motionless in a baked-blue sky. Perpetual snow blanketed the mountains; a sheen of permanent ice imprisoned the waters of the world's most northerly lake; gray-blue char hung suspended in its depths. There was no sound, not even the tinkling of candled ice in the wind.

Away from the lake, the tundra, a vast brown carpet blistered with hummocks and pockmarked by bog water, rolled on to a far horizon. From this distance, the land looked empty, barren, dead.

Life was in little things. At my feet the ground was patterned in myriad shapes; the rocks were clothed in colorful lichens; the tussocks were skirted in moss and grass; tiny flowers were sprouting through impossible cracks. I looked up and, near the skyline, a white rock glistened.

Suddenly, where there had been one rock, there was another, and then one more. Arctic hares? No, too big. Wolves! Pure white tundra wolves. I whispered the words like a prayer; then, as if to confirm their reality, I counted aloud. Four, five, six, seven, eight, nine, ten—ten white wolves in single file, heading toward me on the hunt. On the hunt? For a moment, the old tales surfaced and the thrill of fear shot through the thrill of discovery.

The wolves came closer until they formed a line across my camera's viewfinder. I snapped several pictures, but it was not enough; I wanted to be with them in their world. I tried to howl. They stopped, as one, and stared. Ten pairs of eyes were riveted on mine as I in turn stood riveted to the tundra. It was a magic moment, one that I wanted to last a millennium; yet, too soon, responding to some unseen signal, nine wolves followed their leader to the horizon and beyond. The spell was broken.

But not forgotten. I felt compelled to share what I had seen and experienced. Back at the lake, back beneath those glaciered mountains, the others did not understand. Pilots, miners, traders, they flew over the continent-wide tracts of Arctic wilderness, seeing it as nothingness. They thought it absurd that someone could find such joy in wolves — and even more absurd that someone would worry that numbers of wolves were dwindling. They huddled over their cards and glasses inside a tiny, insulated canvas cocoon and ignored the wonder I tried to express.

What created the enchantment in the brief moments I spent with those wolves? Was it in making contact with wild creatures that had possibly never seen humans? Did the magic lie in a challenge met? Did the wolves represent the life and beauty to be found in barrenness if only one looks and waits? Or was it the wildness that was important? Was it the silence, the solitude, the space that one naturalist called the soul of a country? Was it the feeling of being in a remote spot on the roof of the world, alone with these creatures?

Whatever it was, I do not take it for granted. The magic and the motivation remain. I hope that lady from Nebraska finds her personal wolves.

Epilogue

For most of us, Wild America ended in Anchorage, a touch of civilization before we parted and went our separate ways — to England, to Australia, to Canada, to other parts of the United States. Gus Yaki would be going to Newfoundland, in effect beginning Wild America all over again. I was going to spend the rest of the summer seeking wilderness in Canada's Northwest Territories. For one week some of my companions — Ruth Delaney, Susan Harvey, Anne Macdonald, Jack Bryans, and Gus — would be going there too.

"Going over to Canada, you say?" echoed the pilot as we crowded into the small bush plane for a night flight across the roof of North America. Yes, we were — across the Mount St. Elias Range, across the second-highest mountains in North America, across the most extensive nonpolar icefields in the world. East into the rising sun we would fly from Alaska to the Yukon to the Northwest Territories and the Mackenzie Mountain Barrens. We would travel to the largest uninhabited wilderness mountain range in North America, perhaps in the world.

There was time on the flight to reflect. Not on the 518 species of birds we had seen in ninety days. Not even on our rarities, a Chilean pintail, albino oddities, or a Brandt's cormorant in nuptial plumage. Instead, my mind went back to my first discovery of Wild America. I had come to the New World expecting it to be buried under billboards and parking lots; yet for months I explored its parks and outback areas and almost never saw a freeway. I agreed then with James Fisher, who had been amazed to discover that although North Americans had the power to ravage their land, they had made it "a garden." That was in 1953. Was it a garden now? Would it still be a garden in another thirty years?

Back in the Pribilofs, we had invited Roger Tory Peterson to join us in 2013 for a Wild America reunion. He laughed and reminded us that he would be 105 years old then. So we talked of what Wild America was like now. "Much of it is still wild," he conceded, "but wild in a different way. It's a managed wild now. I think North America is holding up pretty well. Thirty or forty years ago, the grassroots conservationist movement did not exist. But now we have such a body of public opinion that if something is really in trouble, the public is there to make sure it gets help.''

He talked of specifics, of fewer vireos and warblers, fewer loggerhead shrikes and seabirds. He said that yellow-billed cuckoos and blue grosbeaks were in trouble. On the other hand, kites and ospreys were improving. ''There were a hundred pairs of ospreys in a ten-mile circle of our house in Old Lyme, Connecticut, when we moved there in 1954. They were reduced to one and then to only nine for the whole state. Now, through management, they are doing well.'' As one with long experience in the natural world and the politics of conservation, Roger Tory Peterson was generally optimistic about mankind's ability to turn things around.

James Fisher had hoped we North Americans would always hold onto our primitive areas. He had said the English would give their souls to have some of them on their side of the Atlantic. And he had reminded us that people do not appreciate how important wilderness is until they lose it.

Well, James, ours is a managed garden now, a new kind of wilderness. We scrape our beaches so least terns can nest there. We move sea otters and bighorn sheep and bald eagles from areas of abundance to areas of devastation. We remove the last of the ferrets and condors from the wild and try to breed them in captivity. We build nest boxes for wood ducks, leave snag trees for eagles, even dig artificial burrows for auklets. We set fires, plant grasses, and make potholes. We outlaw billboards and join Coalitions for Scenic Beauty. You said we were worthy landlords. We now call ourselves habitat enhancers, wildlife managers.

Patches of wilderness in their primitive sense — roadless tracts where natural ecosystems play out their dramas unobstructed — still remain on your Wild America route. We saw them on the Pribilofs, in the Yukon-Kuskokwim Delta, on the Olympic Peninsula, along the Big Sur coast, high in the Sierras. Scenes of abundance still stir the soul: flocks of wintering shorebirds in Florida, flights of ducks and geese on the Texas coast and central California, forests of bald eagles in Alaska.

Will it be the same in thirty years?

It would be nice to push a button and find out if we are winning or losing in our battle to conserve wilderness and wildlife, or if we are maintaining the status quo. But despite the wealth of data and the sophisticated methods of collecting it compared to those available thirty years ago, there are just too many variables to give an accurate answer. Species vary from place to place. (Sea otters are endangered in Oregon, but not in Alaska.) Populations vary from time to time. (Puffins declined in Newfoundland in 1981, but recouped by 1986.) Data collection methods vary. (John James Audubon counting eggs in 1832 and Roger Tory Peterson watching terns on the Tortugas in 1953 could not provide data comparable to that of ornithologists using replicate transects today; even modern census methods differ in their degree of refinement.) People vary in their interpretation of the data, according to their biases. (Politicians who do not want to upset native hunters on northern breeding grounds will judge the impact of bird hunting differently from opponents of hunting in southern cities.) Not all aspects of the environment receive the same amount of attention. (Politicians provide more funds to study animals that voters are interested in, like wolves, or those that bring economic benefits, like deer or fish, than for the study of some obscure plant or butterfly.) We are not gods, even with today's computers. And most often, especially in a year like the year of El Nino, it is not in our hands at all.

Considering our love of people and all that goes with them—cities, roads, industries—we cannot go back to the good old days of supposedly pristine panoramas, diversity, and abundance. But since Peterson and Fisher traveled Wild America, people have been shocked into action be seeing firsthand, or on their television screens, nasty scenes of oiled seabirds, strangled seals, poisoned lakes, and acid rain. They have seen species reduced to numbers they can count on one hand. They have flocked to join a thousand conservation groups, signed a million petitions. Governments have decreed more national parks, monuments, refuges, even national seashores, rivers, and parkways. Private individuals and groups have donated land for even more sanctuaries. People have voted in wilderness acts, endangered species acts, a myriad conservation bills. Eighty percent of polled Americans support the environmental movement. Eighty-three percent of Canadians believe that protection of the environment is more important then keeping costs down.

Just how successful have we been? Peterson said that less than 0.75 percent of the land area of the United States was protected in national parks in 1953. Since then its national park acreage has increased threefold, its national wildlife refuge acreage fivefold (we now have 143 more refuges than in 1953), and its wilderness forest land has increased fivefold. Since then, the Nature Conservancy has protected almost three million acres of land. The National Audubon Society has provided over 150,000 acres for sanctuaries, and Ducks Unlimited even more. Over 11 percent of the land area in the United States is now protected wilderness. "I think we have done an incredible job of preserving wilderness," said George Kyle of the National Parks Service in Washington, D.C. (And that is despite an increase of 50 percent in human population in the last thirty years.)

Is it enough? Can it possibly be enough when the problems now are global—when tropical forests are being cut down at the rate of 32,000 square miles a year (an area the size of Austria)? Some experts say this will cause the loss to the world of one third or more of all wildlife species over the next century. We have different problems now, James. We might have anticipated that the seabirds on San Miguel Island would die in oil, but who would have thought when you visited that they may also be subjected to sonic boom pressure waves from space-shuttle launches?

Well, on a world scale we are probably losing, but in Wild America, for now, I think we are possibly winning, or at least maintaining the status quo.

Flying over a sea of untouched peaks and glaciers on the roof of North America as we sped eastward to complete the circle of the continent, it seemed appropriate to remember the battles we had won.

In Newfoundland northern gannets have outgrown their nesting sites and are now spilling to the "mainland," seabirds are doing well, humpback whales have increased fivefold, and the right whale has been brought back from the brink of extinction.

In the Northeast farmland is being revegetated, links are being added to a chain of refuges along the coast for migratory birds, nesting bird species have increased fivefold in a refuge like Jamaica Bay, egrets are expanding their range, and ospreys and peregrine falcons are breeding again.

In the Southeast the brown pelican, snail kite, alligator, and Key deer have made successful comebacks, least terns are expanding their range and adjusting to people, wood storks and red-cockaded woodpeckers are showing gains, a government vows to save the Everglades and even build underpasses for panthers, and the ivory-billed woodpecker, now seen in Cuba, may also exist in the Southern United States.

In the Middle South oil industry barons and wildlife seem to be getting along, reddish egrets and black-shouldered kites are increasing in numbers, and the whooping crane has been brought back from near extinction.

In the West wild and ruggedly beautiful landscapes still seem the same, cougars are now valued for themselves, increased populations of sea otters, sea lions, elephant seals, and gray whales show nature's resiliency, ancient laval rocks stand beside newly erupted flows to show an earth still in flux, and destruction is followed by construction to keep us humble and give us hope.

In the North — Alaska — people still have a chance to choose the wisest use of the land before they develop it, Wild America can still be seen as once it was, and a new spirit of cooperation between different interest groups can show itself in wise conservation decisions.

People are making the difference. "Endless pressure endlessly applied," said Dan Heinz of the American Wilderness Alliance. I thought of Peterson and Fisher, of Bob Bateman and Gus Yaki, of Bill Montevecchio and the men from Memorial University in Newfoundland, of Frances Hames in Florida, of Ned McIlhenny in Louisiana, of Judith Toups in Mississippi, of Margaret Owings in California, of Eleanor Stopps in Washington. I remembered specialists like ornithologists, wildlife biologists, and habitat managers now working together with foresters, fishermen, and industrialists. I thought of the media that spread the word and of the governments that respond.

Humans are part of the environment too. There is no place where they have made no mark, but we can still find a "vacation from the human condition," wilderness and wilderness experience in America. We can still find our personal wolves. With eternal vigilance, we can achieve success.

Our Bird List

Order GAVIIFORMES
Family Gaviidae
Gavia stellata (Pontoppidan). Red-throated Loon.
Gavia arctica (Linnaeus). Arctic Loon.
Gavia immer (Brünnich). Common Loon.

Order PODICIPEDIFORMES
Family Podicipedidae
Tachybaptus dominicus (Linnaeus). Least Grebe.
Podilymbus podiceps (Linnaeus). Pied-billed Grebe.
Podiceps auritus (Linnaeus). Horned Grebe.
Podiceps grisegena (Boddaert). Red-necked Grebe.
Podiceps nigricollis (Brehm). Eared Grebe.
Aechmophorus occidentalis (Lawrence). Western Grebe.
Aechmophorus clarkii (Clark). Clark's Grebe.

Order PROCELLARIIFORMES
Family Procellariidae
Fulmarus glacialis (Linnaeus). Northern Fulmar.

Order PELECANIFORMES — Suborder PHAETHONTES
Family Phaethontidae
Phaethon lepturus (Daudin). White-tailed Tropicbird.

Suborder PELECANI
Family Sulidae
Sula leucogaster (Boddaert). Brown Booby.
Sula bassanus (Linnaeus). Northern Gannet.

Family Pelecanidae
Pelecanus erythrorhynchos (Gmelin). American White Pelican.
Pelecanus occidentalis (Linnaeus). Brown Pelican.

Family Phalacrocoracidae
Phalacrocorax carbo (Linnaeus). Great Cormorant.
Phalacrocorax auritus (Lesson). Double-crested Cormorant.
Phalacrocorax olivaceus (Humboldt). Olivaceous Cormorant.

Phalacrocorax penicillatus (Brandt). Brandt's Cormorant.
Phalacrocorax pelagicus (Pallas). Pelagic Cormorant.
Phalacrocorax urile (Gmelin). Red-faced Cormorant.

Family Anhingidae
Anhinga anhinga (Linnaeus). Anhinga.

Suborder FREGATAE
Family Fregatidae
Fregata magnificens (Mathews). Magnificent Frigatebird.

Order CICONIIFORMES — Suborder ARDEAE
Family Ardeidae — Tribe Botaurini
Botaurus lentiginosus (Rackett). American Bittern.
Ixobrychus exilis (Gmelin). Least Bittern.
Tribe Ardeini
Ardea herodias (Linnaeus). Great Blue Heron.
Casmerodius albus (Linnaeus). Great Egret.
Egretta thula (Molina). Snowy Egret.
Egretta caerulea (Linnaeus). Little Blue Heron.
Egretta tricolor (Müller). Tricolored Heron.
Egretta rufescens (Gmelin). Reddish Egret.
Bubulcus ibis (Linnaeus). Cattle Egret.
Butorides striatus (Linnaeus). Green-backed Heron.
Tribe Nycticoracini
Nycticorax nycticorax (Linnaeus). Black-crowned Night-Heron.
Nycticorax violaceus (Linnaeus). Yellow-crowned Night-Heron.

Suborder THRESKIORNITHES
Family Threskiornithidae — Subfamily Threskiornithinae
Eudocimus albus (Linnaeus). White Ibis.
Eudocimus ruber (Linnaeus). Scarlet Ibis.
Plegadis falcinellus (Linnaeus). Glossy Ibis.
Plegadis chihi (Vieillot). White-faced Ibis.

Subfamily Plataleinae
Ajaia ajaja (Linnaeus). Roseate Spoonbill.

Suborder CICONIAE
Family Ciconiidae — Tribe Mysteriini
Mycteria americana (Linnaeus). Wood Stork.

Order ANSERIFORMES — Suborder ANSERES
Family Anatidae — Subfamily Anserinae — Tribe Dendrocygini
Dendrocygna bicolor (Vieillot). Fulvous Whistling-Duck.
Tribe Cygnini
Cygnus columbianus (Ord). Tundra Swan.
Cygnus olor (Gmelin). Mute Swan.
Cygnus atratus (Latham). Black Swan.

Tribe Anserini

Anser erythropus (Linnaeus). Lesser White-fronted Goose.
Chen caerulescens (Linnaeus). Snow Goose.
Chen canagica (Sewastianov). Emperor Goose.
Branta bernicla (Linnaeus). Brant.
Branta canadensis (Linnaeus). Canada Goose.

Subfamily Anatinae — Tribe Cairinini

Aix sponsa (Linnaeus). Wood Duck.

Tribe Anatini

Anas crecca (Linnaeus). Green-winged Teal.
Anas rubripes (Brewster). American Black Duck.
Anas fulvigula (Ridgway). Mottled Duck.
Anas platyrhynchos (Linnaeus). Mallard.
Anas bahamensis (Linnaeus). White-cheeked Pintail.
Anas georgica. (Linnaeus). Yellow-billed Pintail.
Anas acuta (Linnaeus). Northern Pintail.
Anas discors (Linnaeus). Blue-winged Teal.
Anas cyanoptera (Vieillot). Cinnamon Teal.
Anas clypeata (Linnaeus). Northern Shoveler.
Anas americana (Gmelin). American Wigeon.

Tribe Aythyini

Aythya valisineria (Wilson). Canvasback.
Aythya americana (Eyton). Redhead.
Aythya marila (Linnaeus). Greater Scaup.
Aythya affinis (Eyton). Lesser Scaup.

Tribe Mergini

Somateria mollissima (Linnaeus). Common Eider.
Somateria spectabilis (Linnaeus). King Eider.
Somateria fischeri (Brandt). Spectacled Eider.
Polysticta stelleri (Pallas). Steller's Eider.
Histrionicus histrionicus (Linnaeus). Harlequin Duck.
Clangula hyemalis (Linnaeus). Oldsquaw.
Melanitta nigra (Linnaeus). Black Scoter.
Melanitta perspicillata (Linnaeus). Surf Scoter.
Melanitta fusca (Linnaeus). White-winged Scoter.
Bucephala clangula (Linnaeus). Common Goldeneye.
Bucephala islandica (Gmelin). Barrow's Goldeneye.
Bucephala albeola (Linnaeus). Bufflehead.
Mergus merganser (Linnaeus). Common Merganser.
Mergus serrator (Linnaeus). Red-breasted Merganser.

Tribe Oxyurini

Oxyura jamaicensis (Gmelin). Ruddy Duck.
Oxyura dominica (Linnaeus). Masked Duck.

Order FALCONIFORMES
Suborder CATHARTAE — Superfamily CATHARTOIDEA
Family Cathartidae
Coragyps atratus (Bechstein). Black Vulture.
Cathartes aura (Linnaeus). Turkey Vulture.

Suborder ACCIPITRES — Superfamily ACCIPITROIDEA
Family Accipitridae — Subfamily Pandioninae
Pandion haliaetus (Linnaeus). Osprey.

Subfamily Accipitrinae
Chondrohierax uncinatus (Temminck). Hook-billed Kite.
Elanoides forficatus (Linnaeus). American Swallow-tailed Kite.
Elanus caeruleus (Desfontaines). Black-shouldered Kite.
Rostrhamus sociabilis (Vieillot). Snail Kite.
Ictinia mississippiensis (Wilson). Mississippi Kite.
Haliaeetus leucocephalus (Linnaeus). Bald Eagle.
Circus cyaneus (Linnaeus). Northern Harrier.
Accipiter striatus (Vieillot). Sharp-shinned Hawk.
Accipiter cooperii (Bonaparte). Cooper's Hawk.
Accipiter gentilis (Linnaeus). Northern Goshawk.
Parabuteo unicinctus (Temminck). Harris's Hawk.
Buteo lineatus (Gmelin). Red-shouldered Hawk.
Buteo platypterus (Vieillot). Broad-winged Hawk.
Buteo swainsoni (Bonaparte). Swainson's Hawk.
Buteo albicaudatus (Vieillot). White-tailed Hawk.
Buteo albonotatus (Kaup). Zone-tailed Hawk.
Buteo jamaicensis (Gmelin). Red-tailed Hawk.
Buteo regalis (Gray). Ferruginous Hawk.
Aquila chrysaetos (Linnaeus). Golden Eagle.

Suborder FALCONES
Family Falconidae — Tribe Polyborini
Polyborus plancus (Miller). Crested Caracara.
Tribe Falconini
Falco sparverius (Linnaeus). American Kestrel.
Falco columbarius (Linnaeus). Merlin.
Falco peregrinus (Tunstall). Peregrine Falcon.
Falco mexicanus (Schlegel). Prairie Falcon.

Order GALLIFORMES — Superfamily CRACOIDEA
Family Cracidae
Ortalis vetula (Wagler). Plain Chachalaca.

Superfamily PHASIANOIDEA
Family Phasianidae — Subfamily Phasianinae — Tribe Perdicin
Francolinus francolinus (Linnaeus). Black Francolin.

Tribe Phasianini
Gallus gallus (Linnaeus). Red Junglefowl.
Phasianus colchicus (Linnaeus). Ring-necked Pheasant.
Pavo cristatus (Linnaeus). Common Peafowl.

Subfamily Tetraoninae
Dendragapus obscurus (Say). Blue Grouse.
Lagopus lagopus (Linnaeus). Willow Ptarmigan.
Bonasa umbellus (Linnaeus). Ruffed Grouse.

Subfamily Meleagridinae
Meleagris gallopavo (Linnaeus). Wild Turkey.

Subfamily Odontophorinae
Cyrtonyx montezumae (Vigors). Montezuma Quail.
Colinus virginianus (Linnaeus). Northern Bobwhite.
Callipepla squamata (Vigors). Scaled Quail.
Callipepla gambelii (Gambel). Gambel's Quail.
Callipepla californica (Shaw). California Quail.
Oreortyx pictus (Douglas). Mountain Quail.

Order GRUIFORMES
Family Rallidae — Subfamily Rallinae
Rallus longirostris (Boddaert). Clapper Rail.
Rallus elegans (Audubon). King Rail.
Rallus limicola (Vieillot). Virginia Rail.
Porzana carolina (Linnaeus). Sora.
Porphyrula martinica (Linnaeus). Purple Gallinule.
Gallinula chloropus (Linnaeus). Common Moorhen.
Fulica americana (Gmelin). American Coot.

Family Aramidae
Aramus guarauna (Linnaeus). Limpkin.

Family Gruidae — Subfamily Gruinae
Grus canadensis (Linnaeus). Sandhill Crane.

Order CHARADRIIFORMES — Suborder CHARADRII
Family Charadriidae — Subfamily Charadriinae
Pluvialis aquatarola (Linnaeus). Black-bellied Plover.
Pluvialis apricaria (Linnaeus). Greater Golden-Plover.
Pluvialis dominica (Muller). Lesser Golden-Plover.
Charadrius wilsonia (Ord). Wilson's Plover.
Charadrius semipalmatus (Bonaparte). Semipalmated Plover.
Charadrius melodus (Ord). Piping Plover.
Charadrius vociferus (Linnaeus). Killdeer.

Family Haematopodidae
Haematopus palliatus (Temminck). American Oystercatcher.
Haematopus bachmani (Audubon). American Black Oystercatcher.

Family Recurvirostridae
Himantopus mexicanus (Müller). Black-necked Stilt.
Recurvirostra americana (Gmelin). American Avocet.

Suborder SCOLOPACI — Superfamily SCOLOPACOIDEA
Family Scolopacidae
Subfamily Scolopacinae — Tribe Tringini
Tringa melanoleuca (Gmelin). Greater Yellowlegs.
Tringa flavipes (Gmelin). Lesser Yellowlegs.
Tringa solitaria (Wilson). Solitary Sandpiper.
Catoptrophorus semipalmatus (Gmelin). Willet.
Heteroscelus incanus (Gmelin). Wandering Tattler.
Actitis macularia (Linnaeus). Spotted Sandpiper.
Tribe Numeniini
Bartramia longicauda (Bechstein). Upland Sandpiper.
Numenius phaeopus (Linnaeus). Whimbrel.
Numenius americanus (Bechstein). Long-billed Curlew.
Tribe Limosini
Limosa haemastica (Linnaeus). Hudsonian Godwit.
Limosa lapponica (Linnaeus). Bar-tailed Godwit.
Limosa fedoa (Linnaeus). Marbled Godwit.
Tribe Arenariini
Arenaria interpres (Linnaeus). Ruddy Turnstone.
Arenaria melanocephala (Vigors). Black Turnstone.
Tribe Calidridini
Calidris canutus (Linnaeus). Red Knot.
Calidris alba (Pallas). Sanderling.
Calidris pusilla (Linnaeus). Semipalmated Sandpiper.
Calidris mauri (Cabanis). Western Sandpiper.
Calidris ruficolis (Pallas). Rufous-necked stint.
Calidris minutilla (Vieillot). Least Sandpiper.
Calidris fuscicollis (Vieillot). White-rumped Sandpiper.
Calidris bairdii (Coues). Baird's Sandpiper.
Calidris melanotos (Vieillot). Pectoral Sandpiper.
Calidris maritima (Brünnich). Purple Sandpiper.
Calidris ptilocnemis (Coues). Rock Sandpiper.
Calidris alpina (Linnaeus). Dunlin.
Calidris himantopus (Bonaparte). Stilt Sandpiper.
Tribe Limnodromini
Limnodromus griseus (Gmelin). Short-billed Dowitcher.
Limnodromus scolopaceus (Say). Long-billed Dowitcher.

Tribe Gallinagonini
Gallinago gallinago (Linnaeus). Common Snipe.
Phalaropus tricolor (Vieillot). Wilson's Phalarope.
Phalaropus lobatus (Linnaeus). Red-necked Phalarope.
Phalaropus fulicaria (Linnaeus). Red Phalarope.

Suborder LARI
Family Laridae — Subfamily Stercorariinae
Stercorarius parasiticus (Linnaeus). Parasitic Jaeger.
Stercorarius longicaudus (Vieillot). Long-tailed Jaeger.

Subfamily Larinae
Larus atricilla (Linnaeus). Laughing Gull.
Larus pipixcan (Wagler). Franklin's Gull.
Larus ridibundus (Linnaeus). Common Black-headed Gull.
Larus philadelphia (Ord). Bonaparte's Gull.
Larus heermanni (Cassin). Heermann's Gull.
Larus canus (Linnaeus). Mew Gull.
Larus delawarensis (Ord). Ring-billed Gull.
Larus californicus (Lawrence). California Gull.
Larus argentatus (Pontoppidan). Herring Gull.
Larus glaucoides (Meyer). Iceland Gull.
Larus schistisagus (Steineger). Slaty-backed Gull.
Larus occidentalis (Audubon). Western Gull.
Larus glaucescens (Naumann). Glaucous-winged Gull.
Larus hyperboreus (Gunnerus). Glaucous Gull.
Larus marinus (Linnaeus). Great Black-backed Gull.
Rissa tridactyla (Linnaeus). Black-legged Kittiwake.
Rissa brevirostris (Bruch). Red-legged Kittiwake.
Xema sabini (Sabine). Sabine's Gull.

Subfamily Sterninae
Sterna nilotica (Gmelin). Gull-billed Tern.
Sterna caspia (Pallas). Caspian Tern.
Sterna maxima (Boddaert). Royal Tern.
Sterna elegans (Gambel). Elegant Tern.
Sterna sandvicensis (Latham). Sandwich Tern.
Sterna dougallii (Montagu). Roseate Tern.
Sterna hirundo (Linnaeus). Common Tern.
Sterna paradisaea (Pontoppidan). Arctic Tern.
Sterna forsteri (Nuttall). Forster's Tern.
Sterna antillarum (Lesson). Least Tern.
Sterna fuscata (Linnaeus). Sooty Tern.
Chlidonias niger (Linnaeus). Black Tern.
Anous stolidus (Linnaeus). Brown Noddy.

Subfamily Rynchopinae
Rynchops niger (Linnaeus). Black Skimmer.

Suborder ALCAE
Family Alcidae — Tribe Allini
Alle alle (Linnaeus). Dovekie.
Tribe Alcini
Uria aalge (Pontoppidan). Common Murre.
Alca torda (Linnaeus). Razorbill.
Pinguinus impennis (Linnaeus). Great Auk.
Tribe Cepphini
Cepphus grylle (Linnaeus). Black Guillemot.
Cepphus columba (Pallas). Pigeon Guillemot.
Tribe Aethiini
Cyclorrhynchus psittacula (Pallas). Parakeet Auklet.
Aethia pusilla (Pallas). Least Auklet.
Aethia cristatella (Pallas). Crested Auklet.
Tribe Fraterculini
Cerorhinca monocerata (Pallas). Rhinoceros Auklet.
Fratercula cirrhata (Pallas). Tufted Puffin.

Suborder COLUMBAE
Family Columbidae
Columba livia (Gmelin). Rock Dove.
Columba leucocephala (Linnaeus). White-crowned Pigeon.
Columba flavirostris (Wagler). Red-billed Pigeon.
Columba fasciata (Say). Band-tailed Pigeon.
Streptopelia risoria (Linnaeus). Ringed Turtle-Dove.
Streptopelia chinensis (Scopoli). Spotted Dove.
Zenaida asiatica (Linnaeus). White-winged Dove.
Zenaida aurita (Temminck). Zenaida Dove.
Zenaida macroura (Linnaeus). Mourning Dove.
Columbina inca (Lesson). Inca Dove.
Columbina passerina (Linnaeus). Common Ground-Dove.
Leptotila verreauxi (Bonaparte). White-tipped Dove.

Order PSITTACIFORMES
Family Psittacidae — Subfamily Platycercinae
Melopsittacus undulatus (Shaw). Budgerigar.

Subfamily Arinae
Myiopsitta monachus (Boddaert). Monk Parakeet.
Amazona viridigenalis (Cassin). Red-crowned Parrot.

Order CUCULIFORMES
Family Cuculidae — Subfamily Coccyzinae
Coccyzus americanus (Linnaeus). Yellow-billed Cuckoo.

Subfamily Neomorphinae
Geococcyx californianus (Lesson). Greater Roadrunner.

Subfamily Crotophaginae
Crotophaga ani (Linnaeus). Smooth-billed Ani.
Crotophaga sulcirostris (Swainson). Groove-billed Ani.

Order STRIGIFORMES
Tyto alba (Scopoli). Common Barn-Owl.

Family Strigidae
Otus kennicottii (Elliot). Western Screech-Owl.
Otus trichopsis (Wagler). Whiskered Screech-Owl.
Bubo virginianus (Gmelin). Great Horned Owl.
Nyctea scandiaca (Linnaeus). Snowy Owl.
Micrathene whitneyi (Cooper). Elf Owl.
Athene cunicularia (Molina). Burrowing Owl.
Strix varia (Barton). Barred Owl.
Asio flammeus (Pontoppidan). Short-eared Owl.

Order CAPRIMULGIFORMES
Family Caprimulgidae — Subfamily Chordeilinae
Chordeiles acutipennis (Hermann). Lesser Nighthawk.
Chordeiles minor (Forster). Common Nighthawk.

Subfamily Caprimulginae
Nyctidromus albicollis (Gmelin). Common Pauraque.
Phalaenoptilus nuttallii (Audubon). Common Poorwill.
Caprimulgus carolinensis (Gmelin). Chuck-will's-widow.

Order APODIFORMES
Family Apodidae — Subfamily Chaeturinae
Chaetura pelagica (Linnaeus). Chimney Swift.
Chaetura vauxi (Townsend). Vaux's Swift.

Subfamily Apodinae
Aeronautes saxatalis (Woodhouse). White-throated Swift.

Family Trochilidae
Amazilia yucatanensis (Cabot). Buff-bellied Hummingbird.
Lampornis clemenciae (Lesson). Blue-throated Hummingbird.
Eugenes fulgens (Swainson). Magnificent Hummingbird.
Archilochus colubris (Linnaeus). Ruby-throated Hummingbird.
Archilochus alexandri (Bourcier & Mulsant). Black-chinned Hummingbird.
Calypte costae (Bourcier). Costa's Hummingbird.
Selasphorus platycercus (Swainson). Broad-tailed Hummingbird.
Selasphorus rufus (Gmelin). Rufous Hummingbird,

Order TROGONIFORMES
Family Trogonidae
Trogon elegans (Gould). Elegant Trogon.

Order CORACIIFORMES
Suborder ALCEDINES — Superfamily ALCEDINOIDEA
Family Alcedinidae — Subfamily Cerylinae
Ceryle torquata (Linnaeus). Ringed Kingfisher.
Ceryle alcyon (Linnaeus). Belted Kingfisher.
Chloroceryle americana (Gmelin). Green Kingfisher.

Order PICIFORMES
Suborder PICI
Family Picidae—Subfamily Picinae
Melanerpes erythrocephalus (Linnaeus). Red-headed Woodpecker.
Melanerpes formicivorus (Swainson). Acorn Woodpecker.
Melanerpes aurifrons (Wagler). Golden-fronted Woodpecker.
Melanerpes carolinus (Linnaeus). Red-bellied Woodpecker.
Sphyrapicus varius (Linnaeus). Yellow-bellied Sapsucker.
Sphyrapicus ruber (Gmelin). Red-breasted Sapsucker.
Sphyrapicus thyroideus (Cassin). Williamson's Sapsucker.
Picoides scalaris (Wagler). Ladder-backed Woodpecker.
Picoides pubescens (Linnaeus). Downy Woodpecker.
Picoides villosus (Linnaeus). Hairy Woodpecker.
Picoides stricklandi (Malherbe). Strickland's Woodpecker.
Picoides borealis (Vieillot). Red-cockaded Woodpecker.
Colaptes auratus (Linnaeus). Northern Flicker.
Dryocopus pileatus (Linnaeus). Pileated Woodpecker.

Order PASSERIFORMES
Suborder TYRANNI — Superfamily TYRANNOIDEA
Family Tyrannidae — Subfamily Fluvicolinae
Contopus borealis (Swainson). Olive-sided Flycatcher.
Contopus pertinax (Cabanis & Heine). Greater Pewee.
Contopus sordidulus (Sclater). Western Wood-Pewee.
Contopus virens (Linnaeus). Eastern Wood-Pewee.
Empidonax virescens (Vieillot). Acadian Flycatcher.
Empidonax alnorum (Brewster). Alder Flycatcher.
Empidonax traillii (Audubon). Willow Flycatcher.
Empidonax minimus (Baird & Baird). Least Flycatcher.
Empidonax hammondii (Xantus de Vesey). Hammond's Flycatcher.
Empidonax oberholseri (Phillips). Dusky Flycatcher.
Empidonax wrightii (Baird). Gray Flycatcher.
Empidonax difficilis (Baird). Western Flycatcher.

Sayornis nigricans (Swainson). Black Phoebe.
Sayornis phoebe (Latham). Eastern Phoebe.
Sayornis saya (Bonaparte). Say's Phoebe.
Pyrocephalus rubinus (Boddaert). Vermilion Flycatcher.

Subfamily Tyranninae
Myiarchus cinerascens (Lawrence). Ash-throated Flycatcher.
Myiarchus crinitus (Linnaeus). Great Crested Flycatcher.
Myiarchus tyrannulus (Müller). Brown-crested Flycatcher.
Pitangus sulphuratus (Linnaeus). Great Kiskadee.
Myiodynastes luteiventris (Sclater). Sulphur-bellied Flycatcher.
Tyrannus couchii (Baird). Couch's Kingbird.
Tyrannus vociferans (Swainson). Cassin's Kingbird.
Tyrannus verticalis (Say). Western Kingbird.
Tyrannus tyrannus (Linnaeus). Eastern Kingbird.
Tyrannus dominicensis (Gmelin). Gray Kingbird.
Tyrannus forficatus (Gmelin). Scissor-tailed Flycatcher.

Suborder PASSERES
Family Alaudidae
Eremophila alpestris (Linnaeus). Horned Lark.

Family Hirundinidae — Subfamily Hirundininae
Progne subis (Linnaeus). Purple Martin.
Tachycineta bicolor (Vieillot). Tree Swallow.
Tachycineta thalassina (Swainson). Violet-green Swallow.
Stelgidopteryx serripennis (Audubon). Northern Rough-winged Swallow.
Riparia riparia (Linnaeus). Bank Swallow.
Hirundo pyrrhonota (Vieillot). Cliff Swallow.
Hirundo rustica (Linnaeus). Barn Swallow.

Family Corvidae
Perisoreus canadensis (Linnaeus). Gray Jay.
Cyanocitta stelleri (Gmelin). Steller's Jay.
Cyanocitta cristata (Linnaeus). Blue Jay.
Cyanocorax yncas (Boddaert). Green Jay.
Cyanocorax morio (Wagler). Brown Jay.
Aphelocoma coerulescens (Bosc). Scrub Jay.
Aphelocoma ultramarina (Bonaparte). Gray-breasted Jay.
Gymnorhinus cyanocephalus (Wied). Pinyon Jay.
Nucifraga columbiana (Wilson). Clark's Nutcracker.
Pica pica (Linnaeus). Blacked-billed Magpie.
Pica nuttalli (Audubon). Yellow-billed Magpie.
Corvus brachyrhynchos (Brehm). American Crow.
Corvus ossifragus (Wilson). Fish Crow.
Corvus cryptoleucus (Couch). Chihuahuan Raven.
Corvus corax (Linnaeus). Common Raven.

Family Paridae
Parus atricapillus (Linnaeus). Black-capped Chickadee
Parus carolinensis (Audubon). Carolina Chickadee.
Parus gambeli (Ridgway). Mountain Chickadee.
Parus hudsonicus (Forster). Boreal Chickadee.
Parus rufescens (Townsend). Chestnut-backed Chickadee.
Parus wollweberi (Bonaparte). Bridled Titmouse.
Parus inornatus (Gambel). Plain Titmouse.
Parus bicolor (Linnaeus). Tufted Titmouse.

Family Remizidae
Auriparus flaviceps (Sundevall). Verdin.

Family Aegithalidae
Psaltriparus minimus (Townsend). Bushtit.

Family Sittidae — Subfamily Sittinae
Sitta canadensis (Linnaeus). Red-breasted Nuthatch.
Sitta carolinensis (Latham). White-breasted Nuthatch.
Sitta pygmaea (Vigors). Pygmy Nuthatch.

Family Certhiidae — Subfamily Certhiinae
Certhia americana (Bonaparte). Brown Creeper.

Family Troglodytidae
Campylorhynchus brunneicapillus (Lafresnaye). Cactus Wren.
Salpinctes obsoletus (Say). Rock Wren.
Catherpes mexicanus (Swainson). Canyon Wren.
Thryothorus ludovicianus (Latham). Carolina Wren.
Thryomanes bewickii (Audubon). Bewick's Wren.
Troglodytes aedon (Vieillot). House Wren.
Troglodytes troglodytes (Linnaeus). Winter Wren.
Cistothorus platensis (Latham). Sedge Wren.
Cistothorus palustris (Wilson). Marsh Wren.

Family Cinclidae
Cinclus mexicanus (Swainson). American Dipper.

Family Muscicapidae — Subfamily Sylviinae — Tribe Sylviini
Regulus satrapa (Lichtenstein). Golden-crowned Kinglet.
Regulus calendula (Linnaeus). Ruby-crowned Kinglet.
Tribe Polioptilini
Polioptila caerulea (Linnaeus). Blue-gray Gnatcatcher.
Polioptila melanura (Lawrence). Black-tailed Gnatcatcher.

Subfamily Turdinae
Oenanthe oenanthe (Linnaeus). Northern Wheatear.
Sialia sialis (Linnaeus). Eastern Bluebird.
Sialia mexicana (Swainson). Western Bluebird.

Sialia currucoides (Bechstein). Mountain Bluebird.
Myadestes townsendi (Audubon). Townsend's Solitaire.
Catharus minimus (Lafresnaye). Gray-cheeked Thrush.
Catharus guttatus (Pallas). Hermit Thrush.
Hylocichla mustelina (Gmelin). Wood Thrush.
Turdus migratorius (Linnaeus). American Robin.
Ixoreus naevius (Gmelin). Varied Thrush.

Subfamily Timaliinae
Chamaea fasciata (Gambel). Wrentit.

Family Mimidae
Dumetella carolinensis (Linnaeus). Gray Catbird.
Mimus polyglottos (Linnaeus). Northern Mockingbird.
Oreoscoptes montanus (Townsend). Sage Thrasher.
Toxostoma rufum (Linnaeus). Brown Thrasher.
Toxostoma longirostre (Lafresnaye). Long-billed Thrasher.
Toxostoma curvirostre (Swainson). Curve-billed Thrasher.
Toxostoma redivivum (Gambel). California Thrasher.

Family Motacillidae
Motacilla flava (Linnaeus). Yellow Wagtail.
Anthus spinoletta (Linnaeus). Water Pipit.

Family Bombycillidae
Bombycilla garrulus (Linnaeus). Bohemian Waxwing.
Bombycilla cedrorum (Vieillot). Cedar Waxwing.

Family Ptilogonatidae
Phainopepla nitens (Swainson). Phainopepla.

Family Laniidae — Subfamily Laniinae
Lanius excubitor (Linnaeus). Northern Shrike.
Lanius ludovicianus (Linnaeus). Loggerhead Shrike.

Family Sturnidae — Subfamily Sturninae
Sturnus vulgaris (Linnaeus). European Starling.

Family Zosteropidae
Zosterops japonicus (Temminck & Schlegel). Japanese White-eye.

Family Vireonidae — Subfamily Vireoninae
Vireo griseus (Boddaert). White-eyed Vireo.
Vireo bellii (Audubon). Bell's Vireo.
Vireo vicinior (Coues). Gray Vireo.
Vireo solitarius (Wilson). Solitary Vireo.
Vireo flavifrons (Vieillot). Yellow-throated Vireo.
Vireo gilvus (Vieillot). Warbling Vireo.
Vireo philadelphicus (Cassin). Philadelphia Vireo.
Vireo olivaceus (Linnaeus). Red-eyed Vireo.
Vireo altiloquus (Vieillot). Black-whiskered Vireo.

Family Emberizidae — Subfamily Parulinae
Vermivora peregrina (Wilson). Tennessee Warbler.
Vermivora celata (Say). Orange-crowned Warbler.
Vermivora ruficapilla (Wilson). Nashville Warbler.
Vermivora virginiae (Baird). Virginia's Warbler.
Vermivora crissalis (Salvin & Godman). Colima Warbler.
Vermivora luciae (Cooper). Lucy's Warbler.
Parula americana (Linnaeus). Northern Parula.
Parula pitiayumi (Vieillot). Tropical Parula.
Dendroica petechia (Linnaeus). Yellow Warbler.
Dendroica pennsylvanica (Linnaeus). Chestnut-sided Warbler.
Dendroica magnolia (Wilson). Magnolia Warbler.
Dendroica tigrina (Gmelin). Cape May Warbler.
Dendroica caerulescens (Gmelin). Black-throated Blue Warbler.
Dendroica coronata (Linnaeus). Yellow-rumped Warbler.
Dendroica nigrescens (Townsend). Black-throated Gray Warbler.
Dendroica occidentalis(Townsend). Hermit Warbler.
Dendroica virens (Gmelin). Black-throated Green Warbler.
Dendroica fusca (Müller). Blackburnian Warbler.
Dendroica dominica (Linnaeus). Yellow-throated Warbler.
Dendroica pinus (Wilson). Pine Warbler.
Dendroica discolor (Vieillot). Prairie Warbler.
Dendroica palmarum (Gmelin). Palm Warbler.
Dendroica castanea (Wilson). Bay-breasted Warbler.
Dendroica striata (Forster). Blackpoll Warbler.
Dendroica cerulea (Wilson). Cerulean Warbler.
Mniotilta varia (Linnaeus). Black-and-white Warbler.
Setophaga ruticilla (Linnaeus). American Redstart.
Protonotaria citrea (Boddaert). Prothonotary Warbler.
Limnothlypis swainsonii (Audubon). Swainson's Warbler.
Seiurus aurocapillus (Linnaeus). Ovenbird.
Seiurus noveboracensis (Gmelin). Northern Waterthrush.
Seiurus motacilla (Vieillot). Louisiana Waterthrush.
Oporornis formosus (Wilson). Kentucky Warbler.
Oporonis philadelphia (Wilson). Mourning Warbler.
Oporornis tolmiei (Townsend). MacGillivray's Warbler.
Geothlypis trichas (Linnaeus). Common Yellowthroat.
Wilsonia citrina (Boddaert). Hooded Warbler.
Wilsonia pusilla (Wilson). Wilson's Warbler.
Wilsonia canadensis (Linnaeus). Canada Warbler.
Cardellina rubrifrons (Giraud). Red-faced Warbler.
Myioborus pictus (Swainson). Painted Redstart.
Icteria virens (Linnaeus). Yellow-breasted Chat.
Peucedramus taeniatus (Du Bus de Gisignies). Olive Warbler.

Subfamily Thraupinae — Tribe Thraupini

Piranga flava (Vieillot). Hepatic Tanager.
Piranga rubra (Linnaeus). Summer Tanager.
Piranga olivacea (Gmelin). Scarlet Tanager.
Piranga ludoviciana (Wilson). Western Tanager.

Subfamily Cardinalinae

Cardinalis cardinalis (Linnaeus). Northern Cardinal.
Cardinalis sinuatus (Bonaparte). Pyrrhuloxis.
Pheucticus ludovicianus (Linnaeus). Rose-breasted Grosbeak.
Pheucticus melanocephalus (Swainson). Black-headed Grosbeak.
Guiraca caerulea (Linnaeus). Blue Grosbeak.
Passerina cyanea (Linnaeus). Indigo Bunting.
Passerina versicolor (Bonaparte). Varied Bunting.
Passserina ciris (Linnaeus). Painted Bunting.
Spiza americana (Gmelin). Dickcissel.

Subfamily Emberizinae

Arremonops rufivirgatus (Lawrence). Olive Sparrow.
Pipilo chlorurus (Audubon). Green-tailed Towhee.
Pipilo erythrophthalmus (Linnaeus). Rufous-sided Towhee.
Pipilo fuscus (Swainson). Brown Towhee.
Aimophila aestivalis (Lichtenstein). Bachman's Sparrow.
Aimophila cassinii (Woodhouse). Cassin's Sparrow.
Aimophila ruficeps (Cassin). Rufous-crowned Sparrow.
Spizella arborea (Wilson). American Tree Sparrow.
Spizella passerina (Bechstein). Chipping Sparrow.
Spizella pallida (Swainson). Clay-colored Sparrow.
Spizella breweri (Cassin). Brewer's Sparrow.
Spizella pusilla (Wilson). Field Sparrow.
Spizella atrogularis (Cabanis). Black chinned Sparrow.
Chondestes grammacus (Say). Lark Sparrow.
Amphispiza bilineata (Cassin). Black-throated Sparrow.
Calamospiza melanocorys (Stejneger). Lark Bunting.
Passerculus sandwichensis (Gmelin). Savannah Sparrow.
Ammodramus savannarum (Gmelin). Grasshopper Sparrow.
Ammodramus maritimus (Wilson). Seaside Sparrow.
Passerella iliaca (Merrem). Fox Sparrow.
Melospiza melodia (Wilson). Song Sparrow.
Melospiza lincolnii (Audubon). Lincoln's Sparrow.
Melospiza georgiana (Latham). Swamp Sparrow.
Zonotrichia albicollis (Gmelin). White-throated Sparrow.
Zonotrichia atricapilla (Gmelin). Golden-crowned Sparrow.
Zonotrichia leucophrys (Forster). White-crowned Sparrow.
Junco hyemalis (Linnaeus). Dark-eyed Junco.

Junco phaeonotus (Wagler). Yellow-eyed Junco.
Calcarius lapponicus (Linnaeus). Lapland Longspur.
Plectrophenax nivalis (Linnaeus). Snow Bunting.
Plectrophenax hyperboreus (Ridgway). McKay's Bunting.

Subfamily Icterinae — Tribe Dolichonychini
Dolichonyx oryzivorus (Linnaeus). Bobolink.
Tribe Agelaiini
Agelaius phoeniceus (Linnaeus). Red-winged Blackbird.
Agelaius tricolor (Audubon). Tricolored Blackbird.
Sturnella magna (Linnaeus). Eastern Meadowlark.
Sturnella neglecta (Audubon). Western Meadowlark.
Xanthocephalus xanthocephalus (Bonaparte). Yellow-headed Blackbird.
Euphagus carolinus (Müller). Rusty Blackbird.
Euphagus cyanocephalus (Wagler). Brewer's Blackbird.
Quiscalus mexicanus (Gmelin). Great-tailed Grackle.
Quiscalus major (Vieillot). Boat-tailed Grackle.
Quiscalus quiscula (Linnaeus). Common Grackle.
Molothrus aeneus (Wagler). Bronzed Cowbird.
Molothrus ater (Boddaert). Brown-headed Cowbird.
Tribe Icterini
Icterus spurius (Linnaeus). Orchard Oriole.
Icterus cucullatus (Swainson). Hooded Oriole.
Icterus galbula (Linnaeus). Northern Oriole.
Icterus parisorum (Bonaparte). Scott's Oriole.

Family Fringillidae — Subfamily Carduelinae
Leucosticte arctoa (Pallas). Rosy Finch.
Pinicola enucleator (Linnaeus). Pine Grosbeak.
Carpodacus purpureus (Gmelin). Purple Finch.
Carpodacus cassinii (Baird). Cassin's Finch.
Carpodacus mexicanus (Müller). House Finch.
Loxia curvirostra (Linnaeus). Red Crossbill.
Carduelis flammea (Linnaeus). Common Redpoll.
Carduelis hornemanni (Holböll). Hoary Redpoll.
Carduelis pinus (Wilson). Pine Siskin.
Carduelis psaltria (Say). Lesser Goldfinch.
Carduelis lawrencei (Cassin). Lawrence's Goldfinch.
Carduelis tristis (Linnaeus). American Goldfinch.
Coccothraustes vespertinus (Cooper). Evening Grosbeak.

Family Passeridae
Passer domesticus (Linnaeus). House Sparrow.

Acknowledgements

Hundreds of people helped me in my journey around North America, both along the way and while this account of that journey was being written. To thank them all individually would require another volume. My long-suffering editor, Denise Bukowski, faced with the Herculean task of reducing the original manuscript by half to fit the requirements of publication, and a stubborn author who wanted to tell it all, was forced to relegate enough material to fill a second volume to the cutting room floor. Many people I wanted to acknowledge may be found there in name: I carry their faces and their contributions thankfully in my heart.

Above all, I am indebted to Gustave J. Yaki whose idea it was to re-create Roger Tory Peterson and James Fisher's journey around "Wild America" and to invite me to record it. He planned the trip, drove the van, sharpened my powers of observation and generously shared his encyclopedic knowledge. Without Gus, this book would not be.

I appreciate deeply the forbearance of all my travelling companions who had to cope with a writer-photographer-naturalist in their midst but I especially thank Tess Kloot whose encouragement kept me going when sometimes the task and the lack of time to do the subject justice seemed overwhelming. Tess spent months assiduously checking the manuscript and adding insights of her own. Her comparisons with Wild Australia would make another volume. In watching Tess discover Wild America I re-discovered joy I felt in earlier discoveries.

I must also single out Jack Bone who for several years both before and after the journey has given me unselfish and unstinting support— researching, xeroxing, adding to my library, preparing maps and indexes, and in those mad final days of editing, doing all domestic chores so that Denise and I (she sitting in one room cutting out and me sitting in another adding in), could squeak in under the deadline. When editing was done and I was still trying to rush off by helicopter to add another update, both Jack and Denise were sobering influences dragging me back to reality.

Two more people who gave me ceaseless encouragement and advice are worldclass naturalists, Fred Bodsworth and David Stirling. I especially appreciate their flying to my side in the last days of editing, and the camaraderie we shared criticizing the entire "three-volume" manuscript in my Mill Bay "eyrie." I am also deeply grateful to several ornithologists from Newfoundland who painstakingly checked the first chapters and warned me the book would be "huge" if I continued to include as much as I wanted — Bill Montevecchi, John Piatt, Bill Threlfall, Bernard Jackson, Bruce MacTavish and John Wells. They were right! Others who checked parts of the manuscript were my travelling companions, Marie Gillespie, Emily Hamilton, Vi Debbie and my longtime friend, marine mammalogist Michael Bigg. In addition, Marie slaved for weeks in libraries researching details on birds.

Others to whom I am grateful for assistance — in sharing their expertise or for hospitality along the way — I name here alphabetically. Admittedly this is a superficial rendering of my warm appreciation for their contributions, but it is heartfelt: David Acuff, Elizabeth and Henry Allen, Peter Allen (National Park Service), Peter Alden (Lindblad Travel), Asgar Amirzadeh, Lyn Atherton (Florida Audubon Society), Paul and Maria Ayuluk, Melvin Bellinger (U.S. Forest Service), Steve Beissinger (Smithsonian Institution), Joe E. Brown, Chris Belden (Florida Game and Fresh Water Fish Commission), Vernon Byrd (U.S. Fish and Wildlife Service), Mary Bukowki, Harry Butt, Wayne Campbell (British Columbia Provincial Museum), Neil and Betty Carey, Howard and Shirley Cartier, Harley Cochrane, Marti Collins (U.S. Fish and Wildlife Service), Lanny Cornell (Sea World), Ruth Delaney, James Dolan (San Diego Zoological Society), Pam Fletcher, Kay Forbes, Denise Frank (Cornell University), Chuck Fowler (National Marine Fisheries Service), Ray Gauthier, Johnny Guerro, Milt Garb, Bob Giersdorf (Alaska Exploration Holidays), Dan Heinz (American Wilderness Alliance), Bill Henry (U.S. Fish and Wildlife Service), Mindy Jackson, Frank Johnson (U.S. Fish and Wildlife Service), Irma Johnson, Mr. and Mrs. Chuck Kaigler, Al Kramer, Clair Kunkel, George Kyle (National Parks Service), Edwin and Lydia Lindsey, Vicki and John Malone, Lily Miller (McClelland and Stewart), Wally McGregor (Ministry of the Environment, British Columbia), Bruce Moorhead (National Parks Service), Leo and Mary Moses, Roy McBride, Paul McIlhenny, Mike McNall, the Merculieff family, Jacob Nash, Ulric Nayamin, Kathy Newell, Eileen and Telford Norman, David Nysewander (U.S. Fish and Wildlife Service), Lorin Orpwood, Ted Parker (University of Louisiana), Ron Perry (U.S. Fish and Wildlife Service), Stuart Pimm (University of Tennessee), John and Nancy

Pond, Rosemary Porter, Dennis Raveling (University of California), Craig Rieben (U.S. Fish and Wildlife Service), Art Risser (San Diego Zoological Society), Bill Robertson (National Parks Service), John Ross (National Parks Service), Lyn Sanny, Joe Scordino (National Marine Fisheries Service), Harley Shaw (U.S. Fish and Wildlife Service), Gene and Mimi Sherman, Beth Shide, Alexander Sprunt IV (National Audubon Society), Arthur Sowls (U.S. Fish and Wildlife Service), Susan Thorsen, Margaret Thornburgh, Leonabelle Turnbull, Brian Walton (University of Santa Cruz), Doug Webb, Tom Wilson (U.S. Fish and Wildlife Service), Ulrich Wilson (U.S. Fish and Wildlife Service), Vern Wray (U.S. Fish and Wildlife Service), Rita and Antonina Unin, Auwina and Thurlow Weed, Doris Winship — and Jerry and Louie in New York who insisted I take home the massive management plan of Jamaica Bay to learn more about "the boids."

Two friends whose final relegation to "volume two" is not indicative of their true contribution to this book are Bill Day of Canada Trust and his wife, Fiona. Enthusiastically and extemporaneously, they launched the expedition from their home in St. John's, Newfoundland, arranging lectures, interviews, field trips, accommodation, and dealing with delays caused by airline strikes, lightning strikes, storms and malfunctioning radar with typical unflappability. When the story was finally recorded, they helped launch it again.

I am eternally thankful to my friend on a neighbouring island, Robert Bateman, who unselfishly illustrated these chapters despite his own hectic schedule, and Roger Tory Peterson who inspired the idea three decades ago and honoured me with his introduction.

Finally, I thank Canada Council most enthusiastically for a grant which ensured that my research reached the word processor and beyond.

Lyn Hancock
Mill Bay, British Columbia, Canada
August 1986

Index

Canada Goose: eastern extension of nesting area, 24; increase in numbers, 48
Canvasback Duck: decline in, 47
Canyon Wren: 104, 118–19
Cape May Warbler: 28
Cape Sable Seaside Sparrow: 61
Cape St. Mary's Sea Bird Sanctuary (Newfoundland): 4–5; birds of 6; Gannets, 6–7; Murres, 7; Northern Gannets, 5; Peterson and Fisher's visit to, 5
Carlsbad Cavern National Monument (New Mexico): 106; bats, 107–08
Cassin's Sparrow: 98
Cattle Egret: 56, 69–70; expansion of breeding range, 48; increase in, 48
Chincoteague National Wildlife Refuge (Virginia): 29; unusual birds, 29; wild ponies, 28
Chiricahua Mountains: 108–10; Care Creek Canyon, 110; Chiricahua National Monument, 111; Madera Canyon, 111; owls in, 112; Santa Rita Lodge, 110, 112–113; Trogons, 109–10, 112
Chuck-Will's-Widow: 102
Colima Warbler: 102
Cougars: 96, 104–05, 129; population increase in, 97
Crested Auklets: 184

Debbie, Vi: 23
Desert Fauna: 99, 116
Desert Flora: 99, 116
Dickcissel: 29
Dry Tortugas: 69–70
Dusky Seaside Sparrow: 53
Dutton, Marjorie: 43

Eastern Brant: increase in, 48
Eastern Panther: 38, 40; sightings and killings, 39
Elephant Seals: population increase in California, 132
El Nino: effect on Appalachians, 36, 38; effect on California, 138; effect on Oregon, 148; effect on Northern Pacific, 181; effect on Yosemite, 140
Eskimo Curlew: 86
Everglades: 63; environmental damage to, 63; geology of, 62; prospects for, 65; "Save Our Everglades" Campaign, 64
Everglades Kite: 58

Fisher, James: on Grand Canyon, 123; at Walden, 19. See also Peterson and Fisher

Florida: Corkscrew Swamp Sanctuary, 73; Cypress Gardens, 54–55; Dry Tortugas, 67–68; Everglades National Park, 70–72; Florida Keys, 65–67; Fort Jefferson National Monument, 67–70; introduced species, 57; Loxahatchee National Wildlife Refuge, 58; Marineland, 50–51; pelicans, 51; St. Augustine, 50; St. Marks National Wildlife Refuge, 47; Tamiami Trail, 70–71. See also Everglades; Lake Okeechobee; Merritt Island National Wildlife Refuge; Wakulla Springs Wildlife Sanctuary
Florida Key White-Tailed Deer: 66
Florida Panther: 71–72; threat to, 72
Florida Torryea: 43, 74
Forbes, Kay: 115
Frigatebird: 68
Fulvous Whistling Duck: decline in, 48
Fur Seal: 169–176; bulls, 172–73; conservation measures, 178; danger of extinction, 170; decline of, 176–177; main Alaska breeding colony, 172; migration patterns, 174

Gannets: 6–7
Georgia: 43–44; flora, 43. See also Greenwood Plantation
Gillespie, Marie: 79
Glossy Ibis: 48
Grand Canyon National Park (Arizona): 123–25; bird species in, 125
Great Auk: 6
Great Egret: local decline in, 48; northern expansion of range, 20
Greater Roadrunner: 95
Great Smoky Mountains National Park (Appalachians): 33, 35; birds of, 37, 40; plants of, 37; eastern panther, 38–40; warbler migration and decline, 36; warblers, 38; wildflowers of, 37
Great-tailed Grackle: 92–93
Green Jay: 94
Green Kingfisher: 95
Green Turtle: 67
Greenwood Plantation (Georgia): 44; flora and fauna, 45; Whitney Family, 44
Gulf Coast: 74–76

Hames, Frances: 66–67
Hamilton, Emily: 43
Hancock, Lyn: x; and Tabasco the raccoon, 80–81; personal discovery of wilderness, 188–89; *There's a Raccoon in my Parka*, xiv; Wild America now and thirty years ago, 194–197

Harbor Seal: 139
Harp seal: and Newfoundland seal hunt, 11
Hawksbill Turtle: 67
Hooded Warbler: 38
Horned Puffin: 183
Humpback Whale: resurgence of, 12

Ivory-billed Woodpecker: 43, 73–74;
 sighting in Cuba, 74

Jamaica Bay National Wildlife Refuge
 (NYC): 22; bird species in, 23; ospreys
 in, 23
Javelinas: 102–03
Johnson, Irma: 23, 43
Joshua Tree National Monument: 126

Klamath Basin National Wildlife Refuge
 (California-Oregon): 145–147; bald
 eagle, 146; decline of birds in, 147;
 western grebe, 146
Kloot, Tess: xvi, and Brandt's cormorant,
 132; on Chihuahuan Desert, 97; interest
 in birding, 1; on scissor-tailed flycatcher,
 83; on smooth-billed ani, 56; and
 yellow-billed pintail, 144

Lake Okeechobee: 55–57; now and thirty
 years ago, 56
Lapland Longspurs: 158–159
Least Auklets: 183
Least Bittern: decline in, 48
Least Terns: 75–76; decline in, 48; on
 Mississippi coast, 75
Lesser Nighthawk: 103
Lewis's Woodpecker: 119
Limpkin: 46
Little Gull: increase in New World, 20
Loggerhead Turtle: 29, 67
Louisiana: 79–83. See also Avery Island
Louisiana Heron: expansion of breeding
 range, 48

Mallard: increase in, 48
Mangrove Cuckoo: 66
Mangrove Trees: 62-63
Merritt Island National Wildlife Refuge
 (Florida): 51, 54; black skimmer in, 52;
 dusky seaside sparrow, 53; roseate
 spoonbill in, 52–53; sandpiper in, 52
Mexican Freetail Bat: 107–08
Monk Parakeet: 60
Moose: 4
Mountain Lions: See Cougars
Murre: coloration, 7; common vs.
 thick-billed, 8; hunt of in Newfoundland, 8

National Audubon Society: Blue List of
 declining species, 47–48; Corkscrew
 Swamp Sanctuary: 72; on decline of
 wetlands, 47
National Monuments: Canyon de Chelly
 (Arizona), 121–23; Fort Jefferson
 (Florida), 67–68; Joshua Tree (California),
 125–26; Lava Beds (California), 147
National Park System: Big Bend (Texas),
 99–103, 105; Carlsbad Caverns (New
 Mexico), 106–08; Everglades (Florida),
 70; Grand Canyon (Arizona), 123–125;
 Great Smoky Mountains (Appalachians),
 33, 35–40; Olympic (Washington),
 149–50, 152–53; Petrified Forest and
 Painted Desert (Arizona), 119–121;
 Yosemite (California), 139–42; Shenan-
 doah (Appalachians), 34
National Wildlife Refuge System: Anahuac
 (Texas), 83–85; Aransas (Texas), 87–88;
 Brigantine (New Jersey), 24–25;
 Chincoteague (Virginia), 28–29; exploita-
 tion of system, 19; Great Meadows
 (Massachusetts), 18; Jamaica Bay
 (NYC), 22–23; Klamath Basic
 (California-Oregon), 145–47; Loxahatchee
 (Florida), 58; Merritt Island (Florida),
 51–54; origins of system, 18; Parker
 River (Massachusetts), 19–20; problems
 of system, 84; Santa Ana (Texas), 92–93;
 St. Marks (Florida), 47, 49; Washington
 Islands (Washington), 150–151; Yukon
 Delta (Alaska), 156
Nevada: 143–44
New England: Great Meadows National
 Wildlife Refuge, 18; gull sightings, 20;
 Nuttall Ornithological Club, 18; Parker
 River National Wildlife Refuge, 19–20;
 Pine Barrens, 20. See also Boston
Newfoundland: attitude to conservation, 12;
 Butterpot Provincial Park, 3; Cape Race,
 10–11; conservation in, 11; discovery of,
 2; environment compared to thirty years
 ago, 12; environmental dangers, 12–13;
 geology, 3; harp seal hunt, 11;
 introduced species, 3; moose, 4;
 Salmonier Nature Park, 4; See also
 Avalon Peninsula; Cape St. Mary's
 Seabird Sanctuary; St. John's; Witless
 Bay Seabird Sanctuary
New Jersey: 23; Cape May State Park,
 27–28, Nature Conservancy, 23; Stone
 Harbor Bird Sanctuary, 28. See also
 Brigantine National Wildlife Refuge
New Mexico: See Carlsbad Caverns
 National Monument